WITNESSING FOR SOCIOLOGY

Sociologists in Court

Edited by
PAMELA J. JENKINS
and
STEVE KROLL-SMITH

Foreword by Marvin E. Wolfgang
Afterword by Kai Erikson

Westport, Connecticut
London

Library of Congress Cataloging-in-Publication Data

Witnessing for sociology : sociologists in court / edited by Pamela J.
  Jenkins, Steve Kroll-Smith ; foreword by Marvin E. Wolfgang ;
  afterword by Kai Erikson.
         p.   cm.
  Includes bibliographical references and index.
  ISBN 0–275–94852–8 (alk. paper)
     1. Evidence, Expert—United States. 2. Forensic sociology—United
  States. I. Jenkins, Pamela J. II. Kroll-Smith, Steve.
  KF8968.68.W58   1996
  347.73'67—dc20   95-45421
  [347.30767]

British Library Cataloguing in Publication Data is available.

Library of Congress Catalog Card Number: 95-45421
ISBN: 0-275-94852-8

First published in 1996

Praeger Publishers, 88 Post Road West, Westport, CT 06881
An imprint of Greenwood Publishing Group, Inc.

Printed in the United States of America

The paper used in this book complies with the
Permanent Paper Standard issued by the National
Information Standards Organization (Z39.48–1984).

10 9 8 7 6 5 4 3 2 1

Steve Kroll-Smith dedicates this book to his aunt,

Blanche Vandewalle,

for believing

Contents

Foreword

Marvin E. Wolfgang

Expert witnesses have been recorded since ancient times. Consider the trials of Jesus, Socrates, and, later, Galileo. The U.S. Supreme Court heard expert witnesses in the famous *Plessy v. Ferguson* case of separate but equal clauses of conditions of life from education to drinking fountains, buses, and businesses.

How can we trust expert witnesses? We cannot, not easily. We must use the principle of the best available evidence, which means that we must rely on the traditional canons of scientific inquiry.

There is no substitute for the dogged pursuit of testing hypotheses over and over again. The maverick scientist who contradicts the commitments of dozens of carefully researched findings is an unlikely voice of truth. There may be virtue in the challenge of the scientific community, but neither science nor law can count on it until history passes and possesses the accumulation of replications.

We are at a new threshold of significance in the use of expert witnesses. Congress has debated the issue of statistical evidence regarding discrimination in the use of the death penalty. Statistical evidence has been accepted in housing and employment discrimination cases but not in death penalty sentences.

I first testified in Little Rock, Arkansas, in the *Maxwell* case in 1966 and showed the court that there was a systemic, 20-year period of disproportionate (discriminatory) sentencing of blacks to the death penalty when the defendant was black and the victim, white. Baldus and others since have confirmed in brilliant detail what I reported much earlier.

The Supreme Court has listened to but not learned from our researches. The expert witness often is viewed as a biased liberal, despite our efforts to show our commitment to scientific inquiry and methodological objectivity.

Social science is, however, marching ahead on many issues that are arising in litigation and appellate review. Sexual harassment, domestic violence, and racial discrimination are some of these issues.

The expert witness will become more and more important in the traditional court drama. I recommend to my colleagues who may be requested to testify: keep your curriculum vitae up to date; do not speak in absolutes; use probability statements; be calm and never aggressive; sound confident in all your statements; admit you do not know if you really do not know.

A courtroom experience, with a court reporter taking note of every word said, is quite different from a seminar session at the university. One must be careful in language and law to say precisely what is meant. Do not hesitate; do not have gaps of silence. Speak affirmatively and with a sense of authority.

As an expert, you must be a person who knows more than the prosecutor and the defense lawyer about your topic. If you follow these dicta, you may not always win, but you will never lose your dignity.

Witnessing for Sociology is a richly documented account of personal and professional experiences by those who have been called to serve as expert witnesses. This volume has a breadth of topics and a variety of reactions to testifying in court that go beyond any other collections I have seen. I congratulate the editors and all the contributors.

Acknowledgments

There are several people who deserve recognition for their efforts on behalf of this book. Edmund LaTour and Sheila Meyers helped to clarify legal questions and read and commented on several chapters. Lori Kelly, Barbara Davidson, and Dallas McGlinn assisted in keeping us organized and also read and commented on several chapters. Steve Meinhold worked quickly and efficiently during the final days, using his wizardry with computers and a good editor's eye to bring the project to a successful conclusion. Finally, a special thanks goes to Molly Biehl, who, mature beyond her years, read and commented on final drafts, served as our style editor, and gave us the confidence to bring this project to closure.

1

Old Stories, New Audiences: Sociological Knowledge in Courts

Steve Kroll-Smith and Pamela J. Jenkins

If at one time sociology was like a spacious room off the center hall of the academy, today it looks more like a sagging porch flimsily attached to the main house, struggling to remain standing. Sociology is fighting for its legitimacy. Departments are being scaled back or downsized. Graduate programs are being cut. Most disturbing of all, entire departments are being eliminated. Sociology appears to be losing favor with college and university administrators strapped by shrinking budgets and increasing operating costs.

What are the root causes of sociology's current crisis? Perhaps, it is the eclipse of what Gouldner (1970) called "academic sociology" by new left theories, ethnomethodology, and other nonfunctionalist models of social order. These non-Parsonian theories are, after all, less inclined to address the practical problems of adjusting to a late capitalist welfare state and, therefore, are more easily dispensed with. On the other hand, perhaps it is an unintended consequence of an uncritical positivism that, to paraphrase Collins (1975), encourages keen minds to pursue explanatory exercises that fall well below the levels of genuine intellectual concern, or it might be because of the increasing Balkanization of the discipline itself, expressed in the observation that a sociologist is always "a sociologist of (pick one of dozens of substantive specialties)." No longer guided by core theories and questions, it is difficult for others to visualize just what it is that sociologists do. Finally, a less interesting, but plausible cause of sociology's crisis is the post–Reagan-Thatcher impetus that dissuades students from considering careers that require more than a four-year technical or business degree while promoting a balanced budget at the expense of human welfare projects that, by definition, would invite a sociological point of view.

Sociology's crisis will continue to be debated as it shortens the careers and pinches the pocketbooks of scholars from 4-year state schools to the mandarins of Wisconsin, Chicago, and the Ivy League.

Ironically, as the question "Why sociology?" haunts the corridors of academe, sociology itself is becoming an increasingly authoritative voice in tort, criminal, and civil proceedings. As sociology faces a challenge to its claim to a rightful place in colleges and universities, it seems to us an appropriate moment to consider the work of those sociologists who represent their discipline in courts of law. We do not know how many sociologists in the United States work as expert witnesses or expert consultants in legal cases; the number, however, appears to be increasing. Many sociology departments can now identify one or two faculty members, perhaps more, who represent sociology in legal proceedings as far ranging as nuisance suits, toxic torts, capital sentencing hearings, spousal abuse, or civil rights violations. The term "represent" purposely is used here to denote two interrelated processes. The sociologist who serves as an expert witness speaks *for* the discipline of sociology while also speaking *to* the courts about the relevance of sociology for the legal issues in question.

Courts of law are dramatic public stages where moral and material fortunes depend on the capacity of the actors to tell persuasive stories. For many of the participants in these dramas, including defendants, plaintiffs, judges, juries, and attorneys, sociology is an abstract, perhaps arcane, academic discipline with no particular relevance to the important issues before the court. Medicine, psychology, and engineering, on the other hand, are first among those specialties generally recognized as legitimate areas of expertise. Therefore, when a sociologist appears in court or at some juncture in a legal proceeding, she is afforded an opportunity to speak for the culturally redeeming value of sociology to a generally skeptical public in a high-stakes arena. The soci-ologist is, in short, a witness for the explanatory value of sociology but is obviously doing more than representing the discipline.

A sociologist who gives a deposition, testifies in a legal proceeding, assists in preparing a legal brief, or simply consults on a case fashions, to some degree, the opinions of the courts. Sociological knowledge, albeit some small part of it, becomes a perspective for introducing and interpreting certain facts of a case. If it is true that an increasing number of life circumstances and troubles are now adjudicated, it also is true that an increasing number of sociologists are rendering sociological interpretations that have some bearing on the courts' decisions.

As a growing chorus of sociologists speak in court about the relevance of sociological knowledge, sociology is reaching into a critical arena of social and political life. At stake in court proceedings are such critical human resources as money, housing, social standing, and, at times, life itself. Sociological knowledge that contributes in some measure to the redistribution of money or the civil rights to shelter, that enhances or diminishes social standing or complicates the question of capital punishment has political implications beyond the classroom and the occasional journal article or book. Teaching and publishing will continue to be the mainstays of the discipline, but as the chapters in this book illustrate, sociology is reaching beyond the academy to address a real and increasingly visible politic of contemporary life: the courtroom.

In his recent presidential address to the Mid-South Sociological Association, Standford Lyman observed that the future of sociology depends in part on the capacity of sociologists to "tell better and more plausible stories" (1994:224). We would append to Lyman's sage prediction an additional idea: sociologists not only must tell better and more plausible stories, they also must tell these stories to audiences whose lives are changed, albeit in some small measure, by the narration. Although publishing and teaching are the measures by which we judge ourselves, they no longer may be a sufficient justification for our discipline or any other that purports to interpret the human condition. Thus, the chapters in this book do more than describe the rich and varied experiences of sociologists who serve as expert witnesses; they also are modest reasons for optimism as we anticipate the future of sociology.

UNITY IN DIVERSITY: A SHORT HISTORY OF THE BOOK

In the summer of 1993, we wrote a short article for the American Sociological Association newsletter announcing our intention to create a directory of sociologists who serve as expert witnesses. Included in this announcement was an additional appeal to readers who might be interested in contributing a chapter to an edited book on sociologists as expert witnesses. We received over three dozen enthusiastic responses to the book proposal. Shelving the directory for the moment, we decided to devote our limited time to editing a book.

We had three criteria for selecting chapter contributors. First, we wanted only sociologists. Next, we wanted contributors who had full-time academic appointments; we specifically did not want professional expert witnesses. Finally, we wanted the chapters to represent a broad distribution of legal areas in order to illustrate the wide-ranging role of sociology in the courts. We specifically did not use publication records to select authors. Indeed, we took this opportunity to create some space for the voices of sociologists who work as expert witnesses but do not regularly publish. Thus, there are a range of publishing records represented in these chapters. Contributors were asked to write original chapters that described their personal experiences as expert witnesses and to focus attention on specific ways in which sociological knowledge helped shape or fashion the legal questions at issue. Sociologists rarely are asked to write reflexively, to consider themselves as subjects. This proved difficult at first for a few contributors. With suggestions from the editors and considerable work by the contributors, however, readers can discern a reflexive voice in each chapter.

We encountered an unanticipated problem in pursuit of the reflexive stance, however. Reading through the first drafts, we were struck by the diversity of personal experiences. Narrating personal accounts, we quickly learned, resulted in a wide array of story styles. Some contributors chose to focus on one or two cases, while others discussed many cases. Some authors recounted emotions, describing both the tribulations and satisfactions of expert witnessing; others provided a more detached account of events, preferring to keep emotional matters to themselves; still others mixed the two styles. Our response to these mixes of reflexive voices was admittedly simple, if not preordained: we surrendered to it. Perhaps a reviewer or two will critique the project for its diversity of personal stories. Reflected in this diverse array of first-person accounts, however, is a common theme: the personal recollections of a small group of sociologists on a topic of some importance to their professional careers and, by implication, to the career of the discipline.

A second source of unity is the attention each author pays to the specific uses of sociological knowledge in courts. We asked contributors to consider how sociology constructed a part of the legal drama. Each chapter, therefore, addresses a particular way in which the imagination of sociology becomes confounded with the imagination of the courts. Readers will be struck by the seriousness attributed to sociological knowledge in a wide array of legal proceedings. Several authors suggest how sociological knowledge challenges the knowledge claims of psychology and medicine, complicating questions of causality and guilt. Other contributors illustrate ways in which sociology is helping to define the limits of moral accountability in courts of law. Still others show how sociologists teach the courts the meaning of statistics or surveys, at times lecturing hostile judges or naive attorneys on the rudiments of research. Finally, a number of authors direct attention to the uses of sociology in humanizing a defendant by situating criminal behavior in a life-history narrative that does not forgive but helps to explain such deleterious conduct.

Thus, running through each of these chapters is a reflexive voice narrating accounts of how sociology informs the deliberations of the courts. We take this opportunity to thank the chapter authors for their hard and persistent work to address these two themes.

A brief consideration of laws pertaining to the use of experts and expert evidence sets the stage for a more-extended introduction to the chapters.

FRYE, DAUBERT, AND THE EXPERT WITNESS

Expert witnesses aid juries or judges in finding facts that bear on civil, criminal, and tort matters. An expert is not sought because he has observed events or knows the defendant. It is his skillful ability to identify and interpret circumstances, events, and other occurrences that are beyond the ken of nonexperts that makes him an expert.

As with any courtroom procedure, rules guide the use of experts. Trial judges are the first and sometimes final arbiter in deciding whether or not expert testimony is applicable to a particular case. Their decisions are based on general principles that, on the surface, appear straightforward.

First, for the issue(s) to be understood in the courtroom, testimony is required from someone with specialized knowledge. The general test is whether the subject matter is beyond the understanding of the ordinary person. This test constitutes a threshold standard applied to determine when expert testimony can be admissible (Crocker 1985).

Next, whatever it is that the expert claims to know must pass a test for reliability. The test asks, simply, whether or not knowledge or practice in a particular field is sufficiently developed to evaluate the credibility of the expert's testimony. The reliability standard is met if an expert is able to convince the court that his testimony is derived from generally accepted procedures and concepts in the particular discipline.

The reliability standard was established over 50 years ago in the landmark Supreme Court case, *Frye v. United States* (1923). In 1923, a young black man named James Frye was accused in federal court of murdering a white man. His lawyer offered evidence of a polygraph test accompanied by expert testimony. The testimony and the polygraph results were rejected. The court ruled that the novel, newfangled contraption called a "lie detector" was not generally accepted as an appropriate measure of determining the truth. Hereafter referred to as the rule of general acceptance, expert evidence presented to the court must be based on theories or techniques that have near-unanimous acceptance in an appropriate field (Jasanoff 1989).

Although the *Frye* standard has been popular in many state and federal courts, other jurisdictions have used Rule 702 of the Federal Rules of Evidence (1989), adopted by the U.S. Congress in 1975. It is not acceptance by the scientific community that constitutes the *Frye* test, but whether the testimony will help jurors understand evidence or determine a fact at issue. Judges may exclude the testimony if they determine that it might prejudice, confuse, or mislead the jury. *Frye* and Rule 702, in combination with numerous state rules, created a permissive climate that allowed a wide spectrum of disciplines, professions, and specialties to serve as experts.

It was expected that the debate on expert testimony in courts would subside somewhat with the recent Supreme Court ruling in *Daubert v. Merrell Dow Pharmaceutical* (1993). In this case, parents of two children with limb-reduction birth defects sued the manufacturer of the drug Bendectin, alleging that it caused the defects. In the civil trial, Merrell Dow Pharmaceutical submitted an affidavit from an expert who analyzed 30 published studies that involved 130,000 patients who were treated with Bendectin; he concluded that the drug was not a human teratogen. The plaintiffs did not challenge the use of the defendant's research but offered eight of their own experts, who testified that Bendectin does cause birth defects, based on test-tube and live-animal studies, pharmacological studies, and a reanalysis of previously published epidemiological studies (Orr 1994). However, the major studies cited by the plaintiff's experts were not published in refereed journals and, thus, were subject to challenge by the defense using the general acceptance rule (*Frye*).

The district court granted summary judgment for Merrell Dow, and the Ninth Circuit affirmed, based on *Frye*. At some surprise to the legal community, however, the U.S. Supreme Court granted certiorari to determine the appropriate standard for admission of expert testimony. In other words, the Supreme Court agreed to address the issue of expert testimony for the first time in 70 years.

Amicus briefs, or friend-of-the-court statements, were filed with the Supreme Court from states, individual scientists, and a remarkable diversity of scientific and legal organizations. Many of the national science organizations argued that this was an opportunity for the court to rule on "junk science." The American Association of Science, the National Academy of Sciences, and the American Medical Association supported the position of the defendant, Merrell Dow. Other scientists, who supported the plaintiff, were concerned that scientific testimony must pass a test of consensus or that acceptable scientific results must be published in particular forms to be accepted. Amicus briefs for the plaintiff were provided by a group of scientists including Stephen Jay Gould; the American Society of Law, Medicine and Ethics; and the American Trial Lawyers Association.

The Supreme Court ruled that the *Frye* test was replaced by the Federal Rules of Evidence. Moreover, although the rejection of *Frye* lessened the general acceptability rule, the court stressed that trial judges shall play a crucial role in the admissibility of testimony. The court wrote that judges should be "active gatekeepers" who have a duty to ensure that "any and all scientific testimony or evidence admitted is not only relevant, but reliable" (113 S. Ct., 2795). The court did provide general observations to help federal judges decide whether specific evidence is admissible, including whether the theory or technique has been (and can it be) tested, whether the proposed evidence has been subjected to peer review and publication, what is the potential rate of error for the scientific technique at issue, and whether the methodology enjoys general acceptance in the discipline or has been able to attract minimal support in the community (113 S. Ct., 2796-2797). The *Daubert* ruling was expected to create a more flexible approach toward the admissibility of expert testimony. Surprisingly, however, in a review of the federal cases since *Daubert*, half have excluded expert testimony. Moreover, *Daubert* is being used in state courts to limit expert testimony rather than to expand it. In this conservative climate, *Daubert* may represent the changing face of expert testimony and other changes in tort litigation. In the future, sociologists as expert witnesses may face even more stringent tests of credentials.

In summary, when a sociologist decides to become an expert witness, she faces a rugged and often-uncertain challenge to both her status as an expert and to the relevancy of the expertise. In spite of the difficulties, however, sociologists are influencing the courts by applying the perspectives of sociology to a broad spectrum of legal issues from tort to liability to criminal law. Moreover, each chapter in this volume suggests that allowing the discipline into the courts is not a benign exercise. Sociology's influence on legal proceedings might be likened to the occasional college freshman who allows himself to be affected by an introductory course in sociology. In other words, it expands and complicates the range of issues the freshman customarily attends to, assuring that the world is more bizarre, quixotic, and interesting than common sense would have it.

The next several pages introduce the chapters by identifying four ways in which the stories sociologists tell in court are likely to haunt, if not directly challenge, several of the court's entrenched assumptions regarding defendants, victims, criminal behavior, human losses, and so on.

TELLING OUR OLD STORIES TO NEW AUDIENCES

Narrative is reenchanting the academy. Sociologists and, somewhat surprisingly, biologists and, perhaps less surprisingly, physicists (Riessman 1993; Gould 1977; Feyerband 1975) are increasingly referring to their work as story telling, couching their learned conclusions in chronicles intended to illuminate the reader. Joining what some might call the "narrative turn" in the human sciences, we are encouraged to consider the sociologist who serves as an expert witness a storyteller. Like Levi Strauss' bricoluer, the sociologist as expert weaves together a method, a concept, and an interpretation to tell sociological stories about defendants and plaintiffs, environments, religious practices, and pornography, about safe and dangerous locations, and so on to the often skeptical audiences of the courts.

With some exceptions, of course, most sociological stories are told to sociologists. Over time, story telling among confederates assumes the character of ritual, where each participant in the telling knows the story and waits with assurance for the next development. It is not new knowledge that is passed among confederates during a story ceremony but a generally affirming feeling that they are all in this together.

Talking about a research project in a two o'clock session at a regional meeting attended by five or six sociologists sprinkled about a room with 50 chairs, however, is considerably different than explaining and defending sociological knowledge in depositions and trials. Both are story-telling events, to be sure, but one story is told to confederates, insiders who often can anticipate at least the plot sequence, if not the denouement, while the second story is told to an array of audiences, many of whom know very little about sociology.

Moreover, the stakes in the outcomes of the two expressive events are not commensurate. Telling a sociological story to sociologists is, to be sure, risky for the storyteller but is routinely experienced by the audience as at least a benign, if not a tedious, event. Sociologists who tell their stories in legal proceedings, on the other hand, face audiences that are both sympathetic and hostile and not unaffected by the tale. The emotional responses to sociological stories told in court is explained in some measure by the simple idea that degree of attention and affect are likely to increase proportionately to the perception that the stories being told will bear in some measure on the redistribution of important life resources. Such a perception, we dare say, is noticeably absent in a two o'clock paper session at a regional meeting.

The fact that sociological stories are told in courts at all invites comment. Indeed, it could be argued that sociological knowledge is not particularly suitable for the design of the court. Sociological stories routinely complicate the romantically elegant notions that there is a right and a wrong, a good and bad, or an innocent and a guilty party. In this romantic world, the courts reward heroes and punish villains, wrongs are redressed, and the moral order, thrown askew by wayward deeds, is regularly made straight. It is true that this idyllic view does not represent the typical experiences of, say, an overworked, underpaid, and burned out public defender. Nevertheless, at the very least, it expresses the hopes of those whose destinies in some fashion are dependent upon legal proceedings. The truth be known, the frustrations of public defenders probably stem in no small measure from the disjuncture between their vision of the law and their intimate observations of its day-to-day practice.

Belief in an "American legal romanticism," a term borrowed from Robin West (1985:161), is more easily sustained when evidence in courts is limited to the paradigmatic assumptions of medicine, psychology, or engineering, for example, that focus attention on physical systems or individuals and not on abstract, nebulous things like social stratification, attitude distributions, social role, life history, alienation, and so on. There is a certain fit between the tendencies of the courts to think in the polarized logic of innocent or guilty, liable or nonliable, coerced or volunteered, drunk or sober, and so on and the hard, obdurate evidence of bridges, engines, sobriety tests, deoxyribonucleic acid strands, or personality indexes.

Each chapter in this book suggests that sociology complicates the romantic notion that truth is just a fact away from being established. Truth, these chapters remind us, is usually quite messy, confounded by histories, surveys, critical assessments of literatures, scaler method-ology, and sustained arguments with the reductionist assumptions of medicine and psychology. Sociology enlarges appreciably the traditional range of concerns a court must consider to reach a just decision. Its maddening premise that every way of seeing is also a way of not seeing challenges the court to expand its deliberations to include the more abstract but no less real concerns of a sociological imagination.

We identified four story lines in these chapters that represent how sociology is challenging courts to consider an appreciably more com-plicated vision of human behavior and, in turn, a more complicated vision of punishment, liability, moral accountability, and so on. These stories include the numbers game, humanizing the defendant, a benign satire of entrenched knowledge, and expanding the court's traditional boundaries of moral accountability. Although these narratives are not assumed to be inclusive of the ways sociology challenges the courts, we encourage their inclusion in future discussions of sociology's influence on judges and juries charged with a fair and impartial assessment of the "facts."

THE NUMBERS GAME

Sociological knowledge chides the specificity of the law through its most frustrating sleight of hand: statistics. From "split-half reliability" and "Latin-square design" to "halo effects" and "recursive modeling," statistics rests on a foundation of peculiar, if not bizarre, terms. String-ing strange term after stranger term, however, does not result in defini-tive answers. Statistical answers are always contingent. Resting on the uncertain foundation of probability, statistical stories explain by elimination. They seem more interested in what does not explain observed differences than in what does. Not surprisingly, sociologists who wield the statistical stick often face a skeptical and hostile courtroom.

A sociologist works for defense attorneys to design and supervise community surveys to determine local citizen awareness and opinions of defendants accused of committing notorious murders (Jacoby, Chapter 2 in this volume). Popular knowledge of a well-publicized murder often creates a prejudicial climate that makes it difficult to impanel a fair and impartial jury. Use of inferential statistics to demonstrate bias among potential jurors often is challenged by judges and opposing counsel, who question the logic of the representative sample. After all, it is argued, a part is not a whole. It is not reasonable to interview all potential jurors, however. Therefore, a sociologist tries to convince a skeptical judge and an argumentative state's attorney that justice in this case begins with accepting an apparent statistical sleight of hand.

Another sociologist, working for several plaintiffs who are alleging job discrimination, designs a statistical study that eliminates differences in reliability, punctuality, and skills as causes of unequal treatment by an employer (Feinberg, Chapter 3 in this volume). Devising a modified sign test for the regression coefficients for race in each month the discrimination allegedly occurred, he concludes that race remains a critical factor in accounting for the unfair treatment. In this fashion, sociological knowledge probes behind the apparent "facts" of a case to construct a morality play symbolized in ordinary least squares equations.

HUMANIZE A DEFENDANT

Blueprints, test scores, determinations of a body's unique chemistry, and accounts of a person's character measured by standardized questionnaires share at least one common feature: the unit of concern or focus of attention is so defined as to eliminate, or, at best, obscure, the social and cultural backgrounds, settings, and forces that shape events and circumstances. The Manichean morality of criminal, tort, and civil law encourages a focus on the smallest, most exclusive act or event. It is far easier to find light and dark (good and bad) by considering only simple, basic human acts, not the increasingly inclusive, more complicated set of circumstances and "facts" within which a single behavior or occurrence is inevitably situated. The momentum of sociological knowledge, however, is from a discrete act to a more inclusive, more abstract interpretation. In the hands of a skilled sociologist, a defendant, even a convicted murderer, can be fashioned into a human being with virtues and vices and a biography not unlike our own.

To obtain the death penalty after a capital murder conviction, for example, the prosecution will argue vehemently against introducing testimony that locates the defendant in a social milieu that in some small measure explains his or her conduct. The goal of the prosecution is to keep the court focused on the discrete act of murder, but a murderer, as any social scientist will acknowledge, is also someone's son, perhaps a brother, father, husband, employee, rural or urban dweller, and so on — in short, a typical person, often similar to members of the jury. A sociologist who represents defendants convicted of first-degree murder pleads for life rather than death by carefully reconstructing life histories that locate these single horrendous acts in complicated webs of social and cultural influences (Forsyth, Chapter 4 in this volume).

Sociologists do not necessarily look at situations or evidence of which the courts are unaware, but they do look at them in a different way. Recalling the image of the Russian nesting doll, sociology begins with an assumption that a solitary act is more adequately accounted for by nesting it in increasingly broad and more complicated social and cultural patterns. If a criminal lawyer's task is either to match the facts of a case with a law or to argue that a particular law does not apply to certain facts, the sociologist might be just as interested to know what laws the accused is following when he or she behaves in an allegedly criminal manner. Ignorance of a law, of course, is not a legal excuse for breaking it, but one sociologist argues persuasively that knowing a defendant struggles with reconciling one culture's laws with those of another does challenge the court to recognize the all too human experience of living betwixt and between codes of conduct (Steinhoff, Chapter 5 in this volume). Finally, a sociologist expands the identity of a battered woman who kills to include her past history of abusive relationships, and her struggles to carve out a sense of self-efficacy in a violent world and to achieve some closure on a way of life that traps her in a chronic state of danger (Jenkins, Chapter 6 in this volume).

BENIGN SATIRE OF ENTRENCHED KNOWLEDGE

Sociology does more than dare courts to think about equity and fairness in the logic of distributions and probabilities; it also challenges many of the assumptions of psychology and medicine that have become, over time, entrenched truths in courts of law. In its inclination to assume that "things are not what they seem" (Berger 1963:23), sociology challenges the often utilized wisdom of the courts, engaging in what we might call a benign satire of entrenched knowledge. The word "benign" is used here to signal the motive of the sociologist serving as an expert witness. The intention is not to lampoon the court, chiding it for failing to consider a more complex rendering of the "facts" of a case; this trope is likely to be reserved for colleagues and graduate students. The purpose, rather, is to represent sociology to the court as a mode of thought suitable for making sense of a type of behavior, act, or event. In so doing, however, the sociologist trespasses, albeit often unintentionally, on many of the commonsense assumptions of courts and society.

Consider a sociologist who tenaciously rebukes the claims of psychologists (and at least one sociologist) that new religions use brainwashing to attract young adults to their organizations (Richardson, Chapter 7 in this volume). Based on his own research and assessment of the literature, he concludes that young people voluntarily join new faiths, participate for a while, and routinely drop out. This sociologist participated in writing several amicus briefs to, among other judicial venues, the United States Supreme Court, making a case for the nonscientific basis of brainwashing claims.

Exclusive reliance on medical models of chemical dependency is contested in court by a sociologist who argues persuasively for complicating the issues of volition and individual responsibility by nesting drug or alcohol abuse in social and cultural fields (Kinsey, Chapter 8 in this volume). Loss of control, for example, from drug or alcohol use is shown to be closely related to cultural expectations regarding the effects of substances on the body. Drinking norms, often coded in specialized argots, are shown to not only represent behavior but also, in part, determine it. In this fashion, sociology joins physiology to culture to tell a story about substance abuse that ensnares courts in tangled webs of causality that highlight the limitations of the biomedical model.

Finally, a sociologist challenges the courts to develop more sophisticated criteria for gang membership by demonstrating the limitations of a police science model based on naive and unreliable indicators. This same sociologist also disputes the psychological bias of a key concept used to defend women who act violently toward their partners (Bowker, Chapter 9 in this volume). "Battered woman syndrome" (BWS) is a gendered variant of learned helplessness, an acquired incapacity to act effectively when faced with important life troubles. A key problem with BWS, however, is that many women who are abused and arrested for killing or wounding their partners do not necessarily appear helpless. Moreover, to be officially labeled as suffering from BWS is to risk being judged an unfit mother and to lose the right to parent. Embedding BWS in a sociological field focuses attention on severity and levels of abuse (physical, psychological, economic, social, and sexual) and indicators of the interaction patterns between the abused, her abuser, and other immediate social relationships. From a sociological perspective, a battered woman may be quite active, developing strategies to avoid violence while seeking assistance and advice from others. Her violence may be an extreme form of coping that expresses a momentary lapse from other, more benign, strategies of self-protection.

EXPANDING THE COURT'S TRADITIONAL BOUNDARIES OF MORAL ACCOUNTABILITY

If sociological knowledge in courts often ignites debates with medicine and psychology, thawing out a few of the hardened assumptions of body-mind narratives, it also, in the hands of some experts, expands the court's relatively narrow boundaries of moral accountability.

Working on premise liability cases, for example, two sociologists developed and regularly use a "crime foreseeability model" that accounts for a complicated array of variables in determining degree of responsibility in cases where a person is attacked or injured on a specific site (Voigt and Thornton, Chapter 10 in this volume). Their system level analysis combines industry standards of security, profiles of offender and victim, and demographic features of the surrounding area, among several other variables, to complicate considerably the court's assessment of the relative degree of negligence.

If a prosecutor seeks an obscenity conviction based on belief that the public's standards of decency are jeopardized by a film or magazine, a sociologist might determine through a survey of adult attitudes regarding pornography that the local public finds the suspect materials morally acceptable and the state's charge groundless (Holley, Chapter 11 in this volume). An environmental sociologist, on the other hand, argues persuasively that victims of toxic contamination are threatened by more than the presence of toxins in their local biospheres (Picou, Chapter 12 in this volume). Expanding the legal limits of compensable loss into the more nebulous areas of diminution of neighborhood life, separation from significant cultural traditions, and diminished self-esteem, sociology is making it more costly to pollute human habitats.

Housing is another arena where sociology is contributing to an expansion of the court's traditionally narrow range of moral accountability (Silver, Fischbach, and Kaye, Chapter 13 in this volume). With no constitutional right to housing, Americans in increasing numbers are finding themselves homeless. Building shelters to house the homeless typically is resisted by communities, who fear a surge of crime and loss of property values. Residents of one neighborhood in a conservative New England city protested the city's plan to build a modest shelter in their area. Citing a version of the domino theory, that is, one shelter would be followed by others until the neighborhood was a collage of homeless, prostitutes, and unkept public housing, a citizen's group sought to dissuade the city from building the proposed housing. Working closely with two attorneys, a sociologist gathered sufficient statistical data to document discriminatory intent and offered an opinion on the importance of these data based on her familiarity with social science literature on race relations. She, thus, argued that the conflict was not over differences in the changing use of urban land but over an expression of racial discrimination. As a consequence of her testimony, the court permitted the case to be heard as a violation of the federal Fair Housing Act, which makes it illegal to act in a manner that effectively results in housing discrimination based on race, sex, ethnicity, and so on.

SOME CONCLUDING REMARKS

Sociological knowledge complicates the goal of the courts by making it more difficult to reach a decision or verdict. Telling stories that humanize defendants, challenging the physical and individual reductionism peculiar to medicine and psychology, expanding the limits of moral accountability, or, finally, using statistics to reveal patterns of inequity that likely would remain invisible in the absence of probabilities is to invite the court to reconsider its typical modes of reasoning. When a sociologist asks the court to revisit its typical strategies for interpreting human behavior or the contextual circumstances of events, sociological knowledge is momentarily transformed into an ethical appeal to refashion the limits of liability, accountability, motive, and so on.

John Rawls might argue that sociological knowledge pushes justice in the direction of greater fairness, if to be fair necessarily entails treating all sides alike (1971). If justice ultimately is based on impartial judgments of the "facts" of a case, then what "facts" get introduced is itself a moral deliberation on the limits of fairness. Limiting the "facts" of a case to an act, to its physical and, perhaps, psychological representations, is likely to make it easier to reach a verdict. Introducing sociological knowledge in a court of law, however, is likely to increase the range of plausible explanations and perspectives, expanding the opportunity for more fairness while making it more difficult to reach a decision. It is the capacity of sociological knowledge to frustrate the court's traditionally less complicated modes of moral reasoning that prompted a judge to remark during a television interview regarding the O. J. Simpson murder trial, "We can't be social scientists and get our work done."

If sociological knowledge stretches the limits of fairness by encouraging the courts to mull over elaborately interconnected and abstract "facts," it is worth considering how courts should address the problem of priority in determining what is fair. After all, not all "facts" are equal. To know that a defendant was battered as a child and as an adult abused drugs after several failed attempts to find work is plausibly of less importance than the fact that he murdered his wife, but "knowing" the defendant in this more complicated fashion may save his life, an accomplishment some people would view as less than just. Thus, what weight should courts give to sociological observations and conclusions? Society will ask and answer this question in the years to come. We only can observe that, at this juncture in time, sociological knowledge is an increasing part of the court's deliberations.

REFERENCES

Berger, P. L. 1963. *Invitation to Sociology*. New York: Doubleday.

Collins, R. 1975. *Conflict Sociology*. New York: Academic Press.

Crocker, P. L. 1985. The Meaning of Equality for Battered Women Who Kill Men in Self-Defense. *Harvard Women's Law Review, 8*, 121–153.

Federal Rules of Evidence for United States Courts and Magistrates. (1989) St. Paul, MN: West.

Feyerband, P. 1975. *Against Method*. London: NLB Press.

Gould, S. J. 1977. Eternal Metaphors of Paleontology. In A. Hallam (Ed.), *Patterns of Evolution as Illustrated by the Fossil Record* (pp. 1–26). Amsterdam: Elsevier.

Gouldner, A. W. 1970. *The Coming Crisis in Western Sociology*. New York: Basic Books.

Jasanoff, S. 1989. Science on the Witness Stand. *Issues in Science and Technology, 6*(1), 80–87.

Lyman, S. M. 1994. The Bequests of 20th Century Sociology to the 21st Century. *Sociological Spectrum*, *15*, 209–225.

Orr, J. A. 1994. Electromagnetic Field Litigation: The Use and Abuse of Scientific Evidence. National Rural Electric Cooperative Association, G&T Legal Seminar, November 10–11.

Riessman, C. K. 1993. *Narrative Analysis*. Newbury Park, CA: Sage.

Rawls, J. 1971. *A Theory of Justice*. Cambridge: Harvard University Press.

West, R. 1985. Jurisprudence As Narrative: An Aesthetic Analysis of Modern Legal Theory. *New York University Law Review*, *60*(2), 145–211.

CASES CITED

Daubert v. Merrell Dow Pharmaceutical, 113 S. Ct. 2786 (1993).

Frye v. United States, 293 F.1013,1014 (D.C. Circuit 1923).

I

THE NUMBERS GAME

2

"We Don't Deal in Probabilities Here": Tales of a Quantitative Sociologist in Court

Joseph E. Jacoby

Though I am an academic sociologist, I have served as a consultant and expert witness, working with attorneys in Pennsylvania, South Carolina, and Ohio intermittently over a 15-year period. On several of these occasions, I have designed and supervised community surveys commissioned by attorneys representing defendants accused of committing notorious murders for which they could have received the death penalty.

In the small communities where these crimes were committed, the local print and broadcast media had covered the crimes extensively. In each of these cases, defense attorneys believed that pretrial publicity had been so extensive that a fair and impartial jury could not be selected in the jurisdiction where the crime occurred. The attorneys, therefore, sought a change of venue to another county where the publicity about the case had not been so extensive.

My role in each of these cases was to design and conduct a survey of public knowledge and opinion about the case. Questions were included in the survey to determine whether respondents knew details about the crime, had discussed the crime with other people, knew the victim and offender personally, had drawn conclusions about the guilt of the defendant, had determined the appropriate penalty that should be imposed if the defendant were convicted, and had fixed opinions about the use of the death penalty in murder cases generally. I then analyzed the results of the survey and testified about it in a pre-trial hearing.

My courtroom testimony, covering three issues, usually took several hours. I first described the survey (i.e., sample selection, questionnaire construction, interviewer training, and interview procedures). Second, I presented my analysis of responses to the questions. Finally, I testified to my conclusions about the implications of the analysis for the possibility that an impartial jury could be selected. My testimony then was offered by the defense as evidence that pre-trial publicity had promoted such widespread knowledge and opinions in the jurisdiction where the crime occurred that impaneling a fair and impartial jury in that location would be impossible.

Drawing from my experience in working with attorneys, conducting community surveys for them, and testifying as an expert witness, I will explain how the perspective and methods of quantitative sociology diverge from the perspective and methods of the law. The most serious obstacle to bringing sociology into the courtroom is the stark difference between sociologists and lawyers in their orientations toward individuals and groups. Drawing on the language of the market, I would characterize the difference between sociological knowledge and legal knowledge as the difference between wholesale and retail.

Sociology's concerns are "wholesale." When conducting a survey of public opinion, for example, the sociologist tries to answer the question, "What is the pattern of opinions, generally?" The possibility that some people may misrepresent their opinions does not defeat the sociologist's efforts to uncover the underlying pattern of opinions, because the sociologist has strategies for dealing with outliers and estimating the direction and magnitude of misrepresentation. These strategies are based on well-established principles of data analysis and interpretation. They yield results that, to a sociologist, are "reliable" and "valid."

When lawyers use the adjective "reliable," they typically are describing a witness who consistently gives testimony that supports their arguments. In contrast to the sociologist's concern about the general pattern of public opinion, the lawyer asks, "What did a specific person know?" I, therefore, characterize lawyers' concerns as "retail," to signify their focus on the individual.

Consider an example of the differences in perspectives between sociologists and lawyers. There is substantial and unrefuted social science evidence that defendants convicted of killing white victims are significantly more likely to be sentenced to death than are defendants convicted of killing nonwhite victims (for a review of the research, see Nakell and Hardy 1987). Social scientists generally conclude from this evidence that the application of the death penalty is unjustly biased against murderers of whites.

The current legal treatment of allegations of racial bias, however, ignores this evidence. Under current law, a successful demonstration of bias requires showing that a particular defendant was sentenced to death because that defendant's particular murder victim was white (*McClesky v. Zant* 1984). To determine whether bias exists, under such a standard, sociologists would have to expose the motivation of the particular prosecutors, judges, and jurors who made decisions that culminated in the death penalty for a particular defendant, an exercise closer to psychology than to sociology.

Although such an exploration is logically possible, it would be extremely difficult to carry out for two reasons. First, legal actors who acted in a biased fashion would be unwilling to acknowledge that racial bias entered into their decisions. Second, people whose decisions are racially biased may not even be aware they are acting on their biases. Even if they were to answer questions about their decisions "honestly," their answers would not reflect their biases accurately. One of the strengths of sociology's survey methodology is its ability to expose generalized patterns of behavior, such as biased decision making, even though the actors involved are unaware they are engaging in such behavior.

In this chapter, I present a series of experiences that exemplify the difficulties for sociologist expert witnesses created by the "wholesale" versus "retail" perspectives of sociology and law. If the whole is, in fact, greater than the sum of its parts, the possibility of reaching a just decision on the fate of an individual may depend on courts acknowledging the existence of abstract social patterns that affect situated outcomes. All the quotations included herein are taken verbatim from transcripts of actual legal proceedings.

CREATING AN EXPERT WITNESS

My first exposure to the role of expert witness occurred when I was a graduate student. I sat enthralled while my mentor, Marvin Wolfgang, described his presentation of some of the very first criminological evidence offered before the federal appellate courts. Wolfgang and his colleagues persuaded the courts to declare the death penalty for rape unconstitutional (*Maxwell v. Bishop*) because it had been applied in a racially discriminatory manner. Similarly, in *Gregory v. Litton Systems, Inc.*, they persuaded the courts to prohibit the use of arrest records (where there were no convictions) to deny employment to black job applicants, because blacks were more likely to be arrested despite the absence of evidence that they were more often involved in crime (Wolfgang 1974). As Wolfgang described it to his students, consulting involved working with highly skilled attorneys on dramatic cases in which criminological data persuaded the courts to issue decisions that substantially improved the quality of justice.

My first reactions to being asked to work as a criminological expert witness were ambivalent — excitement at the prospect of being involved in a real capital case, tempered by humility. I was not, after all, Wolfgang; I lacked his erudition, his experience, and his reputation. However, I also recognized that no one else was going to do the work if I refused.

The attorney undoubtedly would have preferred to engage the services of Wolfgang or someone of similar stature. His problem was that there was no money to hire experts. The defendant was indigent, and South Carolina law provided a maximum of $2,000 to court-appointed attorneys representing indigent defendants in capital cases. No money was available for consulting of the sort I could provide.

Most people accused of capital crimes are (or quickly become) indigent, so they have no access to high-powered lawyers or experts. Giannelli, following a discussion about contingent fees (i.e., compensating experts only if their clients win in court), states: "Those familiar with criminal prosecutions might be bemused about the discussion of the contingent fee issue — not because they favor such fees, but because obtaining the services of *any* defense expert in criminal litigation is so difficult" (1993: 188). I was "selected" because I was at least minimally qualified, willing to work for free, and available on short notice.

Most of my consulting work is done without financial compensation (which turns out to be both an advantage and a burden to the defense, as I discuss later). The high-powered consulting work I was told about in graduate school was financed by the National Association for the Advancement of Colored People Legal Defense and Education Fund and led by some of the best lawyers and criminologists in the world. Though I work, at times, with fine attorneys, I probably will never enjoy the resources to do large-scale, definitive research on criminal cases. My experience may be as instructive as Wolfgang's, however, because it represents the more common circumstance of sociologists who work with defense attorneys representing indigent clients: we work for free, on short deadlines, and use strategies that challenge the legal process only as it applies to one defendant.

"DID YOU ACTUALLY DO ALL THESE INTERVIEWS?" — SCIENTIFIC VERSUS LEGAL STANDARDS OF RELIABILITY

The sociologist who enters the legal arena must contend with questions and concerns that are irrelevant to good sociological research. In fact, at times, we are confronted by legal logic that makes it impossible simultaneously to do good science and provide legally persuasive evidence. One example of the difference in emphasis between law and sociology is the former's exclusion of data obtained from secondhand sources and the sociologist's dependence on such sources.

The courts generally prohibit the introduction of hearsay evidence (secondhand information, not experienced directly by the person testifying). Sociologists, in direct contrast, customarily depend on data gathered by other people. We routinely employ assistants to carry out surveys and subcontract for surveys to be completed by interviewers whom we do not even know. Our capacity to conduct large-scale surveys is dependent largely on our access to such assistance. The results of any survey conducted by people other than the sociologist testifying may, however, be characterized in court as "hearsay."

In attempts to discredit my testimony and have it excluded from the legal record, opposing attorneys will ask me whether I personally conduct every telephone interview. When I reply that I do not personally call every respondent, they ask me if I can be sure the answers I report to the court are actually the answers given by the respondents. Of course, I am unable to assert that I hear every question asked by every interviewer and every response given by every respondent. Opposing attorneys then attack as hearsay my testimony about the surveys I design, supervise, and analyze.

Sometimes, opposing attorneys do not have to work very hard because the judge attacks my work for them. The following verbatim exchange is from a pre-trial hearing where I was to testify about the results of a community survey. I made a tape recording of the training session I conducted for the interviewers, and before leading me through a description of the survey, the defense attorney was offering this recording as evidence of the training when the judge cut him off:

DEFENSE ATTORNEY: The next exhibit is a cassette player which includes the orientation . . .

JUDGE: What are you talking about? Orientation? You didn't do this survey?

DEFENSE ATTORNEY: No, sir. This will be explained in just a moment. It was done by a survey team.

JUDGE: If he didn't do it, I don't see how he is going to testify about it.

DEFENSE ATTORNEY: We will be getting into that. It was done by 17 different people.

JUDGE: Where are they?

DEFENSE ATTORNEY: Some of them are present here. We have a list of everybody that was involved in it.

JUDGE: You don't know whether they complied with them [the instructions given the interviewers] or not, or do you?

JACOBY: I do have an idea of whether they complied or not.

JUDGE: Not an idea, sir. I want to know, do you know whether they complied fully with this?

JACOBY: Yes, I do, Your Honor.

JUDGE: How do you know that?

JACOBY: If you will allow me to develop the description.

JUDGE: I want to know how you know that.

JACOBY: I feel as though you will be satisfied, Your Honor, that we did do this in a rigorous manner.

JUDGE: I'm not trying to mix you up; I'm not trying to mess you up, but I have to hear testimony that's based on knowledge, not belief or feelings. I'm asking you first, and I'm going to hear the rest of it, but I want to know; I want an answer to it; do you know of your own knowledge whether these questions and all were followed out to your instructions?

JACOBY: Yes, I do.

JUDGE: How do you know that?

JACOBY: I know that as a result of both training the people . . .

JUDGE: Thank you. That's all right.

Survey researchers are highly dependent on the work of other people; we cannot supervise their work closely enough, however, to be able to claim we "know for a fact" the answers we report are the ones actually given by the respondents to our interviewers. As a consequence, most survey research evidence is vulnerable to challenges in this form.

As scientists, we depend implicitly on the integrity of our colleagues. Although we feel free to accuse another scientist's technical judgment (for using the wrong statistical test, for example), only on rare occasions would we challenge a colleague's honesty. When we use the term "reliability," we are referring not to the intellectual integrity of a scholarly work but to the replicability of a finding when the same methods are used on different samples. In the legal context, however, challenges to the integrity of witnesses are standard practice. Thus, when we enter the courtroom, we are confronted by challenges to our integrity that are difficult to fend off with standard technical explanations.

Opposing attorneys, in their attempts to discredit the testimony of survey researchers, are likely to express their disdain for such evidence. In one case in which I conducted a survey, the prosecutor claimed that my testimony was "double hearsay," because the responses I reported neither were my own opinions nor had I actually heard them expressed by the respondents.

PROSECUTOR: Thus, your Honor, the items that we are talking about here and the contents of this alleged survey are clearly hearsay, and not only hearsay one time, but apparently hearsay twice, double hearsay. A statement made by an alleged registered voter to an interviewer is hearsay once, if that person were here to testify. That person is not here. It's hearsay yet a second time from what the interviewer told this particular witness, your Honor.

The sociologist conducting a survey may be inclined to defend himself against this anticipated line of attack by the prosecutor. A defensive strategy that mimics police procedures by scrupulously maintaining the chain of evidence can backfire, however. Survey researchers nearly always promise confidentiality to informants, despite the lamentable fact that such promises of confidentiality are not backed by statute or case law. Courts may issue subpoenas demanding all records related to the research (I have received such a subpoena). In responding to the subpoena, the researcher who has kept records identifying respondents may be forced to reveal their identity (see Picou, Chapter 12 in this volume).

Evans and Scott (1983:197) warn against preserving records that could compromise the identity of informants who were promised confidentiality. A researcher who follows their advice to destroy some research records, however, would be unable to provide a complete documentary history of the research. I might be accused of making my case too strongly; after all, the courts recognize that special circumstances, including standard professional practices, may sometimes override the hearsay evidence rule. The Federal Rules of Evidence (803 and 804) specifically provide for the admissibility of "polls," so it is possible to get the results of social surveys admitted into evidence (*Federal Rules Decisions* 1960:425–431; Federal Judicial Center 1982:Section 2.71,I). The hearsay characterization, by itself, should not be successful in having these results excluded from evidence. The accusation that sociological evidence is hearsay may, nevertheless, diminish its credibility.

Although sociologists who enter the courtroom would anticipate being attacked by opposing attorneys, they might be surprised by the more subtle and potentially more serious problems they encounter in dealing with the attorneys who employ them.

"JUST GIVE ME THE BOTTOM LINE, AND KEEP IT SIMPLE" — RELATIONS BETWEEN SOCIOLOGISTS AND ATTORNEY AND CLIENTS

A sociologist is a scientist with primary allegiance to the truth as revealed through the scientific method; an attorney is an advocate with primary allegiance to a client. These differences in allegiance create real tensions when a lawyer engages a sociologist to conduct research on an issue that has implications for the interests of the lawyer's client. How sociologists resolve the tension has potentially far-reaching consequences, both for an immediate case and for all subsequent expert witness work they may do.

One of the sources of tension between expert witnesses and the lawyers who commission our work is just how closely we should work together. Sociologists writing on this issue typically urge close communication between attorneys and consultants (Evans and Scott 1983). A major source of the credibility of the expert in court, however, is his/her proclaimed allegiance only to a truth, as revealed through science. Excessively close consultation may jeopardize the expert's claim to independence and neutrality. On the other hand, failure to work sufficiently closely may produce misunderstandings that can lead to errors in research design.

As an example of an unsatisfactory resolution of this tension, I once designed a survey for an attorney who wanted me to be the sole author of the survey instrument. He specifically refused to proofread a draft of my questionnaire before I fielded it, so that I would be able to testify to my independence from his influence. One of the multiple-choice questions I included in the interview schedule offered respondents a punishment option that was not available under state law in the jurisdiction of the study. Had my attorney and client been willing to review the interview schedule before it was fielded, he probably would have caught my error. The opposing attorney caught the error and used it in his attempt to discredit the survey.

Lawyers bring scientists into legal conflicts to provide evidence that supports their cases. Social scientists, at best, have relevant data — information subject to many interpretations. Communicating what we can, and cannot, offer is part of our responsibility. "The expert witness must also 'coach' and familiarize the attorneys with the methods of social science research so that they may adequately lay a foundation and pose relevant questions for the expert witness in court" (Evans and Scott 1983:190).

We must educate lawyer clients about the strengths and limitations of sociological analysis. This is sometimes a difficult task, Wolfgang's experience notwithstanding:

With respect to my experience on the witness stand in the *Maxwell* trial, I can honestly say that I never felt frustrated. I was well directed under direct examination, and well prepared beforehand by the very capable lawyers of the Legal Defense Fund. . . . I never had to respond in a simple yes-or-no style. Moreover because of the appreciation and understanding of the role of the social scientist by the Legal Defense Fund lawyers, I never felt that I had to suppress, mute, or otherwise distort any of my findings or any of the scientific inquiry that led to the evidence I ultimately presented. (1974:244–245)

My experience has been that lawyers generally do not want us to educate them about the intricacies of social science and, certainly, about its limitations. They want us to make categorical statements about the meaning of our data, to answer "ultimate questions" with "yes or no" answers favorable to their clients. We can seldom accommodate, in good faith, their need for a categorical response.

The community surveys I conduct typically show widespread knowledge about the cases under consideration for a change of venue. There always are some respondents who profess no knowledge or opinion about a given case. The proportion of people who are acceptable jurors may be small. When I project the results from my sample to the larger population of all people eligible to serve on a jury, the number of acceptable jurors always exceeds 12 (the size of a petit jury). I never conclude that it would be impossible to find 12 people who could serve on the jury.

Defense attorneys who commission my work typically want me to draw a categorical conclusion from my data — that it would be impossible under the conditions documented by my study to impanel a fair and impartial jury. The best that I can do is to state in probabilistic terms the difficulty of obtaining such a panel (e.g., "___ percent of respondents know about the case, ___ percent have drawn conclusions about the guilt of the defendant, and ___ percent have an opinion about the appropriate punishment"). The strongest qualitative characterization I can offer — "It would be *very difficult* to find people who both knew little about the case and had not drawn conclusions about the guilt of the defendant or the appropriate punishment" — falls short of the categorical conclusion desired by the defense attorney.

Because I never conclude that it would be impossible to select a fair and impartial jury, I refuse to say so. This issue creates the most strain in my relations with attorneys. In our prehearing preparations, they ask me what I would say on the stand regarding whether it would be possible to select a fair and impartial jury. I tell them the type of answer I could give, which never satisfies them. Despite these exchanges before the hearing, attorneys always ask during the hearing for my conclusion on the ultimate question and, predictably, are never completely satisfied by my answer.

Another source of pressure is the belief or the wish on the part of the attorney that we have definitive knowledge to bring to bear on a case. Unaccustomed to such blandishments, we are highly vulnerable to developing a bloated perception of our own importance and knowledge. We are susceptible to being manipulated into giving testimony that cannot be supported by our data. The consequences of ego-driven overgeneralization are potentially disastrous for the both the client and the sociologist. A sociologist who generalizes beyond the data in just one case risks destroying the credibility of all the testimony she gives in that case and all subsequent cases in which she testifies.

"TEN DAYS IS NOT MUCH TIME TO DO A SURVEY, IS IT?" — CROSS EXAMINATION

We sociologists defend our research methods and theories as a matter of course. We recognize that works of science always can be improved upon and accept as inevitable that some present or future scientist will find flaws in our work and improve upon it. When we are criticizing the work of other sociologists, we generally restrict our criticism to their scientific theories and methods. Seldom do questions of intellectual honesty arise in the scholarly arena.

We are, therefore, not accustomed to public attack on our intellectual honesty and motives, but that is precisely the type of attack we experience in the courtroom. Sociologists who present expert witness testimony are subject to the same ad hominem attacks as all other witnesses. To persuade a court to accept our scientific evidence, we also must persuade the court of our general integrity and the purity of our motives.

In my experience, opposing attorneys generally do not call in other sociologists to challenge our work by conducting parallel work. Our research methods seldom are subject to serious critique. Rather, attorneys attack our credentials, our motives, and conceptually insignificant aspects of our research.

> No statistical expert witness was ever offered to contradict this evidence. Nor has any statistician, social scientist, or criminologist ever been offered by opposing advocates to contradict or reinterpret my research data. Thus, instead of being asked questions directly related to the scientific limitations of the research, I was asked a series of questions that, from my perspective, had no relationship to the thrust of the inquiry, or to the reliability or validity of the findings. (Wolfgang 1974:244)

If opposing counsel is successful in this line of attack, even the most carefully done scientific study will be discredited.

In the scientific arena, universal recognition of the virtual inevitability of error creates a climate of tolerance for the scientist who makes a mistake. Moreover, our mistakes and approximations usually do not fatally undermine our findings (e.g., we consider regression assumptions to be "robust," so we are willing to accept the results of regression analyses even if the data fail to meet the assumptions underlying the linear regression model).

In the courtroom, in contrast, there is zero tolerance for error. A witness who is caught making any sort of error may find all of his/her testimony discredited. In the context of a long and detailed questionnaire, I included for one question a punishment response option that was not available under the current law. The purpose of asking the question was to determine whether respondents had come to a conclusion on the appropriate punishment, should the defendant be convicted. To answer this underlying question, it made no difference, conceptually, which punishments respondents chose.

Because the error had no conceptual bearing on the results, I considered this to be an insignificant, though regrettable, error. The opposing attorney's reading of the error was entirely different. By pointing out this one error, the attorney was implying that all of my research was flawed by inaccuracies such as this one (even though he found no other similar errors).

If any aspect of an expert witness's testimony is discredited, all of that testimony becomes tainted as the work of either a "hired gun" or, perhaps, simply an incompetent. Even worse, the sociologist who has given discredited testimony can never live it down. Once a legal record of a sociologist's testimony is made, that record is publicly available to any attorney who, in a subsequent case, perhaps years later, seeks to discredit the sociologist's work. I was the target of such an attack when opposing counsel cited the uncomplimentary opinion of a state appeals court (in another state) about studies I did for an unrelated case over a decade earlier. The availability of computerized legal databases makes searching for all prior legal involvement by an expert witness (cited in published court decisions) a quick and simple process.

The capacity of judicial memory to recall our work with a few keystrokes on the computer should make us all the more careful and deliberate, but working within the legal arena often means relinquishing control over the pace of work to judges and lawyers. The scholar is forced to forego the customarily long periods of contemplation and review before putting a research plan into action or presenting the results. Two or three weeks is the typical window within which a research plan must be designed and executed, the results analyzed, and a polished presentation made in court.

Performing under the pressure of a short deadline can produce a curious trap: we must work quickly, or legal proceedings will be conducted without our contribution. While working quickly, we still must be able to demonstrate that we were careful and made no mistakes. The tension between being both quick and accurate was a particular problem in one case where I was commissioned to do a community survey. Opposing counsel pressed hard outside of court to have the results of the survey made available to him within a short time. I did manage to design and conduct the survey in time to present the results at a motions hearing. After I presented the results of the survey in court, on cross-examination, the same attorney asked me how long it took to conduct the survey. When I replied, "About ten days," he asked, skeptically, "That's not very long to do a [good] survey, is it?"

The prosecutor had a good point: ten days is a very short time to do a good survey. Just by asking the question, without even asserting that there were specific flaws in my research, the prosecutor had challenged the quality of my work. Sociological testimony is inherently vulnerable to such attacks in court. Many of the decisions we make in designing and executing research can be questioned. The sociologist who has done good scientific research has nothing to hide, but direct examination usually is not exhaustive. Many details of the research then are brought up on cross-examination in the context of the opposing attorney's attack on the work. Regardless of how hostile questions are answered, the tone of the questions and the frustration of the witness in being forced to give categorical responses to complex questions are likely to diminish the credibility of the testimony.

The best way to deal with the vulnerability of sociological evidence to attack is probably to raise the sensitive issues on direct examination, when the sociologist can explain the underlying rationale in response to friendly questions designed to facilitate this presentation. There is recent experimental evidence supporting the conventional wisdom that stealing thunder from the opposition in this way is a successful courtroom strategy (Williams, Bourgeois, and Croyle 1993).

The courtroom is an advocacy arena, where the expert witness expects to be attacked by opposing attorneys. The judge, however, is supposed to preside over the proceedings with an even hand, giving neither side the advantage. Sometimes the nature of expert witness testimony creates an alliance between the judge and the opposing attorney, as revealed in the next section.

"DO YOU MEAN TO SAY THE DEFENDANT CANNOT GET A FAIR TRIAL IN MY COURT?" — UNFRIENDLY JUDGES

In the community surveys I conduct as an expert witness, I frequently find that a large proportion of people eligible to serve on the jury have substantial information about the case and have already drawn conclusions about the guilt of the defendant and the appropriate penalty. When I present these survey results in court, I am saying to the judge, in effect, "A fair trial cannot be held in your court." Judges, understandably, are likely to take great offense to this. I am, thereby, cast in the unenviable role of enemy of the court as well as the prosecutor. Here, as in our relationship with our attorney and clients, our quantitative methods and concepts press us into confrontations with judges.

A major strength of anonymous surveys is that they provide a forum where people can express their uncensored feelings without worrying about any consequences that might follow if they express the same sentiments in public. Anonymity requires surveying large numbers of people whose individual responses are not disclosed. The logic of legal proceedings is quite different. Again, we encounter the tension between wholesale and retail. The law depends on individual accountability. Every person who testifies in court is identified and sworn to tell the truth. This public identification and swearing has great symbolic importance for our legal process, despite widespread recognition that people lie, even under oath.

The different perspectives of sociologists and lawyers on truth telling is revealed in one courtroom exchange in which I tried to explain the logic behind surveying prospective jurors anonymously about their knowledge and opinions about a case. My argument is that the demand characteristics of voir dire encourage prospective jurors to give socially approved responses. People generally know that they are supposed to be fair. In the formality of the courtroom, under questioning by judges and attorneys, most people would claim that they would be impartial, that they would judge the case only on the evidence presented in court, and that they could render a fair and impartial verdict. The social pressure to appear impartial probably is sufficiently great that most people would claim that they could be impartial even though they held strong prior opinions about a case, making it difficult or impossible for them to be impartial.

Notice, in the following exchange, that it is not the prosecutor but the judge who attacks the reason I conducted the survey:

JUDGE: Then you probably know that these very same questions [included in the survey] . . . would be asked on voir dire?

JACOBY: Yes, Your Honor.

JUDGE: The very same questions that you have here and they would be asked of people who are under oath to tell the truth. Do you know that?

JACOBY: Yes, Your Honor.

JUDGE: Don't you think that [my] survey [voir dire] would be just as accurate as yours?

JACOBY: No, for a number of reasons.

JUDGE: Are you telling me that voir dire is no good and the oath is no good?

JACOBY: I didn't say that, Your Honor.

JUDGE: I want to ask you again. How come the Court couldn't ascertain this on a voir dire just as well as you ascertained it?

JACOBY: I think the intent of this was to determine in the county what the opinions and attitudes of the people were about this case, how they would likely respond on voir dire.

JUDGE: Does that show that you could not get a fair and impartial trial in this county?

JACOBY: I believe our results do, in fact, indicate that it would be very difficult.

The judge, clearly annoyed with me, took over the cross-examination almost completely, doing the prosecutor's job of attempting to discredit my work while the prosecutor sat back and smiled. Through his line of questioning, the judge seemed to place me in the uncomfortable position of asserting that "voir dire is no good and the oath is no good." I never got the chance to articulate the logic behind the anonymous survey in court. The judge's rhetorical questions certainly did not provide the opportunity. My attorney and client also let the matter drop, because trying to explain why an anonymous survey might be superior to voir dire for some purposes would have further irritated the judge.

Even when the content of expert witness testimony is not perceived to be a direct challenge to the integrity of the court, the judge sometimes takes over cross-examination. In the next section, I examine the challenge of explaining inferential statistics to reluctant judges.

"WE DON'T DEAL IN PROBABILITIES HERE" — THE DIFFICULTY OF COMMUNICATING STATISTICAL INFERENCE IN COURT

In one of my first experiences testifying as an expert witness, I presented evidence on the exercise of prosecutorial discretion in requesting the death penalty in murder cases. The defense was trying to show that the prosecutor was much more likely to seek the death penalty in cases involving black defendants accused of murdering white victims. After going through the usual credentialing formalities, I began to describe my research findings with the words: "The probability of. . . ." At that point, I was cut off by the judge, who admonished me, "We don't deal in probabilities here. We deal in facts."

In making that assertion, the judge was communicating to me that the court was unconcerned about patterns of human behavior, other than the behavior of the defendant in the case before the court. It was not difficult for me to restate my findings using the term "proportions," but I certainly was taken aback by the judge's interruption. This was not the only time I was challenged by a judge for using the term "probability." These challenges emphasize the judges' reluctance to accept my efforts to draw inferences from sample statistics to population parameters.

One aspect of sociology that makes our discipline a science is the power of our statistical methods. My attempts to explain inferential statistics in court, however, largely are unsuccessful. Judges and opposing attorneys typically question both the adequacy of the sample I select for community surveys and the generalizability of findings from my sample surveys. Here is an actual case of judicial doubt about sampling and the inferences one may draw from samples:

JUDGE: You are talking to 200 people, I believe, here. How many registered voters are there in [this] county?

JACOBY: About 18,000.

JUDGE: About 18,000, and you are talking to 205, and most of your survey is made up of less than the 200, so you see you lack asking some 17,000 and some odd people.

JACOBY: If the implication of your comment, Your Honor, is maybe if we had talked to more people, we would have gotten different responses or more accurate results, I think reflecting on the fact that the national pollsters like the Harris Poll and the Gallup Poll use a sample of between 1,500 and 2,000 to get a sense of the national . . .

JUDGE: I've never met anybody they have called yet so I don't know where they call. I've never met anybody in my whole life that they have called. Have they ever called you about anything?

JACOBY: Not that I recall, Your Honor. That's not difficult to understand when they are only calling about 1,500 to 2,000 out of over 200 million.

JUDGE: Well, a lot of times I disagree with those polls. If they call me, I would put my say so in it.

This exchange exemplifies the difficulty I typically experience in explaining the concept of statistical inference. One prosecutor ridiculed my efforts at statistical inference by describing them as "boot-strapping," suggesting that I was trying to draw inferences in some casual and illegitimate way. My attorney and client and I could have anticipated this characterization and challenged it by explaining the underlying conceptual model. Though I am willing to explain the assumptions underlying inferential statistics, my attorney and clients do not request that I do so. All an attorney and client wants from me is my expert opinion about the implications of my research. They are not especially interested in how I formed that opinion. To the contrary, it appears that at least some attorneys consider any explanation I might offer about how I draw my conclusions as potential targets for the opposition. In one case in which I suggested to an attorney and client that I present some very elementary multivariate analysis in court, the attorney said he preferred that I not present such an analysis, because it would be "too confusing."

Sociologists may acquiesce to attorneys' preferences for avoiding discussions of the special technical and conceptual tools that distinguish sociology as a science. By doing so, they may, indeed, avoid confusing the judge. The risk in such a strategy, however, is that their work may be dismissed as requiring no expertise at all.

"THIS IS ORDINARY ENGLISH" — THE DIFFICULTY OF COMMUNICATING CONCEPTUAL INFERENCE IN COURT

Some judges are skeptical that sociologists have any specialized knowledge to offer the court. In one case, I was accepted by the court as an expert competent to carry out a survey, but the judge denied that I was an expert in relation to the results of that survey. In fact, he went beyond denying my expertise; he denied the need for any specialized knowledge at all to determine the meaning of the survey results:

JUDGE: The answers to these questions are not some scientific evidence such as a percentage of alcohol in blood which may have no meaning to someone who is unacquainted with chemistry and other issues and therefore needs interpretation. This is ordinary English language from ordinary citizens from which many people can draw a conclusion. . . . Therefore, I'm separating his expertise into two areas. One is the ability to devise and carry out a survey. Two is his ability, in his opinion, to decide what that means. I think that [the second area] infringes on the court and the counsel's prerogatives in the case to attempt to draw a jury and therefore I am not going to allow that evidence [i.e., his opinion about what the results of the survey mean].

Communicating that sociologists are, indeed, "experts," with a unique body of knowledge and skills, is a special challenge, because we are caught in a double bind: if we use straightforward, nontechnical language to explain our procedures, our work appears to require no special skill. If we adopt the opposite strategy, using a technique such as multivariate analysis, the court's inability or unwillingness to understand those procedures makes our testimonies vulnerable to the accusation that "anyone can lie with statistics."

The following exchange exemplifies a court's unwillingness to accept, or even listen to, the logic underlying the construction of a questionnaire. I had omitted the question, "Could you render a fair and impartial verdict in this case?" I was trying to defend the omission on the grounds that the socially approved response would be so evident that responses to the question would be invalid. I wanted to present inferences from my analysis of respondents' answers to questions about their knowledge and opinions about the case as indicators of their ability to be fair and impartial jurors.

JUDGE: The main purpose of this is to find out whether he [the defendant] can get a fair and impartial trial. Why didn't you ask that?

JACOBY: Well, Your Honor, there are kinds of principles that people understand very well, and I'm sure that the people of [this] county understand them as well, that when someone asks you, "Do you think a person can get a fair and impartial trial in your county?" the way you are expected to respond is, "Certainly; of course the people of [this] county are fair."

JUDGE: You don't know that until you take the survey in this county, do you?

JACOBY: No, but once having gotten the responses to that question . . .

JUDGE: But I just want to know why you didn't put it in there just for information.

JACOBY: Because, Your Honor, I just didn't feel that the results would be that meaningful.

JUDGE: So you picked out what would be meaningful in your opinion and what would not?

JACOBY: That's right, Your Honor.

JUDGE: And you don't think being fair and impartial was meaningful?

Of course I thought that "being fair and impartial was meaningful." Determining whether a fair and impartial jury could be chosen was the entire purpose of my research. My sociological understanding of the interview situation told me that I would get more valid replies from respondents if I did not ask directly the question whose answer I sought. In the way I approached the problem and the judge's criticism of my approach, the contrast between the sociologist's preference for inference from indirect questions posed to many anonymous respondents and the lawyer's preference for direct questions posed to witnesses sworn to tell the truth is evident.

In the next section, we return to the ad hominem attacks discussed earlier. This time, however, the scope of the attack is broadened from the work done on a particular case to the general character of the expert witness.

"IN HOW MANY CASES HAVE YOU TESTIFIED?" — EXPERIENCE, MOTIVATION, AND CREDIBILITY

Sociologists enter the legal arena as consultants because they have specialized knowledge relevant to a particular point of law or legal conflict. Although we strive for value neutrality in our search for truth, the topics we choose to study are likely to express our individual interests and biases. Under other circumstances, such interests would be viewed as desirable. We want scholars to be driven by their ideals, not just by the promise of extrinsic rewards.

When we enter the legal arena, however, our idealism works against us. My interest in the death penalty, for example, makes me suspect as an expert witness in capital cases. According to the typical standard of expertise, greater experience suggests greater skill. The more often a particular sociologist works as an expert witness, however, the more suspect that particular scientist's motives become.

When I am (inevitably) asked by the opposing attorney, "In how many capital cases have you testified?" no matter what my reply, I am vulnerable to being discredited. If the answer I give indicates I have testified often, I may be labeled either a "hired gun" or an "ideologue." If I indicate that I have not testified often, I could be challenged for being inexperienced.

Sociologists often donate their services. We offer our survey skills to community groups, speak to civic associations, and give interviews to the media about changing social conditions. We are unaccustomed to selling our services for a fee. As a consequence, we tend to undervalue ourselves and underestimate the value of our scholarship. The existence of a market for our services and the awareness that our services have currency in the marketplace is reassuring for us and informs the public that we have something of value to offer.

Other professional service providers who subscribe to high ideals of service, justice, and truth receive substantial monetary compensation for their work, apparently without suffering any taint to their reputations. In a society where value is typically expressed in monetary terms, it makes good sense for sociologists to accept such compensation for our services.

At least some of the lawyers with whom we consult evidently apply this conventional standard of value in their dealings with us. Evans and Scott urge social scientists to charge "market rates" for consulting because "We have also noticed a direct relationship between how much we charge and the cooperation and respect we receive from legal firms. When we charge as much or more than the attorneys typically bill, we have sensed better cooperation and respect" (1983:189).

Of course, the paid expert witness almost certainly will be challenged for receiving compensation, with the implication that he or she is merely a hired gun. The solution might appear to be to work for free. Offering sociological services without financial compensation potentially causes as much trouble in court as accepting pay. If a sociologist performs a professional service (as an expert witness) for free, opposing counsel may still discredit the witness by impugning his motives. Why, after all, would someone work for free except to advance a cause? The obvious rejoinder "that the cause of justice is worthy of advancing, even without payment" sounds quaint and weak in the context of our materialistic society, even if the witness believes it ardently.

"SHOULD I DO THIS KIND OF WORK?" — THE COSTS AND BENEFITS OF BEING AN EXPERT WITNESS

Unfortunately, helping to achieve justice as an expert witness does not win the sociologist much popularity. The legal consulting and expert witnessing I do usually is commissioned by defense attorneys representing clients charged with murders so atrocious that the state is attempting to execute them. Testifying in such cases carries the risk that the sociologist may be viewed publicly as sympathetic to the defendant.

The personal and professional costs of expert witnessing, particularly in support of unpopular cases, can be high. Winfree (1987) surveyed 140 criminologists who had worked as expert witnesses. Fully 22 percent reported that they had experienced problems in their local communities, and 29 percent reported problems at work in response to their expert witnessing. My own position as an untenured assistant professor of criminal justice at the University of South Carolina was terminated before I reached the tenure-decision year primarily because I did expert witness work for attorneys representing capital defendants. Though part of my job included providing consulting service to the local criminal justice community, the dean of the academic unit within which I worked evidently had a conception of community service in which the only acceptable clients were law enforcement and corrections officials. Though I did consult with these other criminal justice officials, my work with criminal defense attorneys brought political pressure from law enforcement officials, pressure that the dean wanted to avoid. Two of us persisted in consulting with defense attorneys, with the same terminal consequence for our academic careers at that university.

Most social scientists do their work while comfortably insulated from any real-world consequences of their scholarship. The legal setting provides an exciting contrast, where someone's life, liberty, or property is at stake. The immediacy of expert witness work focuses the mind and sharpens the intellect. Furthermore, doing this work reassures the scholar and the public that sociology has practical applications and implications as a knowledge system in the courts of law.

CONCLUSIONS

The problems I encountered as an expert witness in capital cases emphasizes the differences in orientation of lawyers and sociologists. Lawyers focus on specific acts by specific persons. I characterized this concern as "retail." Sociologists study patterns of behavior common to large groups of people, an orientation that I called "wholesale." The two perspectives come into conflict when sociologists bring their perspective into the courtroom to be confronted by the logic and rules of legal evidence.

This characterization of the differing concerns of lawyers and sociologists can be used to explore the role that sociologists will play in future legal battles, particularly in light of court decisions about the persuasiveness of sociological data. Decisions by federal courts since the mid-1980s largely closed off the broad attacks on death penalty laws most amenable to sociological investigation. For example, I analyzed the responses from two of the community surveys I conducted and found a pattern of conviction proneness on the part of potential jurors who favored the death penalty (Jacoby and Paternoster 1982). In *Lockhart v. McCree* (1986), a federal appeals court accepted the validity of 15 such social-psychological studies that demonstrated that "death-qualified" juries are conviction prone. The court then ignored those studies and held that death qualification of jurors was permissible in capital cases.

At least as discouraging to sociological attacks on the death penalty was the federal court's response in *McClesky v. Zant* (1984) to data on racial disparities in the application of the death penalty. Though the data showed gross racial disparities in the use of the death sentence, the court concluded that showing of disparities alone cannot prove discriminatory motivation in general or in an individual case.

Sociological evidence of the sort described here is currently unpersuasive to the majority of appellate court judges. As a consequence, most sociologists who get involved in criminal defense consulting in the foreseeable future will be working "retail" rather than "wholesale" — assisting one defendant at a time, as I have done, rather than challenging the law or legal process.

My experience in doing consulting work without financial compensation also is likely to typify such work in the foreseeable future. Most capital defendants are indigent. Michael Radelet, who has done much research on the death penalty and testifying in capital cases wrote:

"Defense experts in capital punishment cases must recognize that those who need this expertise are rarely in a position to be able to purchase it at market rates. In fact, I have never met (nor heard of) any death row or potential death row prisoner who could afford to hire experts out of his (or his family's) pocket" (1987:130). State and federal statutes guarantee legal representation to indigent defendants, but little more. The kind of expert assistance that may be purchased with state funds often is limited to psychiatric evaluation, and the dollar amount made available commonly is very low ($250–300 in some states; $1,000 in federal courts [Giannelli 1993:119]).

The courts currently are unsympathetic to the claim that some defendants need the assistance of experts in order to obtain a fair trial. The leading U.S. Supreme Court case requiring the provision of experts to indigents, *Ake v. Oklahoma* (1985), apparently guarantees only payment for psychiatric evaluations. Even this right is curtailed by some state and federal courts' interpretations of the *Ake* opinion (Giannelli 1993). In a highly critical analysis of the limitations on expert assistance to indigents, David Harris specifically excluded providing assistance of the type sociologists are best qualified to offer (1992:522). The likelihood that legislatures or courts will declare that indigent criminal defendants have a right to assistance by sociological experts seems remote indeed.

In summary, indigent criminal defendants currently have no right to state-furnished sociological expert assistance, and the courts generally are unreceptive to "wholesale" sociological attacks on the law or legal process. The consulting work I have done — usually for free and involving localized research in support of individual defendants — exemplifies the "retail" scale that sociological consulting in criminal cases will typically take for the foreseeable future (see Forsyth, Chapter 4 in this volume).

REFERENCES

Evans, S. S., & Scott, J. E. 1983. Social Scientists as Expert Witnesses: Their Use, Misuse, and Sometimes Abuse. *Law and Policy Quarterly*, 5, 181–214.

Federal Judicial Center Staff. 1991. *Manual for Complex Litigation*, 2d ed. St. Paul, MN: Federal Judicial Center.

Federal Rules Decisions. 1960. Vol. 24–26. St. Paul, MN: West.

Giannelli, P. C. 1993. "Junk Science": The Criminal Cases. *Journal of Criminal Law and Criminology*, 6, 105–128.

Harris, D. A. 1992. The Constitution and Truth Seeking: A New Theory on Expert Services for Indigent Defendants. *Journal of Criminal Law and Criminology*, 83, 469–529.

Jacoby, J. E., & Paternoster, R. 1982. Sentencing Disparity and Jury Packing: Further Challenges to the Death Penalty. *Journal of Criminal Law and Criminology*, 1, 379–387.

Nakell, B., & Hardy, K. A. 1987. *The Arbitrariness of the Death Penalty*. Philadelphia: Temple University Press.

Radelet, M. L. 1987. Sociologists as Expert Witnesses in Capital Cases: A Case Study. In P. R. Anderson & L. T. Winfree, Jr. (Eds.), *Expert Witnesses: Criminologists in the Courtroom*, (pp. 119–134). Albany: State University of New York Press.

Williams, K. D., Bourgeois, M. J., & Croyle, R. T. 1993. The Effects of Stealing Thunder in Criminal and Civil Trials. *Law and Human Behavior, 17*, 597–609.

Winfree, L. T., Jr. 1987. All That Glitters is Not Necessarily Gold: Negative Consequences of Expert Witnessing in Criminal Justice. In P. R. Anderson & L. T. Winfree, Jr. (Eds.), *Expert Witnesses: Criminologists in the Courtroom*, (pp. 138–153). Albany: State University of New York Press.

Wolfgang, M. E. 1974. The Social Scientist in Court. *Journal of Criminal Law & Criminology, 65*, 239–247.

CASES CITED

Ake v. Oklahoma, 470 U.S. 68 (1985).
Lockhart v. McCree, 106 S. Ct. 1758. (1986).
McClesky v. Zant, 580 F. Supp. 338 (1984).

3

Shadowboxing with Mark Twain: Self-Defense of the Statistical Expert

William E. Feinberg

As a quantitative social scientist, I have served as a statistical expert for the plaintiff in about ten civil cases (although I would not refuse to consider working for the defense, and I now act as a statistical consultant for a defendant[1]). In this role, I have been identified to the court as a statistical expert, with passing mention of my training as a sociologist. All of my cases have involved suits alleging either race or age discrimination. These are areas in which statistical analysis has come to be an (almost) obligatory part of plaintiff's evidence. I have presented data analysis specific to each suit rather than giving sociological testimony about general patterns of such discrimination in U.S. society.

The major task of the social scientist as statistical expert is to ask statistical questions that complement and enhance the legal issue that is being contested: whether discrimination occurred in the specific situation. One must consider especially whether the data provide evidence leading to statistical conclusions that resist explicit attack from the other side (and sometimes, as we shall see, from the judge). In theory, the task comprises extensions of what a quantitative sociologist does in sociological research. In practice, the changes in milieu from the university to the courtroom and the shift to a contest that involves money and similar considerations rather than an exchange of sociological ideas are important in determining how the task is performed.

Surprisingly, my professional identification as a sociologist has been largely ignored by opposing counsel despite the relatively poor reputation of sociology (compared with economics, for example) in the general populace. Perhaps I perceive no malice toward my identification as a sociologist because I have testified in only one jury trial, but I believe it more likely that opposing counsel regards skepticism about statistics as the point of attack for attempting to discredit my testimony. That does not mean that other potential points of attack are ignored, however. During my lengthy deposition as the plaintiffs' expert in a race discrimination suit, for example, one opposing counsel asked me whether I belonged to either the National Association for the Advancement of Colored People or the American Civil Liberties Union. I am still uncertain whether he asked these questions because of my being a sociologist, because of the nature of the suit, or in an attempt to annoy a witness for later advantage in cross-examination, a practice one attorney I know calls "lawyering."

LIARS, DAMNED LIARS, AND STATISTICIANS

Mark Twain allegedly said, "There are lies, damned lies, and statistics,"[2] although this saying is sometimes perverted from a complaint about the substance of public policy debates into a condemnation of the debaters themselves as "liars, damned liars, and statisticians." Unfortunately, too many people involved in legal proceedings — attorneys, judges, jury members — subscribe to the original sentiment and often share that skepticism about the import, validity, and reliability of statistical evidence, as well as about the statistician's honesty. It is ironic that attorneys and judges, instructed by the U.S. Supreme Court to be appropriately mindful of statistical evidence, should be so wary and skeptical of such evidence.

Sometimes that skepticism is reinforced by innumeracy or, often worse, by the proverbially dangerous "little bit of knowledge" about statistical procedures. One judge grew rather angry with me because I could not answer his ill-informed question, "What is a statistically significant sample size?" When I tried instead to explain how sample size is related to the reliability of estimates (which I assumed to be his point), he seemed quite angry, probably because he perceived that I was questioning both his authority and his claim to statistical expertise in front of a fairly large audience. Despite my attempts to inform him, I managed instead to convince him either that I was trying to avoid his question (because he believed it was devastating to the point I was attempting to make) or that I was not the expert I was purported to be.

Although general skepticism is a necessary part of such legal proceedings, suspicions about statistical evidence *as evidence*, about the conclusions that can be reached from such evidence, and, ultimately, about the statistician's veracity when offering and interpreting such evidence go beyond that general skepticism. Despite the abundance of questions (scientific and otherwise) about the reliability of eyewitness testimony, Mark Twain never spoke out, as far as I know, against "lies, damned lies, and eyewitness testimony."

SELF-DEFENSE TACTICS OF THE EXPERT

How does the statistical expert defend against such prejudice and lack of knowledge? I wish to argue that the expert must call on classroom skills to have any chance that his or her statistical evidence will be judged fairly and on its own merits. These didactic skills include those used in tutorial sessions that are necessary for educating the attorneys who have retained you. Other didactic skills are those used in lecture and discussion courses and in presentations at professional meetings. These skills provide one's *second* line of self-defense; the first line consists — obviously — of conducting a sound statistical analysis of the data, which leads to a scientifically defensible judgment. That defensibility is at the heart of the expert's interactions with attorneys, judges, and jury members.

Unfortunately, there is no guarantee that being a good teacher will bring success in convincing judge and jury. It seems more likely, however, that the bad teacher will fail. Overcoming skepticism about the evidence is difficult but not impossible, even when one faces rigid views or prejudice against the efficacy of statistics. Some years ago, for example, I testified in a bench trial of a race discrimination suit. The judge's written opinion explicitly rejected as unconvincing *all* the statistical evidence presented, but his opinion for the plaintiff emphatically cited conditions in the plaintiff's work environment, which, according to plaintiff's counsel, were available only in the statistical evidence that I presented. At least the outcome was right, and the judge was able to maintain his skeptical facade. Depending on with whom the expert is interacting during a case, considerably different teaching skills are required. In addition, the adversarial character of our judicial system strongly constrains how the interactions usually proceed. Self-defense is needed throughout, especially when opposing counsel makes it appear as if the expert is on trial.

My use of the term "self-defense" is intentional; I want to emphasize that, often, one is defending that part of the self that is defined in relation to the professional identity of a social scientist. Self-defense here is primarily an issue of impression management,[3] as Goffman (1959) has discussed it. My task is to manage an impression of myself that convinces judges, juries, and attorneys of my competence as a statistical expert. Numbers and probabilities are frequently contested, however, and I must use all of the rhetorical tricks at my disposal to make a persuasive argument.

My initial encounter with an attorney is often in the form of a simple teaching exercise. Attorneys in these first meetings typically offer numerical evidence that they consider quite meaningful and wish to have confirmed as statistically significant. I have dealt with highly intelligent attorneys who know little about statistics and often want to know only "the bottom line," whether the evidence is significant at the .05 level. They often are puzzled as well as disappointed when they learn that their numbers are not necessarily so damning as their common sense led them to believe. My task in that tutorial situation is to explain convincingly why their numbers are not necessarily significant, statistically or otherwise.

One attorney, with whom I had worked successfully on a previous case, called me about an age discrimination case for a plaintiff. The plaintiff was 48 years old and had been dismissed from an important supervisory position in a manufacturing operation that had undergone a large reduction in force. The attorney told me that about 45 percent of those supervisors who lost their jobs were in the protected age class of 40 and above; to him, such a large percentage provided prima facie statistical evidence that his client and others had suffered from age discrimination. When I asked about the age distribution of the supervisory workforce that had been at risk of termination, he did not immediately see the relevance of that information. Once he understood and accepted the explanation (and overcame his skepticism), we went on to discuss what kinds of data we needed to examine in order to establish a statistical case supporting plaintiff's legal arguments and eliminating the alternative explanations (some of which the defense was likely to offer).

STATISTICAL EVIDENCE AND THE COURT

The statistical expert works with counsel to pose statistical questions asking whether the data in the case provide sufficiently strong evidence to warrant defensible conclusions that support counsel's client. The expert-counsel interaction is most successful when the expert is consulted early in the case and is given the responsibility for establishing one or more databases. The expert can minimize the problems of data analysis and inference and then can use the more intimate knowledge of the data to raise additional statistical questions that contribute to the legal arguments. Expert and counsel then can interact to produce mutually reinforcing statistical evidence and legal arguments.[4]

This interactive process produced a successful result in one age discrimination case in which counsel called on me to set up a statistical database for analysis. The process included helping counsel to formulate the items to be included in a set of interrogatories directed at the defendant company. The responses to these interrogatories then would provide the basis for the database to test whether there was evidence of age discrimination. It did not appear to me that the information requested from the company was overwhelming in its scope or volume, but the company sought to avoid compliance with its obligation during the discovery phase of the suit by arguing that fulfilling our request for data was burdensome.

Because the defendant company refused to comply with any part of the request, the judge in the case held a hearing on the motion to produce the data. At the hearing to force compliance, I testified about why the requested data were necessary for our analysis. The defense attorney argued that I did not need the data because, he said, I was retained by the plaintiff's counsel and, therefore, believed the company was guilty. The judge said that, when this case came to trial, it was part of the jury's task to weigh any evidence I might present to "consider its probative value"; it was not his task to prejudge my motivation or work. Defendant's attorney then tried to show how burdensome our request was by calling on a personnel officer in the company to testify about the difficulty of fulfilling that request. She stated that she had directed an employee in the personnel office to gather the requested information for a limited number of the cases we had identified; on the basis of that limited gathering, the personnel officer projected that it would take one employee working full-time 10 weeks to comply fully with the request. The judge ruled quickly against the company, directing it to hire an additional employee for the purpose of gathering the requested information; inferring that two employees should have been able to complete the task in five weeks, the judge allowed the company six weeks to comply. The company settled the suit seven weeks later, after the data had been gathered but before I had begun data entry and analysis.

Unfortunately, a professionally satisfying interaction with counsel does not always produce the anticipated, desirable outcome in interaction with judge, jury, or opposing counsel. This can be illustrated by my experience in a case in which I acted as expert for 26 black plaintiffs who were suing their trade-union local for race discrimination in assigning jobs during a time when there were few jobs. They claimed that those who received assignments were disproportionately white. Not all blacks in the union were willing to enter the suit, however. As a result, the possibility of a class action was obviated, and the trial lasted more than five weeks.[5]

The defense argued in its opening statement that "black members and minorities who would establish reputations for reliability, punctuality, skills, and ability and a good work attitude and ethic"[6] enjoyed the same job opportunities as did white members of the local. Plaintiffs' counsel and I had anticipated this defense argument when we were discussing what statistical investigations would be necessary to test the allegations of race discrimination in the union's operation of its hiring hall. The "reputation" argument offered by the defense could be made moot by the reasonable assumption that good reputations were distributed proportionally among blacks and whites. Yet, we were uncertain whether the court would be satisfied with a rebuttal by assumption, however reasonable the assumption might seem to us. We decided to avoid the assumption, if possible, by finding a way to test whether disparate outcomes for blacks and for whites remained after good reputations were taken into account, even if attribution of good reputation might have been affected by race. Yet, the construction of a reasonable test for the defense's argument, fraught as it was with racial stereotyping, was neither quick nor easy because of the amorphousness of "reputation," "good work attitude," and "strong work ethic." It is important to emphasize that counsel had to agree that the test was both reasonable and persuasive before we would consider presenting it. Without a measure for reputation, race had a large and statistically significant effect in ordinary least squares (OLS) regressions (which also included experience, age, and skill) for "predicting" compensated hours in 65 successive months; OLS regression is a standard statistical procedure confirmed by the Supreme Court as quite appropriate in such suits. Was this finding because of discrimination or the desirable but amorphous reputational characteristics?

The test I devised eliminated the effect of reputation. I considered only instances in which compensated hours surpassed the equivalent of four 40-hour weeks in a month, assuming that 160 hours in a month when opportunities to work so many hours were scarce offered sufficient evidence that the worker had the necessary reputational characteristics. I argued that restricting the range of the outcome variable eliminated the effect attributed by the defense to the reputational characteristics that were not measurable; "good reputation" was now a constant and, thus, incapable of statistically explaining any remaining variation. Then, with this restricted sample, for each of the same 65 months, I used the identical OLS regression procedure for compensated hours predicted from race, age, experience, and skill to assess the remaining effect of race, even after accounting for or eliminating reputational characteristics and other possible measured influences. I then devised a modified sign test for the regression coefficients for race in each of the months: a negative coefficient meant that blacks were predicted statistically to receive fewer compensated hours than were whites, after the other factors were taken into consideration.

To eliminate race as a significant predictor, then, we should find that about half (or 65) of the coefficients for race should be positive and half negative; significantly more negative than positive coefficients would mean that blacks were still at a disadvantage in relation to whites, even among those with the best reputations, and that race still played a significant role. Because there were many more negative than positive coefficients (and because several of the negative ones were statistically significant), this sign test led to the conclusion that race was still a significant factor in varying the compensated hours; this was a consequence of differential job assignment even among those who presumably had good work reputations. By implication, the finding meant that race probably played a role in attributing reputations for many of the blacks in the union.

The defense attorneys objected quickly to our presentation of these findings, contending that the union never alleged a race difference in reputation and work habits. The court initially sustained the objection, interpreting the opening contention by the defense to refer only to some of the plaintiffs while averring that plaintiffs' "work habits as a group are impeccable."

During subsequent discussion between the court and plaintiffs' counsel, the court expressed shock that the issue of race differences in work habits was "being injected in this case by the plaintiffs. . . . I thought that bogus position was put to rest years ago." Plaintiffs' counsel agreed about the bogus position but argued that the position was the import of the defense's contention. We were allowed to continue presenting (albeit very briefly) the finding that, even for the subset of instances of high numbers of compensated hours, "blacks are at some disadvantage with respect to whites," that is, race rather than reputational characteristics had produced a significant difference in outcomes.

The court responded quickly and angrily, apparently still believing that counsel and I were appealing to the stereotype rather than trying to dispel it and its consequences because we had anticipated that it would be central to the defense's argument. We succeeded in our goal; the court affirmed our position that differential work habits at least could not explain the observed differences. Still unclear, however, was the cost of that affirmation, because the court disapproved so strongly in attributing to us the injection of the very race issue we were trying to dispel. That we had not needed to address the stereotype became apparent only in the court's reaction to our presentation.

Unfortunately the judge found against the plaintiffs, ruling mainly that the demonstrated race differences in job assignments and, thus, in compensation occurred because of sound business practices having no connection with race. Plaintiffs failed on appeal as well.

CREDIBILITY AS AN EXPERT

How do experts convince audiences that they have something credible, important, and statistically defensible to say? In examining what makes a good witness, Chesler, Sanders, and Kalmuss (1988:91) point out two related factors that contribute to an expert's credibility: actual expertise, usually based on credentials, and the appearance of persuasiveness as part of the expert's behavior, including what is said and how. The courts generally are quick to certify that the expert has expertise, especially if he or she has been certified already by another court. How a judge admits an expert to testify also can affect how persuasive the jurors (the audience) find the expert to be, no matter how well or how badly the expert presents the statistical evidence.

The Judge

In the first case in which I served as an expert, involving an allegation of age discrimination, the federal district judge disparaged me even while granting certification. The disparagement preceded any substantive testimony on my part, so I still do not understand why he did it. He instructed plaintiff's attorney presenting my qualifications to "select those portions that you want the jury to take into consideration" and commented further that, in "my experience, most expert witness's [sic] curriculum [sic] vitae are very comprehensive and normally list everything they've ever written, every institution they've ever visited, whether officially or unofficially." After counsel recited highlights of my career and moved for my designation as "an expert in the area of statistics," the judge responded, "With all the qualifications, the jury can decide whether they are persuaded if he's an expert. I'm not going to tell them he's an expert. He can certainly proceed now that his minimal qualifications of an expert have been established. They'll have to decide how much of an expert he is." Curiously, the judge did not make the same disclaimer when the defense's expert was presented.

Plaintiff's counsel could not have anticipated and, thus, could not have prepared either me or herself for that kind of treatment or for the judge's subsequent comments and quarrels as I attempted to present my statistical argument and evidence to the jury. Because that experience was so unusual and because it influenced so strongly my view of the process as being dominated by self-defense, I wish to describe further what happened during my testimony.

I began to present some statistical evidence contained in a chart. The judge interrupted several times to ask many questions about the specific numbers in the chart and then said, "Better give it to me again. I'm having trouble. If I'm having trouble, maybe the jury will have trouble. They may be smarter than I am but I would like to understand it before we get them to understand" (see Jacoby, Chapter 2 in this volume). This request was followed by more testimony, essentially about the chart, and more questioning by the court, including the comment "You bother me." Having had my professional identity[7] attacked, I then entered into a lengthy argument with the judge, in front of the jury, about what to expect with the numbers and how those expectations related to a legal argument about differences in the treatment of the protected (age 40 and above, as defined by law) and unprotected age groups.

In case I have been unintentionally but unconsciously biased in my selection of statements from the transcript, the extent of the judge's interference also can be considered quantitatively by counting in the official transcript the numbers of lines attributed to his comments and questions. These numbers are contrasted with similar counts for the testimony of the expert for the defense, all within direct examination, cross-examination, and redirected examination, as well as in questioning the other expert about the statistical meaning and legal interpretation of changing differences.

In my testimony, numbers and percentages of lines attributed to the judge in the official transcript of the trial reinforce my argument:

	Plaintiff's Expert (self)	*Defense's Expert*
Direct	366 of 1,201 lines (30.5%)	6 of 186 lines (3.2%)
Cross	3 of 307 lines (1.0%)	72 of 429 lines (16.8%)
Redirect	155 of 295 lines (52.5%)	No redirect testimony
By Court	None	43 of 83 lines (51.8%)
Total	524 of 1,803 lines (29.1%)	121 of 698 lines (17.3%)

I had found a significant difference between the unprotected (under-40) age group's experience of lowered termination rates between two time points and the protected (40+) age group's experience of no change in rates during the same interval. The judge wanted the expert for the defense to confirm that my finding was insufficient for demonstrating relative change in the treatment of the protected age group; the judge insisted that the members of that group had to experience worsening rates in order to prove discriminatory treatment, whatever the younger group's experience. This does not sound like a supportable legal argument, and certainly it is a peculiar statistical argument about contrasts involving control groups, but my fellow expert, a veteran of many court appearances, chose to agree with the judge.

After I finally completed my testimony, which was fragmented badly by the judge's interruptions, he told me, "You know what you did and why you did it. . . . The jury will have to decide how much weight to give to your conclusions. That's their job." When my testimony and that of the opposing expert were completed, the judge declared a recess. In the courtroom, on his way to the restroom, he began to argue with me publicly but out of the jury's presence about my statistical testimony; the argument lasted about a half-hour. Plaintiff's counsel said he had never seen anything like it in all his years of practice. Not surprisingly, the jury found quickly for the defense.

Plaintiff appealed, primarily because of the trial judge's behavior; eventually, in a two to one decision to remand for retrial, the Sixth Circuit Court of Appeals found that the judge's "comments and actions seem more appropriate for a cross-examiner than a fair and impartial judge." Moreover, the appellate judges agreed that plaintiff had "presented enough evidence which *could have* supported a jury verdict in his favor *if* that evidence had been considered by the jury without tainted commentary from the court" [emphasis in the original appellate opinion]. The suit then was settled without retrial.

The Jury

A mute court still leaves one with the task of overcoming a jury's skepticism about statistical evidence. Ironically, plaintiff's counsel had retained me as an expert for this case because I was reputed to teach statistics well (and, thus, by implication, could instruct and persuade a jury about an arcane subject). However, we, counsel and I, did not have a chance against such skepticism when it was reinforced by a vocal and intrusive court. Jurors, however, or judges in a bench trial are not required to accept or even pay attention to what the expert is trying to teach them, unlike most students, who usually face an examination. Not only is the authority structure of the classroom absent; it is the expert who is being examined. Moreover, courtroom procedure allows the expert scant opportunity for a "revise and resubmit."

Defense counsel in this case believed he could rely on jurors' skepticism, just in case the judge's contribution was insufficient. In his cross-examination, counsel raised the following question about some result I had presented: "Forget your expertise for one second. Does not common sense tell you that there's not a great deal of difference between seventeen and twenty?" I replied, "If all we had to rely on was common sense, then we would not need statistics." His response — "You know what Mark Twain said?" — did not elicit the alleged quote from me, and he did not attempt to introduce it himself. I am sure he believed, probably correctly, that enough of the jurors already were familiar with it and that he had made his point effectively.

This opposing counsel, badgering and particularly sourfaced during deposition, inspired a third line of self-defense: a private mantra. Imagine the calming effect of uttering over and over to myself Shakespeare's admonition: "The first thing we do, let's kill all the lawyers." Somehow I think Mark Twain would have approved of this mantra.

BALANCE BETWEEN ADVOCACY AND INTEGRITY

Typically, the most difficult self-defense situations arise in less than obvious circumstances and are not resolved through appeal to the usual teaching skills. These situations occur when counsel is preparing an expert to present the statistical evidence and the conclusions drawn from that evidence. Counsel wants the expert to make the most conclusive assertions in the strongest possible language; that language usually is dictated by the phraseology of previous appellate and Supreme Court decisions. The expert, however, wants to express conclusions in a scientifically tentative way. As Chesler et al. suggest, "The expert's problem is to find the appropriate balance between party advocacy and neutral presentation" (1988:100).

The problem of finding that appropriate balance is compounded by the formal and informal interactions between expert and counsel, often occurring over a long period, that have preceded this preparation for trial. The search for balanced presentation creates considerable tension between the two parties, although they are on the same side in an adversarial proceeding, because the search for mutually agreeable language involves considerable conflict and negotiation.

When the expert elects to speak in the formulaic language desired by counsel rather than speaking in the cautious, contingent language of probability, he or she risks creating mistrust of the testimony among those responsible for rendering judgment. The formulaic language sounds ritualistic and rehearsed because it is decidedly different from the language used to describe the expert's findings. Moreover, such presentations can contribute to the general mistrust of experts: I once responded to a judge's question about one "nonfinding" by saying that I did not know why, nor could I immediately hypothesize a reasonable explanation. He muttered sarcastically that he thought experts were supposed to have all the answers. Obviously, some experts who have gone before have spoiled others' expectations for future occupants of the role. This is not surprising when we remember the adversarial nature of these proceedings.

Even the honest expert has at least an obligation to the client not to harm the client's case. That obligation usually is fulfilled by counsel's avoiding questions that have potentially damaging consequences. For a case involving the contested maintenance of affirmative action procedures in a municipal workforce, counsel had asked me before trial about some earlier statistical research that had been used to establish the affirmative action procedures. That earlier research had used the normal approximation to the binomial distribution to examine racial disparities in a number of aspects of the workforce; the normal approximation saves a great deal of computation time when it is used appropriately, that is, when certain assumptions for its use are met. Unfortunately, those assumptions often were not fulfilled in that earlier research, as I pointed out to counsel, and more appropriate tests would not have supported all the original findings of statistical significance used to justify the affirmative action procedures. That argument does not mean that the affirmative action program was unjustified, only that the evidence for its establishment was hardly unequivocal. Counsel had expected me to testify about these earlier findings and how they affected the current dispute, but he avoided the subject in my subsequent testimony.

THE UNINTENDED CONSEQUENCES OF MY TESTIMONY

Not all cases are difficult, however, either in statistical practice or in presentation of the evidence. Yet, the case I found easiest to prepare also may have had the most undesirable consequences. A minority inmate at Lucasville, a maximum-security state prison in Ohio, alleged racial discrimination in the assignment of cellmates, and the inmate's court-appointed attorney asked me to calculate probabilities for the observed racial mix of cellmate pairings at three different dates. Those probability calculations were to supplement the convincing legal brief against these segregation practices that had been crafted by plaintiff's counsel. Large proportions of the cells were occupied by inmates of the same race at each time point. The state contended that such segregation was required to avoid violence between cellmates of different races, many of whom allegedly belonged to racially exclusive groups that sought to protect and maintain their members' interests with violence. Plaintiff argued that racial segregation by the state was unconstitutional, even in penal institutions; he also argued that the degree of segregation observed was considerably greater than was to be expected, even when one allowed for the presence of many inmates violently opposed to sharing a cell with inmates of another race.

I estimated the probabilities of the observed numbers of racially mixed cells among all the shared cells, given the race composition of the prison population. Rather than basing the probability calculations on the continuing process of random assignment of inmates to open cells as new inmates are brought in, I simplified the calculations — using the normal approximation to the binomial distribution — by assuming random assignment of all the prison population available on a particular date. The simplifying assumption was noted explicitly in my subsequent report, which eventually was submitted to the judge. I also estimated these probabilities of racially mixed cells when assuming that increasing proportions (up to 40 percent) of the blacks and of the whites in the prison population were racially violent and, thus, ineligible for sharing a cell with an inmate of the other race. The observed numbers of integrated cells fell significantly below expectations, except when at least 40 percent of the population was assumed to be violent (a percentage that apparently was unrealistically high).

The results were presented in a written report to plaintiff's counsel and later were appended to one of plaintiff's briefs to the court. In response to the legal precedents and (presumably) the statistical evidence, the state avoided a trial and chose to enter into a consent decree, agreeing to follow racially neutral procedures for cell assignment for inmates not documented officially to belong to racial hate groups.

The agreed-upon procedures for cell assignment were put in place. Several months later, nine inmates and one guard were killed in a riot and subsequent week-long siege in one cellblock at the Lucasville prison. There were strong allegations (as well as strong denials) that the effort at racial integration arising from this case was one of the primary grievances of the inmate groups and a major cause of the riots, because one inmate demand for ending the siege was the removal of the new procedure for assigning cellmates. An easy case, you might think: no deposition, no oral testimony, no jury, a relatively easy statistical analysis. However, even this case, because of its alleged consequences, requires self-defense — in this instance, in recurrent interaction with myself. Did I do good while doing right?

CONCLUSION

Serving as an expert in such cases has been intellectually challenging and exciting, if not always completely satisfying. I have learned much about how the law operates and new ways in which statistical evidence can be treated and mistreated. I hope that in carrying out my task as an expert I have treated the evidence fairly while serving my clients well. Ultimately, however, I have learned that in shadowboxing with Mark Twain, on the average, the best verdict one can hope for is a draw.

NOTES

I acknowledge the invaluable help of Karen Feinberg for her substantive comments and copyediting of this chapter, as well as for her forbearance during my legal "education." For propriety's sake, I will maintain the anonymity of the many attorneys and judges who contributed to that education.

1. Statistical consultants have the privilege of confidentiality for their analytic work and their interactions with attorneys with whom they are consulting; consultants need not be identified to the opposition. The protection of confidentiality is forfeited, however, once the consultant is identified as an expert who is scheduled for testimony.

Working as a consultant does not always result in being retained as an expert. As a consultant, I have had to advise attorneys in several instances that their statistical evidence either was weak or did not support the argument they were making.

2. Bartlett's compendium of famous quotations states that Benjamin Disraeli attributed the statement to Mark Twain, but the attribution to Twain cannot be confirmed.

3. The term "impression management" seems to imply the possibility, however remote, of attempting to manipulate interactions in some dishonest way, but obviously, I wish to avoid that implication.

4. I am assuming that the statistical evidence is not being obfuscated but clearly supports the legal arguments.

5. In a class-action suit, it is usually necessary for only one or two members of the class to testify as representative of the class. Otherwise, as in this case, each of the plaintiffs must give testimony and be subject to cross-examination.

6. This and subsequent quotations from trials are taken from the official transcripts.

7. I assumed that my professional identity rather than my personal identity (or integrity) was being attacked, so I was able to maintain my composure.

REFERENCES

Chesler, M. A., Sanders, J., & Kalmuss, D. S. 1988. *Social Science in Court: Mobilizing Experts in the School Desegregation Cases*. Madison: University of Wisconsin Press.

Goffman, E. 1959. *The Presentation of Self in Everyday Life*. Garden City, NY: Doubleday Anchor.

Shakespeare, William. 1952. *King Henry the Sixth, Part II*. Cambridge: Cambridge University Press.

II

HUMANIZING THE DEFENDANT

4

Sociology and Capital Murder: A Question of Life or Death

Craig J. Forsyth

Since the U.S. Supreme Court's landmark ruling in *Furman v. Georgia* in 1972, states have struggled with the problem of how to impose the penalty of death on those convicted of capital murder without running afoul of the Constitution. The court has repudiated mandatory death sentences for capital crimes. Individualized sentencing is required for meeting the requirements of due process. In response to the mandates of the Supreme Court, the individual states have adopted statutes that provide for two trials in capital cases (Hall and Brace 1994).

The first trial is to determine the guilt or innocence of the defendant. If the defendant is found not guilty or guilty of a lesser offense, the trial ends. If a defendant is found guilty of capital murder and is not legally insane, a second trial begins with the same judge, jurors, and attorneys as the first trial. As in the first trial, there are opening and closing arguments by both sides. The difference between the two trials is that the second one determines whether the defendant will live or die.

Evidence is offered on any matter the judge regards as relevant to sentencing and must include matters relating to certain legislatively specified aggravating and mitigating circumstances. The prosecution and the defense present opposing arguments on the moral and legal grounds for imposing the death penalty. The jury deliberates aggravating and mitigating circumstances before imposing a sentence of death or life in prison without parole. It is not hard to imagine how awkward this decision is for the jury. After all, these 12 individuals just have found beyond a reasonable doubt that the defendant committed first-degree murder.

The prosecution argues its case for the death penalty by identifying aggravating circumstances. These are actions or occurrences that increase the seriousness of a crime but are not part of the legal definition of that crime (Oran 1983). Included among aggravating circumstances are the intentionality of the act, the propensity of the murderer to kill again, and the heinous, atrocious, and cruel nature of the murder. The most consequential ingredients for the defense are mitigating factors. Mitigating circumstances are facts that do not justify or excuse an action but can lower the amount of moral blame and, thus, lower the criminal penalty for the action (Oran 1983). They are life conditions and situations that arguably are beyond a defendant's control but act to influence and shape conduct. Interpreted in this fashion, a theory of mitigating factors often is more sociological than medical or psychological, though it may include insights from all.

Louisiana law recognizes any relevant evidence as plausible mitigating testimony. Issues generally considered include that the offender has no significant prior history of criminal activity; the offense was committed while the offender was under the influence of extreme mental or emotional disturbance; the offense was committed while the offender was under the influence or under the domination of another person; the offense was committed under circumstances that the offender reasonably believed to provide a moral justification or extenuation for the conduct; at the time of the offense, the capacity of the offender to appreciate the criminality of the conduct or to conform his conduct to the requirements of law was impaired as a result of mental disease or defect or intoxication; the youthful age of the offender at the time of the offense; and the offender was a principal whose participation was relatively minor.

The argument for life or death is focused on two basic adversarial positions: the specific circumstances of the crime versus the social-psychological character of the defendant. The jury or the trial judge must decide if the nature of the criminal behavior is so violent or heinous that it eclipses the importance of the defendant's biography or if the defendant's biographical circumstances might, in some degree, explain the act. If the jury or judge can be convinced that the act of murder is not independent of the biographical circumstances of the defendant, a convicted murderer is likely to get a life sentence rather than die in the electric chair.

Sociologists with skills in charting life histories are instructing juries on capital murder sentencing (Radelet 1987). Sociology expands the biophysical and psychological boundaries of mitigating factors, akin to moving from C. Wright Mills' (1959) "issue" to a "trouble," an essential tool of the sociological imagination. A key logic of sociology is to embed individual acts into more abstract, but no less real, structures that do not excuse behavior but encourage a more complicated view of it. My job is to narrate a convincing story about a defendant's life that cannot be understood apart from social and cultural factors that ensnare personal guilt in a complicated web that he did not spin.

A sociologist who chooses to serve as an expert witness in capital murder sentencing trials is apt to find the experience stressful and time-consuming. I recall the first time I met a convicted murderer. I was sitting in the cafeteria of a local jail waiting to meet my first client. I wondered what he would look like. My mind conjured up all kinds of stereotypical monsters. He, along with another fellow, had raped and beaten to death a woman and her male companion. The only other person in the room with me was a small, cute kid with blonde curly hair. He looked like someone's little brother. The two of us sat in the room for about 15 minutes before I mentioned to one of the deputies that I was still waiting for my client. He pointed to the cute, curly headed kid.

I am forced to confront my feelings about retribution and punishment. A person (or persons) is murdered. Another person is responsible. Often, the victim is an innocent: a store clerk, a neighbor, perhaps a child. The state is considering whether or not to kill again, to execute the murderer. I admit that there are moments when I feel that a second killing will somehow serve to assuage the pain and loss of the first, but these are moments when I am not thinking sociologically. The fact is, state executions do not deter violent crime, and it is the poor and minority defendant who is more often killed by the state. Moreover, accounting or explaining murder, like explaining almost any human act, requires a sociological imagination. It is not simply "the facts" of the case, as the prosecution argues. Whatever "the facts" might be, they represent a complex culmination of biographical or mitigating circumstances that a jury or judge must, by law, hear before deciding that one death requires another.

The key element in the penalty phase is to explain the criminal behavior of the client so that he will not be sentenced to death. Before an expert can address the bench or the jury, he or she must qualify to testify. Every appearance in court, no matter how numerous are previous appearances, has a qualification sequence for each expert that occurs immediately before their testimony. To the observer, it would appear to be part of their testimony, because the qualification sequence immediately blends into testimony. It is for me the most stressful part of the proceedings. After all, in disqualifying an expert before a judge or jury, a district attorney establishes her credentials as a good prosecutor. Thus, there are sufficient reputational gains in discrediting an expert to prompt vigorous, lively, and, at times, mean-spirited argument from good prosecutors. After successfully qualifying as an expert, I am ready to testify for the life of the defendant.

THE SOCIOLOGIST AND OTHER EXPERTS: BUILDING A CASE FOR LIFE

Two things will keep a person convicted of first-degree murder alive: good expert witnesses and a good defense attorney. Inexperience, failure to prepare, or failure by any participant to be persuasive in court likely means the client will die in about eight years, the time it takes to exhaust the appeals process.

There are at least two other experts who always make up the mitigation team in each death penalty case: a psychologist and a prison expert. A psychologist (who has extensive criminal experience) describes the defendant's intelligence, personality traits, and behavior patterns. A prison expert will offer information about the defendant's adaptability to the prison environment as a long-term inmate (for most capital case defendants in Louisiana, this would mean natural life at the Louisiana State Penitentiary in Angola). The prison expert also describes the prison environment of the state penitentiary for the jury.

Several other experts may be involved, depending on the circumstances of the case. In some cases, a psychiatrist is called first to assert the need for other experts. Also, substance abuse experts may provide additional testimony describing the relationship of addiction to behavior. Often, a neurologist who conducts physical examinations of the defendant may testify that nervous system disorders or impairment of the brain are interfering with the defendant's thought processes. Neurological data often are used to support the testimony of other experts. For example, if a sociologist talked to family members and friends who repeatedly stated that the defendant changed after an accident or changed during the course of an event, be it as abrupt as an accident or as long-term as drug addiction, a neurologist may be brought in to do brain scans. Thus, two pieces of evidence, one sociological and the other biophysical, are joined to create an explanation that something happened to the client, who, therefore, is not in complete control of himself.

Defendant's counsel ordinarily will meet with all the experts for several pre-trial discussions. Initially, each expert collects data and theorizes within his or her respective discipline. Meetings are used to compare findings and discuss theories that fit the various data. Gradually, there emerges a theory of the case. The goal of the attorneys and the various experts involved in a particular case is to present one explanation to the jury that has distinct but complementary parts.

In my experience, attorneys expect sociologists to knit together the opinions of the other experts, to create a whole cloth that explains the relationship of neurology, psychology, social work, and so on to the life of the defendant. More inclusive than the other areas of expertise, sociological knowledge is suited for the task of telling a life story that a judge or jury can understand. Indeed, it is a rare capital murder sentencing case in Louisiana that does not use sociological knowledge to plead for life.

Psychological profiles are important, of course because they relate personality to behavior. However, juries are reluctant to accept a psychological explanation in the absence of other, complementary explanations. Likewise, a neurologist is not very effective in documenting brain damage unless there is some change in behavior. The social caseworker might enumerate important life troubles, such as juvenile delinquency or family of origin problems. Each of these areas of expertise is important in making a case for life, but offered alone, or discretely, they probably will not stop an execution.

The reader should not be too surprised by the importance of sociology to capital murder sentencing hearings. After all, it is sociology, with its theoretical emphasis on the social and cultural contexts of behavior and its life history method, that will tell the more convincing story to a judge or jury by weaving together the stories of the defendant and other experts into a convincing narrative of mitigating circumstances. The sociologist describes the life of the client, focusing on those events that together construct a life story and are supported by the testimony of other experts. The testimony of the sociologist is shaped by legal theory and by the knowledge that there are 12 individuals, who are neither lawyers nor experts, who will decide whether the defendant lives or dies. The sociologist must be a good teacher, taking a judge or jury back and forth between theory and data in terms a nonexpert can understand.

Following are summaries of two capital murder cases tried in Louisiana criminal courts. The two cases I selected are sufficiently different from one another to suggest the range of sociological reasoning that is used to convince a jury that life, rather than death, is the appropriate sentence.

MURDER DURING ARMED ROBBERY

Don is a 35-year-old African-American male. He is married and the father of two young daughters. He committed a murder during an armed robbery. He was 33 at the time of the crime. The client shot the victim when he went for his gun and then shot the victim again as he lay on the floor. The client had committed two armed robberies before the murder, all within a 16-hour period. He was arrested for his first two armed robberies, plea bargained to one count, and was sentenced to 25 years at Angola State Penitentiary. At the time of his arrest, the authorities were not aware of the third crime. He was at Angola serving his sentence when a police detective matched the gun he used in the armed robberies with the bullets in the body of the murder victim. At that time, he was indicted for first-degree murder. He pled not guilty.

When I took this case, it seemed a lost cause. Although many of these cases do at first, this one seemed to be particularly unsalvageable. Not only was the defendant robbing a man, his third robbery of the day, but also, he shot him twice. He shot the man once when he thought the victim was going for a gun. Then, with the victim on the floor writhing in pain, he walked behind the counter of the store and shot him again, as the prosecution would say, "to make sure he was dead." It was this second shot that could persuade a jury to impose the death sentence.

If a defendant is already serving another sentence in prison when he is charged with an additional crime, he usually is moved to a local facility to be more available to the attorneys and experts working on his case. I first interviewed Don in the Lafayette, Louisiana, Parish jail. Background information, details of the crime, and names of family, friends, employers, and so on were recorded during these initial interviews. In the course of many visits, I developed a working relationship with the defendant. Indeed, during the two and one-half years it took to bring this case to trial, I had more contact with the client and his family than any of the other experts.

I interviewed over 30 family, friends, and employers of the client and examined school, hospital, and jail records. His addiction to cocaine would be an important part of my testimony. However, his addiction to drugs, as important as it was to his case, would have to be located in a more generalized context to persuade the jury that it was a mitigating circumstance sufficient to warrant life rather than death. The story I decided to tell is a classic sociological tale: a good rural man goes to the city and becomes a bad man.

The client grew up in a rural, nurturing family environment. He worked hard and put his wife through college. Enticed by the Louisiana oil boom, he moved his family to an urban area to find a good-paying job. He found a job and was making a good adjustment to the city. Then, the bottom fell out of the oil market, and southern Louisiana lost thousands of jobs. People could not pay their mortgages and abandoned their houses. Banks closed. My client lost his job. Gradually, he became addicted to cocaine and began to commit petty burglaries to pay for his habit.

I would tell a story about a farm boy who comes to the city and is overwhelmed by the sudden and unpredictable changes in his life. I created a family tree to show the normal family life of the client, and good character data were used to set the stage for his transformation by addiction to drugs. The story is a variant of a classic sociological narrative found in the work of the early Chicago School; it joins social disorganization and social control theories, forming a sociological model of drug addiction. The premise of the story is that people who move from the country to the city frequently experience some personal and social disorganization because traditional values and social practices no longer seem to work in an urban milieu (Akers 1994). Social disorganization hinders or undermines informal social controls and is likely to pose more serious problems for personal adjustment during periods of rapid economic decline. The absence of social controls is the key explanatory component in the link between social disorganization and crime (Bursik 1988; Sampson and Groves 1989).

I qualified in this case in the typical manner. The prosecutor challenged my credentials to make statements regarding the drug addiction of the client. He argued that I was not qualified to draw a conclusion regarding drug addiction. He was right. I was not qualified to make a clinical diagnosis. The judge, however, disagreed with the prosecutor, concluding that I was constructing a sociological theory of drug addiction, as opposed to a diagnosis.

I started my testimony by describing the data I gathered for the story I was about to tell. Using nontechnical language, I described how most parents protect their children from the evils of the environment. A young child is easy to shield, but as the child gets older, the parents' ability to protect or shelter the child diminishes. However, their loss of control often, particularly in traditional rural areas, is supplanted by that of friends and community. This second tier of young adult socialization did a commendable job with Don and would have continued if he had remained within its influences.

His younger brother and sister, both of whom stayed in this rural area of Mississippi, are successful adults. They strongly suggest what the client would have become had he stayed in his hometown. Indeed, their appearance as character witnesses embodied Don's lost opportunities for the jury. Additional character witnesses confirmed this idea, each attesting to the fact that, prior to moving to the city, the client was a good father, husband, worker, neighbor, and son. When Don moved to the city, however, his life changed dramatically. Rural, familial norms were replaced by the uncertainty that follows relocating in a new cultural area, particularly one that is experiencing marked economic decline. My sociological story makes a plausible link between the defendant's preurban life and his behavior after moving to the city, particularly his addiction to drugs.

I explained to the jury that Don's status as a convicted murderer is inconsistent with his behavior pattern prior to his involvement with drugs. Next, I linked his drug addiction to the murder using the concepts of criminal and drug careers. A person typically enters a criminal career between the ages of fourteen and seventeen and finishes this career track between the ages of twenty-one and thirty. Only career criminals are left at later ages. Those who enter a criminal career at a later age typically are responding to a crisis. Drug addiction is a common crisis that pushes a person into an adult criminal career.

Thus, I explained to the jury that defendants over 30 are likely to have long track records of criminal activity. The few who commit their first serious crimes as they are approaching mid-life, however, typically are not career criminals. Rather, they are guilty of a discrete act or acts that occurred, in large part, because of a particular crisis they could not in some manner avoid. I described Don's addiction to cocaine as such a crisis. Don was 33 years old when he robbed and murdered. He was

living in the city and addicted to cocaine when he committed these
crimes. He entered his criminal career when most people exit theirs.

A time line of the client's life was shown to the jury. It was a visual
documentation of my argument that Don was an ideal citizen for most
of his life. For the first 24 years of his life, he was a normal child, boy,
and young man growing up in Mississippi. For the next seven years, he
was a good family man and citizen. I asked the court to understand my
point: for 31 of his 33 years, Don was an ordinary, law-abiding citizen,
just like every member of the jury. The next two years of his life are far
less than ordinary and law-abiding. From age 31 to age 33, Don wrote
several bad checks and was arrested for possession of a small quantity
of marijuana. At age 32, he committed more serious crimes, like burglary. Also, as the jury was now aware, in a 16-hour crime spree, Don
committed three armed robberies and killed a man. I asked the jury to
compare these 27 months of Don's life with the 399 months of his total
life. Less than 7 percent of his total life was involved in illegal activity,
most of it minor offenses, and, importantly, he was a violent person for
only 16 hours of his life.

Next, I used a sociological theory of drug addiction that put the
client's drug life into a four stage model (Faupel 1991). As I moved
through the model for the jury, I pointed to three factors that mark the
severity of drug addiction: the more addicted the person becomes, the
more drugs he or she uses; the sequence of finding money for drugs is to
exhaust one supply and go to another, and in each sequence, he becomes
a greater risk taker; the addict shifts associations from nonaddicted
friends and associates to fellow addicts. I told my story this way:

In 1984, Don was an experimental user, taking drugs on a few
occasions. In this stage, drugs are incidental to his life. He gradually
becomes a social recreational user. He does not seek out drugs at this
second stage but will use them at parties and other social occasions. At
this point, drugs still are not significant to his life. He spends little
money on drugs, and the money that he spends is his own. He has not
lost contact with extended family and friends yet, but the friends
associated with his drug use are engaging more of his time.

During 1985, the client becomes an involved user. Drug related
behavior assumes more and more of his time as he begins to actively
seek drugs. He is laid off from work. He exhausts all of his own money
and starts getting money from family and friends who do not know he
is a drug user. It does not take these people long, however, to learn that
Don is a drug addict and not the same person they knew and loved.

In 1986, he goes to jail for bad checks and other minor crimes. He is
now well into the involved user stage. His friends have changed; they
are all drug users. By 1987, he is entering the final stage of drug
addiction: the dysfunctional user. At this stage, drug use is organizing
his life. Don now is spending most of his time seeking cocaine. He begins
a pattern of petty burglary and breaks off all contact with relatives and

old friends. On waking one day, for the first time in his life, he is both sick and alone. He never has been this sick before. His preaddiction friends and family are not around, nor are his new addict friends. In the recent past, he was with other, more experienced criminals; now, he must get drugs on his own, but he is physically and emotionally impaired. He is both desperate and inexperienced at burglary. This is an important point because it suggests that he is not a career, or professional, criminal.

Addicts usually get caught when they get out of their pattern of behavior, when they attempt to maneuver in an unknown arena and become more venturesome. Don's lack of criminal expertise is apparent in this last day of life outside of jail. He always attempted to keep both crime and criminals separated from his family. On this day, however, he takes his youngest daughter with him and commits three armed robberies in 16 hours. The first two robberies are committed at his daughter's day-care center and at a business owned by a friend of Don's wife. In both robberies, there is little potential for money and guaranteed identification of the perpetrator.

Concluding my narrative, I asked the jury to consider that these are the actions of a drug addict who is an inexperienced criminal. Transformed by drugs, he could not even accomplish a petty robbery. In the third robbery, the nice, polite man from rural Mississippi kills a man.

My testimony lasted for 75 minutes. The prosecution's approach was to focus on his crimes, rather than to make the crimes part of his addiction. The jury was asked to ignore the "rural man gone bad in the city" story. The jury deliberated on the life and death question for nine hours. He was given a life sentence, but as one juror told us, "It was not a justice verdict . . . it was a merciful one."

FATHER MURDERS DAUGHTER

Fred was 23 years old when he murdered his 2-year-old daughter with a knife. At the time of his trial, he had been in jail for four and one-half years. During this period of incarceration, he added about 50 pounds of muscle to his once normal frame. In addition, he had developed the jailhouse pallor characteristic of those living in county or parish jails. Fred now looked like a criminal.

Constructing a story for life in Fred's case was a considerably different exercise than constructing the story for Don. Fred murdered an infant, and he was never an ideal citizen. After interviewing more than 50 people over a 3-year period, some more than once, I decided to use learning theory to account for how Fred became a violent person.

Learning theory refers to knowledge and habits that develop as a result of the interaction of the individual with the environment (Vold and Bernard 1986). Its central premise is the idea that human beings always develop in relationship to an already developed social and cultural world. Moreover, it assumes that human beings are more dependent on learning than other animals because they are born into the world with comparatively few instincts to insure their survival. Human survival depends primarily on learning the ways of life practiced by a person's family of origin, friendship network, intimate other, and so on.

Applied to criminal behavior, learning theory suggests three processes important to understanding how someone might normalize violence. The first process regards the types of messages a person receives from important others regarding appropriate and inappropriate ways of behaving. It is an extension of Sutherland's theory of differential association (1947): criminal behavior is learned by association with criminal elements and involves the normal learning processes. A second process focuses on the values that people attach to behavior. "Is what I am doing wrong, right, or without moral meaning?" Learning theory suggests these values derive from differential reinforcement: a process of affirmation or disapproval of conduct issuing from important others that helps a person discriminate between good and bad acts. Finally, "imitation" refers to a process of fashioning patterns of action that correspond to the actions of significant others. Learning theory would help me explain Fred's routine use of violence to respond to life's troubles.

I talked to the jury in calm and measured tones about Fred's life. First, I established that the defendant was raised in a family that affirmed violent responses to a broad range of everyday behaviors. In his first 17 years, the client saw his father repeatedly hit his mother. The mother then would leave for a brief period. On those occasions when the father found the mother, he frequently would put a gun to his head and threaten to blow his brains out if she did not come back to him. She always returned. Dad got what he wanted, and Fred internalized this apparently efficacious method of problem solving.

Not infrequently, Fred's father would chase his mother with a knife, threatening to cut her if she did not shut up. The client witnessed this behavior. His father taught him that an appropriate response to women crying is to threaten them with a knife. I asked the jury to consider this particular learned behavior as critical to their deliberations on Fred's life. After all, he murdered his baby girl, who was crying in her crib, as babies are likely to do. He tried to shut her up by sticking a knife into her face.

Returning to Fred's family of origin, I described in graphic detail other episodes of violence in Fred's family. Fred's father watched his father (Fred's grandfather) shoot himself in the head with a gun. Fred's paternal uncle was killed by his son defending his mother from a severe beating. I described instances of Fred's father kicking his older sister with cowboy boots until she lay bleeding on the floor. Believing her life was in danger, Fred lay his body across the bleeding body of his sister to ward off additional blows. Fred began sleeping with a weapon when he was nine years old, afraid that his father would hurt him while he slept. On several occasions, the mother and the children hid under the house all night to escape their dad's assaults. Earlier in the trial, Fred's mother described these events to the jury, and the court clerk started to cry.

I explained to the jury that Fred exhibited strange and quixotic behaviors as a child. He started to kill and torture animals at a very early age. He destroyed property for no apparent reason. He regularly urinated in the middle of restaurants. No one seemed to pay any attention to these behaviors, however.

I continued to pile episodes of violence and bizarre behaviors one on top of the other, hoping the jury believed my argument that Fred's early and formative life was extremely brutal. Violence in his family was expected and planned for. Hitting and kicking were normal adult male behaviors. Indeed, violence was a key strategy for coping with life's frustrations. Invoking the ideas of differential association and reinforcement, I described how Fred learned to be violent. The idea of imitation helped me explain why Fred saw guns and knives as legitimate tools for acting on the world.

During what I termed the second phase of Fred's life, his father has a stroke, and their relationship changes. The client is 17 years old. The father is now physically dependent, unable to work, and unable to be violent. Fred starts to care for his father. The father now becomes focused on doing what he thinks is best for his son. The client becomes emotionally dependent on his father, because the father runs his life. Fred does relatively well during this period.

At this point, his father advises him to marry a woman because she is pregnant with Fred's child. The client's father dies soon after the marriage. Fred's extraordinary dependence on his father is perceptible at the funeral: he jumps into his father's open grave, hugging the casket; it takes several individuals to pry him off the coffin. He subsequently tries to dig up his father's grave. The marriage does not work out. Fred simply is unable to function without his father.

At this point, the third phase of the client's life begins. Fred's father is no longer there to abuse and control his son. His mother starts living with other men. The client starts to drink heavily and is fired from several jobs. He attempts suicide. Fred's family responds by placing him in two 28-day drug treatment programs. I summarize the discharge records of the treatment facilities for the jury. The first summary found Fred "violent, depressed, alcohol dependent, stressed out, and manifesting bizarre behavior and drug induced psychosis — which means when he drinks he goes crazy or he has a mental disorder." The second summary concluded that Fred has "limited social living skills, is dependent, lacks assertiveness, made no progress, is unable to change, and should be referred to another long term program."

After his last discharge from a substance abuse hospital, he begins sleeping on the floor next to his mother's bed. Fred stabs his mother's bed because she is living with a man. His family responds by sending him to live alone on a family farm. Fred becomes more disturbed on the farm. He nails his father's clothes to the wall behind his bed. He tortures animals again. On three occasions, he barbecues live dogs. He is allowed to see his daughter, but only with supervision.

Two months before the murder, the client breaks into his sister's house and steals several guns. She presses charges, and he is put in jail. The sister puts him in jail as a way of keeping him off the street. She eventually drops the charges because he will be sentenced if she does not. This is 17 days before the crime and marks the final phase of his life.

The only reason he is on the street is because his family did not want him in jail. He begins 17 days of drinking. On the night of the crime the client is drinking. He has recently attempted suicide with drugs. In spite of his volatile and bizarre behavior, he is put in charge of his 2-year-old daughter.

It was understood among family and friends, of course, that the child was *never* to be left alone with the client. The maternal grandmother showed extraordinarily bad judgment leaving the baby with Fred. She tells Fred the baby is sleeping and she will come back and get her after she wakes up. The baby wakes up before the grandmother returns. Fred's daughter is crying. He is under the influence of alcohol. He pulls a knife from his "cultural bag." After all, a knife was enough to stop his mother from crying. The toddler, of course, does not recognize the threat of the weapon. "She is an infant and he is an idiot" were my words to the jury. She will not stop crying. The knife, meant to intimidate not to kill, goes too far, slipping into her body.

My testimony was the story of an abused, low-functioning individual who learned to be violent and alcoholic. It was a family of victims. In my final statement I asked the jury to consider Fred's heinous crime in the context of growing up in a horrific family that mistook violence for love, where caring was expressed in hitting. I testified for 90 minutes. The jury voted for life.

It might seem peculiar for someone's mother to embrace an expert to the court and say "thanks" because her son will be in prison the rest of his life, but her son's life was spared, in part through the testimony of a sociologist.

CONCLUSION

Capital murder sentencing trials invite the perspective of sociology. If justice is more than retribution, an eye for an eye, then a single horrific act must be understood in its complicated relationship to biography. Perhaps this more historical understanding will not persuade a jury to spare the life of the murderer, but I believe a jury must, nevertheless, be made aware of those moments and themes in a defendant's life that presaged an act of murder.

Capital punishment is a source of seemingly endless and heated debate. Sociology can contribute a reasonable voice to this controversy in classrooms, through journals and books, and in courts by its careful reconstruction of the life stories of murderers. Humanizing defendants, especially those most likely to be seen as less than human, is a task suited to the methods of sociology.

In closing, I periodically visit Don and Fred in prison. Don recovered from his addiction and enjoys frequent contact with concerned family members. He is making a good adjustment to a life in prison. Not surprisingly, Fred is doing poorly. His family has abandoned him, and he is not adjusting well to prison life. I do not know whether he is thankful to be alive.

REFERENCES

Akers, R. L. 1994. *Criminological Theories*. Los Angeles: Roxbury Publishing Company.

Bursik, R. J. 1988. Social Disorganization and Theories of Crime and Delinquency: Problems and Prospects. *Criminology, 26*, 519–551.

Faupel, C. E. 1991. *Shooting Dope: Career Patterns of Hard-Core Heroin Users*. Gainesville: University of Florida Press.

Hall, M. G., & Brace, P. 1994. The Vicissitudes of Death By Decree: Forces Influencing Capital Punishment Decision Making in State Supreme Courts. *Social Science Quarterly, 75*, 136–151.

Mills, C. W. 1959. *The Sociological Imagination*. New York: Oxford University Press.

Oran, D. 1983. *Oran's Dictionary of the Law*. New York: West.

Radelet, M. L. 1987. Sociologists as Expert Witnesses in Capital Cases: A Case Study. In P. R. Anderson & L. T. Winfree, Jr. (Eds.), *Expert Witnesses: Criminologists in the Courtroom* (pp. 119–134). Albany: State University of New York Press.

Sampson, R. J., & Groves, W. B. 1989. Community Structure and Crime: Testing Social Disorganization Theory. *American Journal of Sociology, 4*, 774–802.

Sutherland, E. 1947. *Principles of Criminology*. Philadelphia: J. B. Lippincott.

Vold, G. B., & Bernard, T. J. 1986. *Theoretical Criminology*. New York: Oxford Press.

5

When Murder May Be Suicide And "Yes" Means "I Heard You": The Sociologist as Cultural Interpreter

Patricia G. Steinhoff

The wife of a Japanese businessman living in California was distraught over her husband's unfaithfulness. She walked with her two small children into the ocean, intending to drown with them in a family suicide. A good Samaritan rescued the woman; the children, however, drowned. The woman was charged with first-degree murder for the deaths of her children and faced a possible death penalty. The case aroused such deep concern in the Los Angeles area Japanese community that 4,000 people signed a petition to the district attorney asserting that the woman's actions would be regarded very differently in Japan (Sherman 1985).

Expert testimony was introduced in the pre-trial hearing about the frequency of mother-child suicides in Japan and the logic that underlies them. A cultural interpreter explained to the judge that, in Japan, suicide is an acceptable, even honorable, way out of certain insoluble problems. Because mothers feel so emotionally bound to their small children, it would be unthinkable and irresponsible to abandon the children when she died. The woman was still subject to U.S. law for her acts, but the cultural interpreter's testimony helped the judge see those acts in a radically different light, and she was permitted to plead guilty to voluntary manslaughter (Galante 1985). The case prompted considerable debate over the appropriateness of a "cultural defense" argument in the U.S. legal system. In this system, the only defense that may be viewed from a cultural perspective is the legal insanity defense (Sherman 1985; Woo 1989; Kawanishi 1990; Choi 1990).

The U.S. legal system holds every sane person accountable as if we all participated in the same shared system of meanings, but in our shrinking, multicultural world, this assumption sometimes does not hold. Cultural differences may affect a variety of critical issues in the adjudication process. The cultural definition of a situation affects its emotional and symbolic significance to the individual, and this bears directly on that person's motives and intent in a criminal case. The impact of an injury on the victim may have a significant cultural component that requires explanation in order to obtain a fair assessment of damages in a civil suit. In any legal case, linguistic and cultural barriers may distort the judge's or jury's perceptions of a person's character and behavior.

The task of the cultural interpreter is to explain differences in everyday social practices, cultural definitions, and the symbolic and emotional significance of situations and behaviors that may affect the judge's and jury's interpretation of the facts of the case. This chapter examines the role of the sociologist as cultural interpreter within the U.S. legal system, drawing on my experience as an expert witness on Japanese society. Through working as a professional sociologist on legal cases, I also have become, unwittingly, a participant observer of the interface between the worlds of social science and the law. The analysis will, therefore, consider both the sorts of cultural differences that a cultural interpreter can explain to the court to assist in a particular case and some of the cultural differences between academic social science and legal practice in the contemporary United States that affect the way such cultural information can be discovered and analyzed.

Although I did not participate as a Japanese cultural expert in the Los Angeles family suicide case, I have worked on a variety of criminal and civil cases in Hawaii. The population of the state of Hawaii (currently about 1 million) is so multicultural that there is no majority or predominant ethnic or racial group. Everyone belongs to a minority, and each person's ethnic heritage becomes a social referent in ordinary conversation. The largest single group, Caucasians, represent only about one-third of the nonmilitary resident population, with Japanese-Americans a close second. Filipinos, Chinese, Koreans, Hawaiian, part-Hawaiian, and Samoans are recognized ethnic subgroups, and each enjoys a population large enough for statistical counts. A Portuguese ethnic minority also is identified socially as being historically distinct from the rest of the generic Caucasian category. Hawaii's sizeable military contingent increases the Caucasian population, and also contributes to the small black and Native American populations. Aside from the native Hawaiians, who have been present for over 1,000 years, many of these ethnic groups have been in Hawaii for several generations. Despite all these self-conscious ethnic minorities, the fastest growing category in the state is persons of mixed ethnicity. The majority of marriages in Hawaii now cross ethnic or racial lines, and the majority of children born in the state have mixed ethnic backgrounds.

At the same time, there is continuous new immigration into Hawaii from Asia and the Pacific, and a substantial part of the resident population is not native-born. Hawaii has a steady flow of immigrants from Asia and the Pacific, who come to Hawaii to work, attend school, or join family members. In addition, the state's main industry is tourism, and

East-bound tourists from Asia are the fastest growing segment of the tourist market. Asian professionals work in tourism-related industries, and Asian businesspersons and investors are now part- or full-time residents of the state.

Under these circumstances, the people and the public institutions of Hawaii are highly sensitive to cultural differences in behavior and outlook, although the complicated interplay of multiple cultures is, admittedly, difficult to apprehend. The state's unusual demographic composition and awareness of diversity produces a need for cultural interpreters in the legal system, and the same factors also make the legal system quite receptive to the use of such experts.

It may seem strange that a Caucasian woman from the Midwest should be needed as a cultural interpreter in Hawaii, when a quarter of the population is of Japanese ancestry and the tourist industry employs thousands of people who speak Japanese. I came to Hawaii fresh out of graduate school in 1968, hired by the University of Hawaii sociology department as a specialist in Japanese society precisely because of the local demand for knowledge about contemporary Japan from a student body that was heavily Japanese-American. Then, as now, very few U.S. sociologists specialized in Japanese society, and even fewer departments sought such a specialist. I consider myself extremely fortunate to have found an academic home in which my unusual specialization is treated as a legitimate and essential facet of sociology. Yet, just as my classrooms are filled with third- and fourth-generation Japanese-Americans who learn their ancestral language and culture at the university, Hawaii's courtrooms are filled with lawyers, judges, and jurors who feel some Japanese cultural identity but do not understand necessarily how people think and act in contemporary Japan. Their frames of reference are U.S. culture and the Japanese-American culture of Hawaii. Their ethnic identity may be an important personal experience, but it is not the same as expert knowledge about Japanese culture.

A cultural interpreter also is not simply a person who is familiar with a particular culture or speaks its language. There are many native Japanese in Hawaii who understand perfectly well how people think and act in Japan, but they may not be able to analyze and present it effectively for the court. The cultural interpreter must have a systematic comparative understanding of how the foreign culture differs from U.S. culture and must be able to explain these differences clearly to the lawyers, judge, and jury. Sociological and anthropological concepts about social interaction, social organization, and cultural values provide the analytical tools for such a systematic comparison. Because the courtroom participants have little patience for arcane academic discourse, the cultural interpreter must be able to translate foreign cultural concepts into plain English explanations, using cultural references that are familiar to the audience.

More importantly, in order to meet the legal standard of an expert witness who can testify in court, the cultural interpreter must present these explanations as a credible expert on the basis of "knowledge, skill, experience, training or education," as the Federal Rules of Evidence put it (Fed.R.Evid.702). My academic degrees in Japanese language and sociology and published sociological research on Japan, plus my years of teaching sociology courses about Japan at the University of Hawaii, can be offered to the court as evidence that I meet this standard. I have qualified as an expert at both the state and federal levels, and my credentials were not challenged, which speaks as much to the general acceptance of the need for cultural interpreters in Hawaii as it does to the content of my curriculum vitae.

THE COURT'S VIEW OF THE CULTURAL INTERPRETER

The question of the cultural interpreter's expertise is secondary, however, to the issue of whether that testimony will help to resolve a significant or disputed issue in the case. The testimony of cultural interpreters as expert witnesses is admissible in court in principle but must be determined by the judge on a case by case basis. The decision is based, first, on the relation of the proposed testimony to the issues in the case and, second, on whether the expert is qualified to give meaningful assistance.

There is little case law on the subject of cultural interpreters as expert witnesses. Because the purpose of case law is to clarify the legal reasoning in disputed cases, the cases that have been decided on appeal do not clarify the sociological task of describing the parameters of situations in which cultural interpreters are used. In a criminal case, the admissibility of expert testimony on cultural matters would reach appellate courts only if the defendant appealed a conviction after being denied the opportunity to call an expert witness. The cases that reach the appeals courts are, therefore, a highly selected sample in which the credentials of the expert witness or the nature of the rejected testimony may be most open to question. In a civil suit, the defendant might appeal if the plaintiff's expert witness had been allowed to testify and the defendant had lost the judgment. This would produce a better sample of the kinds of cases in which the courts have permitted expert testimony regarding culture, but it still would not encompass criminal cases in which the testimony of the cultural expert witness contributed to an acquittal. (I am indebted to Walter K. Horie for this legal reasoning and for his very helpful critique of an earlier draft of the chapter.) The case law, thus, defines the outer limits of acceptability of cultural expert witnesses but does not reveal either the extent to which cultural experts are being used or the kinds of situations in which their relevance and credentials are unproblematic.

At the federal level, the Ninth Circuit has acknowledged the admissibility of testimony by cultural expert witnesses based on Rule 702 of the Federal Rules of Evidence, if such testimony will "assist the trier of fact to understand the evidence or determine a fact in issue" (*United States v. Beneveniste* 1977). In 1991, the Ninth Circuit Court of Appeals (whose jurisdiction includes Hawaii) affirmed the use of cultural expert testimony in a civil action brought by a group of Hmong women against the state of Washington. A Laotian employee of the state employment agency (Xiong) allegedly raped Hmong women when they contacted him about employment. The plaintiffs' conduct in not reporting the rapes and, in some cases, returning to the employment office and being subjected to further rapes was an issue that required some understanding of their culture. The court had permitted an anthropologist (Marshall Hurlich) to testify generally about Hmong culture but did not permit him to give his opinion regarding the specifics of the case, such as whether rapes occurred or why these particular plaintiffs did not report them immediately.

The appeals court opinion outlines the expert witness' contribution to the case in some detail:

At trial, Hurlich explained that Hmong women are generally submissive, and are raised to respect and obey men. He described the role of Hmong women in marriage; their attitudes toward sex, discussion of sex, and extramarital affairs. Most significantly, Hurlich explained that upon fleeing from Laos, Hmong refugees were reliant on government officials for their needs and would not survive in the United States without government assistance. Because of this reliance on government assistance, the Hmong have developed an awe of persons in government positions. (*Vang v. Toyed* 1991:481)

The appeals court decided that the district court did not abuse its discretion in deciding that the testimony was relevant. It found that:

In a hearing that preceded the evidentiary ruling the court said "Hurlich is . . . the only expert that either side has located who can explain to the trier of fact who these people are, where they came from, and why they have responded the way they have in these various functions and various relationships." The testimony was relevant to assist the trier of fact to understand certain behavior of the parties here that might otherwise be confusing, and to explain the cause, effect and nature of long term Hmong reliance on governmental agencies for support. (*Vang v. Toyed* 1991:481)

In a footnote to the phrase "might otherwise be confusing," the appeals court added the following comment: "For example, plaintiffs continued to have contact with Xiong after he raped them. Hurlich's testimony regarding the place of Hmong women in that culture was helpful in understanding plaintiffs' actions after Xiong's attacks" (*Vang v. Toyed* 1991:481n).

This case suggests the kind of situation in which the testimony of a cultural expert could clarify "behavior of the parties . . . that might otherwise be confusing." The language of the ruling also suggests that the expert's testimony is not simply an everyday presentation of expert knowledge such as a professor might offer in a classroom or when a newspaper reporter calls with a question. The task of the cultural interpreter is to bring expertise about a culture into the very different world of the legal system.

THE LEGAL SYSTEM'S MODEL

In order to understand what the cultural interpreter can and cannot do, we must first understand how the cultural interpreter fits into the legal system's own model of its world. Normally, the legal proceedings for a particular case involve two interaction frames, and the case itself is defined at the point of their initial intersection. The first frame is a series of social encounters that brought the client into the U.S. legal system. Possibly included in these encounters are cultural factors that bear on the outcome of the case. These encounters, or precipitating events, constitute the essence of the client's legal problem and are extracted from the flow of everyday life experience when the legal system retrospectively defines and constructs an interaction frame around them in order to create the case. Different readings of this past can be built from the available materials, depending in part upon the cultural understandings one applies.

The second interaction frame is the legal system itself, which encompasses all of the interactions that take place once the case enters this system. The actors within this frame have fixed roles and are expected to follow established procedural rules. As a professional advocate for the client, the lawyer's job is to extract material related to the precipitating events of the case and to present the client's case as effectively as possible within the rules of the legal system. As part of this advocacy effort, the lawyer also may bring in experts who did not participate in the precipitating events of the case but whose knowledge enables them to contribute additional material that may be relevant to the deliberations of the triers of fact. The expert's knowledge is, thus, presumed to be more or less independent of the facts of the case.

How does a lawyer recognize the need for a cultural interpreter as an expert witness? Typically, a lawyer will contact me because a Japanese client or the client's translator tried to explain a situation by describing a practice that the lawyer finds exotic. The lawyer wants me to testify that the practice in question is a cultural phenomenon, a predictable behavior, albeit culturally specific. Because the lawyer does not understand the cultural context and knows only what the Japanese client or translator reported, the problematic cultural practice usually is defined very narrowly. If the lawyer is fortunate, that narrow description may be an example of some significant cultural difference for which I can provide a useful explanation. However, what the lawyer describes may be obscure or trivial, not something about which I could testify comfortably as an expert witness. On one occasion, I was interviewed by a lawyer whose Japanese client was charged with violation of U.S. immigration laws for failing to report an arrest record on his visa application. The lawyer wanted me to testify that it was common Japanese practice for travel agents to fill out the form for the traveler to sign, as part of a defense that the defendant did not knowingly make the false statement attributed to him. Although such a practice would be fully consistent with Japanese attitudes toward forms and signatures, I did not know anything about travel agents filling out visa applications for their tour customers until the lawyer told me about it. It was not a point on which I wanted to stake my professional expertise.

Even when this initial interview with the lawyer is successful and I agree to assist in a case, we are still a very long way from the witness stand. In the legal system's own model, as described above, the lawyer brings the cultural interpreter into the legal system's frame of interaction to offer certain expert knowledge that will contribute to a more effective presentation of the client's case. The cultural interpreter must understand how expert testimony fits into the procedural rules of the legal system and cooperate with the lawyer to ensure that the testimony is admissible, but the cultural expert also must remain the guardian of his or her own expert knowledge, including how it is acquired and how it is used.

THE LEGAL MODEL AND PROFESSIONAL INTEGRITY

Although I have no direct knowledge as a witness to the original series of natural social encounters that comprise the client's legal problem, I may have broad independent knowledge through which these events can be interpreted. In many instances, I could provide testimony about cultural practices without knowing the facts of the particular case, but I have learned that it is risky to do so. Once, early in my work as a cultural interpreter in the legal system, I was asked how Japanese collect rent. The case was a bail hearing for a Japanese defendant seeking permission to return to Japan until his trial date.

I explained that, because personal checks are not commonly used in Japan, the renter pays either by making a bank transfer into a particular savings account designated by the landlord or by paying the landlord directly, but these two methods are not freely interchangeable. If the landlord is paid directly, it is part of a ritualized face-to-face monthly interaction that helps maintain goodwill and, therefore, requires the regular participation of both parties. I agreed to testify on that point at a federal court hearing and went through the necessary preparations without learning anything more about the client or the case.

On the day of the hearing, I was introduced to the client and two other men in the elevator going up to the hearing room, but we did not speak beyond a brief formal greeting, and we did not exchange the customary name cards that help to locate people socially by giving their work affiliation and position. The three men dressed formally in suits and ties did not quite look like middle-class "salarymen" from a large Japanese corporation — the cut of their suits and their sideburns were a bit too continental — but I was more concerned about what I would say to the court.

I testified briefly about the traditional practice of collecting rent in a face-to-face ritual over a cup of tea, being careful to add that not all rent was collected in this fashion in contemporary Japan but that many interactions are still handled in the traditional way. In response to cross-examination by the U.S. attorney and further questioning by the judge, I explained that a person who collected rent in this face-to-face manner could not simply send someone else in his place or ask that it be paid by bank transfer on some occasions, because the whole point of the ritualized encounter was to maintain a direct personal relationship of trust between the landlord and the tenant. What made my testimony as a social scientist different from that of any native Japanese who could have described this ritual of rent collection was the explanation of the significance of the ritual in analytical terms that U.S. legal professionals could comprehend as culturally different but important, which, in turn, made plausible the client's need to return to Japan.

A few days later I was shocked to read in the morning paper that a major Japanese organized crime figure or *yakuza* was granted permission by a federal judge to return to Japan pending the start of his trial on several felony charges. I was relieved that the article did not mention my name and appalled that the practice I characterized as a benign traditional ritual of rent collection might well have been an equally traditional *yakuza* device for extorting protection money from defenseless small shopkeepers. I decided that I would no longer testify as an expert witness unless I had a clear idea of the specific details and overall dimensions of the case.

My reaction was a combination of professional embarrassment for naively lending my credibility to an unsavory cause and character, moral embarrassment for likely facilitating the client's subsequent criminal behavior, and intellectual embarrassment at the mismatch between the explanation I presented and the interpretation I probably would have made if I had investigated the circumstances more thoroughly. In this instance, I could have avoided the first and second problems by asking the lawyer a few questions. The lawyer's ethic is that every person deserves full and fair representation in court, but I am not a lawyer and, therefore, am not obliged to place my professional expertise and reputation in the service of an individual or cause for which I feel no sympathy. I have no idea what kind of rent the client in this case was actually collecting, but I have no desire to assist Japanese organized crime. I now routinely screen for *yakuza* cases in the first conversation with the lawyer and reject them out of hand.

The third issue has much broader ramifications. Even when the case does not involve *yakuza*, if one relies on the lawyer's understanding of the case and his or her view of what the cultural interpreter can contribute, it is quite possible to wind up testifying about a cultural phenomenon that does not fit the circumstances. It is the lawyer's duty to use whatever strategies will best defend the interests of the client, including the presentation of a theory about the case that may not fit the evidence. Such a practice would fundamentally violate the ethical integrity of a scholar, who advances a theory because it offers a plausible fit with the data. In order to go into court as an expert whose knowledge derives from my career as a professional scholar of Japan, I must be persuaded that the cultural factors in question are essential to a correct understanding of what happened.

I now believe I can serve most effectively as a cultural interpreter if I have full access to both the documentation and the client. With access to both the record and the person, I can apply my expertise to identifying cultural aspects of the case and the internal evidence that substantiates them. I then can testify about cultural practices and cite the external sources of my knowledge, in full confidence that what I say applies to the circumstances of the case. The court is not interested in my professional opinion about what actually happened; I was not a direct observer of the precipitating events. It treats my cultural testimony as potentially useful information for its own determination of what happened. However, I have to satisfy my own ethical standards before I can testify in court, and my standards demand that I consider the evidence carefully before I advance a cultural explanation that will be utilized by the lawyer to build a theory about that evidence.

A SOCIOLOGICAL MODEL

The legal system governs case preparation and what happens in court and, therefore, affects my behavior on the witness stand. However, before I reach the stand, I am guided more by the discipline of sociology than by the law. This observation suggests a third interaction frame important to understanding the relationship of the cultural interpreter to the courtroom. In addition to the first frame that brought a person into the U.S. legal system in a manner that includes a cross-cultural problem and the second or legal frame that determines the steps taken in adjudicating the alleged offense, there is a third interaction frame: the relationship of the sociologist to both the evidence and the client. It is here, in this frame, that I work as a symbolic interactionist, interviewing the client and his or her relatives, friends, and associates. I want to hear from them the words they use to comprehend or understand the event or act in question. These words are symbolic evidence, traces of intention and motive embedded in vocabularies not necessarily identical or compatible to those the U.S. legal system is accustomed to recognizing. I also examine documentation specific to a case, looking for convergence and divergence between spoken words and written records. Finally, I often look at literatures specific to particular cultural practices, locating these practices in time-honored traditional activities. My work as a cultural interpreter is not unlike the gestalt therapist who knits together a complex array of issues, people, and history into a coherent image that helps clients visualize their troubles. I, too, seek to create coherent and defensible images of the complex relationships between competing cultures and human actions. Permit me a more concrete word or two on how I work as a sociologist on legal problems that, arguably, require two cultures to comprehend.

FOCUSED INTERVIEWING AND
INTERPRETIVE DISCOVERIES

The actions and events of a particular case happened in the past, outside of my direct personal experience or observation, and I cannot replicate them experimentally. The cases I deal with generally involve unique circumstances and small numbers of people, so they also do not lend themselves readily to quantification. Given these limitations, the most appropriate research tool for discovering the traces of culture is the focused interview. Part of my special research expertise lies in my ability to conduct focused interviews in Japanese that elicit sociologically useful information and to interpret that information using a combination of cultural knowledge and sociological concepts.

The lawyer can interview the client but does not know what cultural clues should be pursued in the client's narrative and does not have the tools to interpret them. Moreover, a U.S. lawyer ordinarily is not fluent in Japanese. A Japanese native speaker, on the other hand, can interview the client in Japanese and understand the cultural aspects of the story but may not know how to assemble them into a sociological interpretation or to convey their significance in English. It is the combination of these linguistic, cultural, and sociological skills that constitute the cultural interpreter's expertise in identifying relevant information for the cultural aspects of the case. These skills must be combined within one person because of the nature of focused interviewing as a research process.

I prepare for an interview with the client in much the same way that I would prepare for any focused interview in my research on Japan. First, I read carefully all of the documentation the lawyer can provide.

Depending on the case, this may include police reports, related evidence, and transcripts of earlier interviews with the client and other witnesses, either in the police report or in the form of depositions. The lawyer provides a general outline of the case and the questions I should address.

From available biographical information, I construct a life history time line that joins the person's life experience to rapid changes in recent Japanese history. A time line allows me to locate a defendant in a generational context that permits an interpretation of behavior in cultural (and not simply personal) terms. I note any aspects of the client's story of the incident that require clarification and any points that suggest potentially significant cultural attitudes and behavior. I also look for any entry points that I can use in the interview to understand more about the client's personality and character. At this point, I also may do some library research to ensure that I have sufficient background knowledge to interview effectively. Sometimes I look up specialized terms in Japanese to make sure that I can follow the technical details of the client's story and that my own questions are precise and well-informed.

For example, in one case, a lawyer told me a client claimed to be a descendant of one of the 47 *ronin*, who were participants in a famous historical incident in feudal Japan. The story of the loyal retainers who pretended to be disloyal in order to carry out an elaborate plot to avenge the wrongful death of their feudal lord has taken on mythological proportions and is the subject of many Japanese novels and movies. I was suspicious of the claim because, in the story, the loyal retainers' lands are taken away, their families are banished, and they commit ritual suicide together after avenging their lord's death. In the lawyer's brief account, which he gleaned through a Japanese-speaking interpreter with very little cultural knowledge of Japan, it was not at all clear what relevance the 47 *ronin* might have to the case. I originally thought the client might be misrepresenting himself to impress the lawyer.

To prepare for the interview, I reread the story of the 47 *ronin* and watched a movie version that happened to be showing on campus at the time. I already knew the general outline of the story and the cultural values of loyalty, duty, and honor it extolled, but for my interview preparation, I concentrated on the names and roles of the participants and the historical details of the story. I noted the client did not come from that part of Japan where the actual historical incident took place.

When I was introduced to the client in the lawyer's office, he initially was quite interested in my academic credentials, which served to establish my credibility as a useful participant in his case. Thinking that it would be an equivalent icebreaker that might catch him in a pretension, I casually asked the man about his connection to the 47 *ronin*. To my surprise, he told me precisely from which person he was descended, a high-ranking retainer of the central character, and explained that the wives and children of the high-ranking retainers of the disgraced feudal lord had been given protection by another powerful feudal lord who was sympathetic to their cause. This man's family had lived in the former feudal domain of that feudal lord down to the present day. He went on to explain that, because of this unusual family background, he was brought up with a traditional Japanese sense of duty and honor. His obligation to act in a dutiful and honorable manner was related to the particulars of his legal predicament. He launched into a narrative of his case, making a connection between his deeply felt Japanese code of conduct and the charges against him.

The client's claim was verified, and I learned important information about his character. He brought up his connection to the 47 *ronin* in order to explain how betrayed he felt in his present legal predicament, but the significance of this connection was not understood by the lawyer or the translator. As the interview proceeded, I learned more about other seemingly unrelated events in his life history that offered additional evidence of his unusually strong sense of loyalty, duty, and honor. These bits of information bolstered my interpretation of his character and its significance for the case. In this instance, the information was potentially useful for presenting the client to a jury as a sympathetic figure, a person caught between two cultural worlds.

DIFFERING THEORIES OF KNOWLEDGE AND CULTURE

The discovery of new information in a legal case is not the normal province of the cultural interpreter, nor does such material have the same importance it would have in one's own research, even though it arises naturally in the course of a focused interview. In most instances, whatever the client told me about what happened in a case would be hearsay and, therefore, not admissible in court. However, if a lawyer elicited the same information from a client on a witness stand, it would be admissible. Aside from reporting it to legal counsel, a cultural interpreter can use this new information primarily as internal evidence of the applicability of a cultural pattern whose existence can be established without reference to the facts of the case.

For a symbolic interactionist, managing data in this fashion reverses the usual research orientation of generating interpretations out of a close reading of the internal dynamics of a social situation. In my own research on radical groups in Japan, I first try to reconstruct the dynamics of a social situation and then look for the general or universal social and behavioral patterns that might help explain those dynamics. Only after this step do I ask what is specifically cultural or Japanese about the situation. I use this strategy in order to avoid invoking culture as an all-purpose explanation for everything, when there might also be important noncultural factors involved. Thus, although I am quite accustomed to picking out cultural elements from the written and oral accounts of a social situation, as a researcher, my emphasis is on the internal evidence of culture in the situation and how the cultural elements interact with other factors within that specific context to bring about certain consequences.

By contrast, the court's rules of procedure imply a more positivist, deductive view of knowledge as independent of the situation. Applied to culture, this easily can lead to reification of cultural patterns as somehow independent of, rather than generated by and through, human interaction. As a cultural interpreter, my basic job is to describe the cultural pattern that applies to the case, rather than to interpret the details of the case by reference to the cultural pattern. If I am fortunate, I will have the opportunity to do both and, thus, to remain true to my sociological understanding of how culture is constructed. However, if the court takes a narrow view and restricts my testimony on the basis of its own positivist assumptions, I cannot get into a philosophical debate about epistemology with the judge. I simply have to accommodate to the court's theory of knowledge as well as I can without violating my own.

SEEING AND HEARING CULTURE THROUGH NATURAL LANGUAGE

Despite the potential constraints on how such material can be used in court, I still have to approach each case by trying to understand how the client viewed the situation. Only by understanding how the client interpreted events and responded to them can I locate the traces of culture that may be embedded in the interaction. Interviewing in Japanese often is essential in order to get a coherent account from the client of what happened in the case, particularly when the circumstances are subject to radically different cultural understandings.

I was asked to assist in an attempted murder case involving a young Japanese male cook who had been arrested in the bedroom of a married Japanese woman in the middle of the night. Police were called to the scene by a neighbor who had heard the disturbance. The man had a pocketknife and a cut on his hand, the woman said he had tried to kill her, and the police had charged him with attempted murder.

The lawyer questioned me about Japanese attitudes toward suicide and said he thought that there were some discrepancies in the police report and that it might not have been attempted murder. I thought he was probably grasping at straws but agreed to look at the police report and to talk to the cook, who spoke very little English. The police report was cryptic, and the major irregularity seemed to be that it was the cook who was cut, not the woman.

The cook was visibly relieved when he met me and was able to tell his story in Japanese. It turned out that he and the woman, the young and beautiful wife of a wealthy elderly businessman, had been lovers. The cook, who had previously lived and worked in the woman's household, became upset when the woman broke a date with him, ostensibly because of her husband, but then went out with someone else. The cook and the woman quarreled over this incident, and she broke off their relationship, returning a ring he had given her. He then got drunk and went to her house to beg her to take him back. When she coldly rejected him, he pulled out a pocketknife and threatened to kill himself if she would not marry him. She had tried to grab the knife while he loudly begged her to kill him if she would not marry him, and at that point, the police had arrived. Caught in very compromising circumstances, the woman quickly claimed he was an intruder who was trying to kill her.

As the cook described how deeply hurt he was by his lover's sudden cold indifference, he jumped up from his chair and showed me, with the characteristic sloppy movements of a Japanese under the influence of alcohol, how he had dramatically threatened to kill himself and how the knife he had pointed at his own body had grazed his hand when she tried to take it from him. Either he was a marvelous actor or he was telling the truth.

I probed for his feelings about death and suicide and elicited the very traditional Japanese cultural view that a dramatic suicide is an honorable way to express one's feelings of betrayal or frustrated commitment. He related how he could have accepted the painful loss of his lover if she had shown him any warmth and sympathy but ruefully acknowledged that, if he had not been drunk, he would not have had the courage to kill himself.

The episode had cultural fingerprints all over it. In predictable Japanese fashion, his emotions led him to this particular course of action. However, a cultural interpreter may not be permitted to testify about the defendant's state of mind at the time of the alleged crime. My job was to explain the Japanese cultural ideas about suicide and honor that underlay his actions so that a U.S. judge or jury could appreciate the seemingly incredible notion that he had been trying to kill himself, not the woman.

The cook's lawyer arranged a plea bargain under which the cook was to plead guilty to a misdemeanor and then return to Japan. As part of this arrangement, his lawyer requested that I write a letter to the judge explaining the cultural basis for interpreting his actions as suicidal rather than murderous. I explained that suicide is often viewed in Japan as the honorable, active way to express one's total commitment to a goal that has become impossible to attain or to a relationship of trust that has been broken by the other party. Although committing suicide on someone's doorstep is not an everyday occurrence, there is ample cultural support in historical incidents, traditional literature, and contemporary popular culture for the idea of doing so. I added that this sort of dramatic suicide is an extreme extension of the everyday

Japanese social interaction pattern in which someone tries to elicit sympathy and care from another by displaying how the other person's lack of attention has wounded him. Culturally, it was far more likely that the cook had threatened to kill himself in that situation than that he had threatened to kill his lover.

In this case, there was minimal documentary material available and the cook spoke very little English; therefore, interviewing him in Japanese was the only way I could find out if there was any cultural element to the case. Even when the Japanese person involved in the case speaks English well, I always prefer to interview in Japanese so that I can hear the words the respondent uses, which can be potentially significant as markers for certain cultural concepts. Sometimes it is the shift of language itself that reveals significant information.

In one case, I interviewed a young Japanese woman who was sexually assaulted by a chiropractor to whom she had gone for treatment. The lawyer asked me to testify about the doctor-patient relationship in Japan and the cultural ramifications of such a sexual violation. Because the victim was an attractive college student who spoke quite unemotionally about the incident in English, the lawyer was worried about how she would come across in court.

I know a great deal about doctor-patient relations and sexuality in Japan, but I wanted to hear in the woman's own words, in Japanese, how she had experienced this event and how it had affected her family. When I began interviewing her in Japanese, I discovered that, although she was able to discuss the incident with clinical detachment in English, when she spoke about it in Japanese, she cried. The incident traumatized her and her family. She could narrate her experience calmly in English because she felt no emotion about the English words she needed to use; in Japanese, the words immediately triggered deep shame and humiliation. Moreover, the legal proceeding itself, which she initiated at the urging of her U.S. roommate and other U.S. advisors, was a source of deep shame and conflict for her family and herself. There was some question about how I might be able to use this material in my testimony as a cultural interpreter, but it was very useful to the lawyer in deciding how to present the client to the jury. Fortunately, the case was settled successfully out of court, and both the young woman and her family were spared the embarrassment of a trial.

The course of a focused interview is quite unpredictable, and the interviewer must be alert to both linguistic and nonverbal cues in addition to the actual elements of the client's narrative. This is particularly true for interviews in Japanese, a linguistic culture in which normal social interaction relies very heavily on nonverbal communication.

I assisted in one civil case in which the dispute hinged in part on whether the Japanese client, who spoke some English, had understood an insurance agent's presentation and knowingly agreed to the insurance contract terms. According to the agent's deposition, he provided the necessary information in the written insurance documents and in his English presentation, and the client did not stop him to seek clarification or say that he did not understand. When the client told me his version of the incident in Japanese, he made a simple gesture with his hand that would signal clearly to any Japanese his anger and inability to understand. It was apparent to me that the agent, a third-generation Japanese-American, would not have noticed or comprehended this gesture and misread the client's silence for comprehension and agreement, when it meant the opposite.

Sometimes a cultural explanation is necessary to prevent misunderstanding of the English text of evidence that was translated from Japanese. In a case described elsewhere in this chapter, involving a Japanese tourist and a Japanese police informer, part of the government's evidence consisted of bilingual transcriptions of conversations with the defendant that were secretly tape-recorded with the assistance of the police informer. In the English translation, the informer presented a series of arrangements, to which the tourist repeatedly replied "yes," implying his agreement to the terms. However, the expression *hai*, which was translated into English as "yes," commonly is used in Japanese conversation to signal the fact that the listener hears and understands what the speaker is saying, without necessarily implying assent. On the witness stand, I pointed out that this difference in language usage is frequently a source of misunderstanding for U.S. businessmen, who think that they have successfully negotiated a contract, when their Japanese counterparts are only communicating that they understand what the American has said. This is not simply a problem of translation but a cultural difference in communication style that affects the meaning of the words even if the translation is literally correct.

All of these examples suggest the close connections between culture and language and the importance of language skills for the cultural interpreter. I interview the client in Japanese and read the Japanese materials in Japanese in order to get a full picture of the cultural factors in the case. Next, I check any translations, transcripts, or English language evidence about the same event to see what significant cultural or linguistic details, if any, were lost in the translation. Only then can I report to the lawyer what cultural factors seem relevant to the case and outline the cultural knowledge about which I could testify.

WORKING WITH THE LAWYER

My presentation to the lawyer at this stage is relatively brief and informal, but a substantial amount of research and thought has preceded it. I generally prepare a simple list of cultural points I have found in my review of the case materials and interviews with the client;

then, I describe orally the cultural relevance of the case material and briefly outline the cultural explanation I would make for each item. The list includes my findings on whatever specific issues I was asked to explore, plus anything else I turn up that might be helpful. The lawyer then considers which of these points will be useful, and we discuss any additional research that may be necessary. We may decide that another interview would be helpful or that I need to check the research literature on a particular point. In this phase, it is clearly the lawyer who is the expert, filtering what I have to say in terms of how the case can be presented most effectively and what material will be admissible. The lawyer's aim is to select the points that fit the overall argument of the case, but there also may be technical considerations that the cultural interpreter does not know about.

In one case, for example, the cultural factor concerned Japanese attitudes toward sexuality and nudity in connection with the widespread inclusion of nude photos in Japanese mass market magazines. (The case involved some young women in Honolulu who had modeled for cover photos in a Japanese weekly magazine and who sued all the individuals and agencies involved when they discovered by chance that the magazines contained some nude photos.) I suggested and carried out a small content analysis of certain magazine issues to demonstrate that the magazines in question were ordinary weeklies with a broad range of content. I also did some quick research during a trip to Japan on the range of magazines containing nude photos or sketches and how they were displayed for sale at newsstands and in neighborhood bookstores.

When I presented this information, the lawyers asked me to go to several bookstores and newsstands in Honolulu that sell the same Japanese magazines to see whether they were displayed in the same way and, if possible, take pictures of the displays. I could not understand why I should run around Honolulu taking pictures of newsstands and wondered why the lawyers could not do it themselves or send their assistants. They explained that they could not introduce it into the trial and neither could the client, an agency involved in arranging the photo session in Honolulu, because the information was not directly connected to the precipitating events of the case two or three years earlier. Because I was to testify both about the magazines themselves and about their cultural context, they could ask me on the witness stand how the magazines were displayed in Japan and in Honolulu.

FINDING TRUTH AS AN ADVERSARIAL PROCESS

When I present myself to the court as an academic sociologist with cultural expertise, I come with my own professional orientation to knowledge, but as a witness, I am subject to the court's unusual distinctions and unfamiliar methods of handling information. Because of the superficial similarities, it is possible to participate in the legal system without noticing the difference. The role of expert witness must be grounded firmly in the sociologist's professional expertise and credibility as a research scholar, but the requirements of the legal system place a new and different set of demands on the scholar-teacher, not the least of which is to be brief and answer only the question that was asked. The legal system incorporates the sociological expert witness into its own research process, with its own distinct set of procedures for determining truth and testing the reliability of evidence and propositions.

The U.S. legal system structures its decision making as an adversarial proceeding between two theoretically equal opposing sides (prosecution or plaintiff and defense) that is played out before an impartial audience (judge and jury). The guiding assumption is that all the relevant information necessary for the impartial judge and jury to make a fair decision will emerge if each side in the adversarial encounter has a full opportunity to present and argue its own case and to weaken the other side's case through cross-examination. The goal is a fair decision, but the procedural language speaks of "facts" and "truth" as though the products of the adversarial encounter were solid quantities of absolute knowledge. By contrast, the goal of academic research is knowledge that is true rather than fair, but contemporary social scientists are much more hesitant to speak of "facts" and "truth," even though their procedures aim at the discovery of these elusive phenomena. This linguistic confusion can lead both academics and lawyers to think their assumptions are more similar than is in fact the case.

I worked on a number of cases without appreciating many of the differences between academic sociology and being an expert witness, until my participation in one case was challenged. A Japanese national was arrested at Honolulu Airport while trying to board a plane to Japan with a cheap handgun in his possession. It turned out that he had bought the gun at a highly inflated price from an undercover government agent, after a Japanese national working as a freelance police informer had arranged both the purchase and the transfer of the weapon inside the airport's security perimeter. The prosecution's version of the case was that the defendant had come to Honolulu to purchase a gun and take it back to Japan illegally, in order to collect a debt. The defense contended that he was an innocent tourist who was entrapped into purchasing a gun he did not want by an unscrupulous police informer who befriended him on the streets of Waikiki at a vulnerable moment and offered to serve as his personal guide.

The lawyer contacted me initially to help make sense of the defendant's account of why he had suddenly come to Honolulu but encouraged me to look for cultural factors in the whole sequence of events. Two interviews with the defendant and careful study of the evidence being used against him not only convinced me that the defendant's version was the more plausible account but also revealed the cultural dynamics involved in the defendant's inability to extricate himself from the situation.

The case materials included several transcripts of phone conversations and meetings with the defendant that had been secretly tape-recorded by the government with the cooperation of the police informer. (It came out in the trial that the government expended substantial resources on this case on the assumption that the defendant was a *yakuza* but then found he was not.) The tape transcripts revealed clearly the common Japanese cultural patterns of emotional dependency and aversion to conflict in interpersonal relations, which together make it almost impossible for a person who is dependent on another to resist that person's demands. An American could easily reject an unwanted offer and walk away from the situation, but a Japanese would find it very difficult to refuse the persistent suggestion or request of someone who had done them a considerable service.

The prosecution vigorously contested the use of a cultural expert witness, so I was called to testify at an evidentiary hearing. As I was outlining the subjects about which I would testify, the judge broke in to ask, "What does that have to do with a man who came to Honolulu to buy a handgun in order to collect a debt?" I was taken aback by the judge's question. It was fundamentally different from my reading of the evidence, and my cultural testimony, of course, did not fit his scenario. The defense attorney then intervened to protest that this was the prosecution's view of the case and outlined the entrapment defense he intended to offer. The judge subsequently issued a ruling that did not permit me to say anything directly about the case, but I was allowed to testify about general cultural patterns. In court, because of further objections from the government's attorney, I was not even allowed to let the jury know that I had any knowledge about the case or that I had interviewed the defendant. It was only when I was radically constrained by the court from making the normal social scientist's connections between my research methods and procedures, my research observations, my general knowledge, and my interpretations or conclusions that I realized how much the court's assumptions about these connections differed from my own. It would be quite ridiculous for an academic to give a research presentation that simply asserted general knowledge, without indicating either the research methods or the specific research observations and without drawing any direct conclusions from the evidence; yet, that is essentially what the court required me to do. Although the lawyer in this case insists that the judge's ruling on my testimony was an unusually narrow reading of the law, the experience led me to rethink my own previous assumptions and behavior as a cultural expert witness and to realize that I had been acting under the illusion that academia and the legal system treated facts, knowledge, and truth in the same way.

Ironically, although the judge's ruling prevented me from testifying about any specifics of the actual case, it is generally permissible for an expert witness to be asked a hypothetical question or to give a hypothetical example. I could, therefore, respond to the defense lawyer's hypothetical questions about how a lone Japanese tourist who spoke no English might respond to a Japanese stranger who offered to take care of him. Later in my testimony, I used a hypothetical example to explain how in Japanese society a person who was being pressed to do something he did not really want to do might offer various vague excuses and hope the matter would be dropped. I explained that, if the other person persisted, most Japanese eventually would capitulate and comply, because there was little cultural support for individual resistance or direct confrontation in such a situation. My example closely paralleled what had transpired in the actual interaction recorded in the government's transcripts of the "wired" informer's meetings and telephone calls with the defendant. The device of the hypothetical situation seemed terribly artificial when the case offered a real-world example, but it preserved the formal separation between the expert's knowledge and the facts of the case that the judge demanded.

Even though I was not permitted to testify about the details of this case or even to reveal that I knew anything about them, I could not have given the cultural testimony I did present if I had not personally investigated the facts of the case in some detail. Although the defendant, translator, and lawyer all had some sense that the police informer pressured the defendant to buy the gun, they could only present the defendant's vaguely expressed personal feelings. My cultural testimony explained why the defendant could not say "no," without saying anything about this particular defendant, by linking the whole interaction to a Japanese cultural pattern.

THE IMPACT OF CULTURAL INTERPRETATION
ON THE CASE OUTCOME

Legal cases have real-world consequences for the people who are caught up in them as plaintiffs or defendants. That may be part of the attraction of legal work for academic sociologists, whose activities are rarely as momentous. Yet, a legal case is made up of many pieces of information, and it is difficult to assess the contribution that the cultural interpreter makes to the whole. The cultural interpreter can find interesting cultural factors that seem relevant to the situation, but they may be irrelevant to the legal case as the lawyer plans to pursue it.

At a more academic level, it sometimes is possible to infer what role the cultural information played from the specifics of the decision. There may be several counts in a criminal case, and the court's specific findings may provide clues about whether and to what extent cultural testimony affected the court's decision. Because civil suits tend to be settled out of court at the eleventh hour, it usually is more difficult to evaluate the actual or potential impact of cultural information on the outcome of the case. In some instances, the fact that there is a cultural expert witness may be more important than any specific thing he or she might say, while in other instances, the expert may be entertaining but ultimately irrelevant.

For example, I participated in a civil case that actually did go to trial on one of Hawaii's more rural islands. The suit involved an automobile accident in which the first son of an elderly Japanese man was killed. The elderly Japanese man was not involved in the accident, but he died not long after. The surviving members of the family, the sisters of the man who was killed in the accident, sued the driver of the vehicle that hit their brother. The first son was actually the youngest child in the family, but his position as first son had cultural significance in Japanese tradition. In this case, the first son was brain damaged in an earlier industrial accident and lived with his elderly widowed father. The family claimed that the father's death was hastened by the shock of the untimely death of his beloved eldest son.

I was called in to testify about the significance of the first son in a Japanese family, which seemed less plausible in light of this son's previous accident and mental impairment and his birth order as the youngest child in the family. To supplement my general knowledge about the significance of the first son, I arranged to fly a day early to the island where the trial was being held so I could interview the surviving family members about the family relationships. I learned that the son indeed had been accorded the full treatment of a first son and had played a significant role as caretaker and companion to his elderly father, in effect retaining his position as eldest son despite his mental impairment. I testified for about half an hour to a very attentive judge and jury about the role of the first son in Japanese culture and its applicability to the dynamics of this particular family and had little difficulty dealing with an aggressive cross-examination. The lawyers were pleased at what seemed to be a virtuoso performance that would help their case.

When I called from Honolulu a few days later to find out the outcome of the case, the lawyers were crestfallen. There were two separate issues to be determined in the case: whether the driver of the vehicle caused the son's death, and if so, what the damages ought to be. My testimony, of course, related to the damage issue. The jury found that the driver did not cause the death of the son by hitting him with a van. An eyewitness to the accident testified that, when the son stepped into the path of the vehicle and the van was just about to hit him, the son's soul could be seen rising up out of his body. The jury decided on the basis of this testimony that the son was already dead when the van hit him. Thus, the issue of the driver's liability for damages was not considered! I would like to think that the jury would have found my explanation of Japanese culture as persuasive as the eyewitness's account of angel feathers, but unfortunately, the first finding precluded the second.

APPLICATIONS FROM LAW TO
SOCIOLOGY AND BACK AGAIN

The work of the cultural interpreter as expert witness, resembling and yet differing subtly from normal academic research, raises anew the basic questions of how we know what we know, how reality is constructed and reconstructed, how the judging observer's cultural baggage distorts what is observed, and how the research account reflects the communicative requirements of its medium and audience. The legal system's objectives and definitions differ from those of academics, offering yet another perspective on the core questions of the social science research enterprise. Analyzing the cultural interpreter's work in a legal setting, thus, helps to illuminate what the sociologist as cultural interpreter does in the classroom and as a research scholar.

At the same time, my work as a cultural interpreter for foreign nationals within the legal system also raises questions about the need for cultural interpretation to bridge similar gaps in understanding within multicultural U.S. society. Underlying the work of the expert witness as cultural interpreter is the philosophical question of how much the U.S. legal system can and should attend to cultural differences. For foreign nationals who become entangled in the U.S. legal system, an ability to reach a just decision may depend, in part, on the participation of a cultural interpreter.

The United States is a multicultural society, still struggling to find ways to respect internal cultural differences while ensuring that the laws apply equally to everyone. Cultural interpretation in the legal system, thus, goes beyond the problem of providing a fair legal environment for foreigners and raises disturbing questions about how far we can go in this direction with our own citizens and permanent residents. Like the insanity defense that is now coming under fresh scrutiny and our changing attitudes toward alcohol consumption and legal liability, these are questions of public policy and legal philosophy that cannot be resolved by sociologists. Yet, by participating as expert witnesses in real cases that move through the legal system, we leave our own footprints as part of the evidence upon which these issues will be determined.

REFERENCES

Choi, C. 1990. Application of a Cultural Defense in Criminal Proceedings. *UCLA Pacific Basin Law Journal, 8*, 80–90.

Federal Rules of Evidence for United States Courts and Magistrates. 1989. St. Paul, MN: West.

Galante, M. A. 1985, November 4. Mother Guilty in Drownings. *The National Law Journal*, 8(8), 10.

Kawanishi, Y. 1990. Japanese Mother-child Suicide: The Psychological and Sociological Implications of the Kimura Case. *UCLA Pacific Basin Law Journal*, 8, 32–46.

Sherman, S. 1985, August 5. Legal Clash of Cultures. *The National Law Journal*, 7(47), 1.

Woo, D. 1989. The People v. Fumiko Kimura: But Which People? *International Journal of the Sociology of the Law*, 17, 403–428.

CASES CITED

United States v. Beneveniste, 564 F.2d 335 (9th Cir. 1977).

Vang v. Toyed, 944 F.2d 476 (9th Cir. 1991).

6

Contested Knowledge: Battered Women as Agents and Victims

Pamela J. Jenkins

The stories of victims of domestic violence can have an unusual power and authenticity. Sometimes, there is something in the telling that can bring listeners to empathize and understand the victims' pain, thoughts, and actions. However, some listeners simply dismiss these stories by blaming the victims, misinterpreting their actions or trivializing their pain. In this way, the voices of women who are victims often are denied their authenticity, and they must find a way to convince others that their stories and their pain are real. One way to tell their story is to have an expert interpret their voice and speak for them. Consider the following:

In a custody hearing in New Orleans, Louisiana, Mrs. S. was fighting for custody of her five-year-old son. Two years previously, after years of battering and intimidation, Mrs. S. left with her small child and stayed underground for two years. After her husband's private detective found her, she was charged with federal kidnapping and spent several weeks in a local jail before the charges were dropped.

At the trial, Mrs. S. and two other ex-wives described physical, emotional, and psychological abuse they all had experienced. Witnesses testified to the fear Mrs. S. had expressed of her husband. Shelters allowed their records describing her experiences into the court proceedings. I testified as a sociologist with expertise in domestic violence and spouse abuse. I attempted to place her experience in the social context of abuse — living conditions that were explosive, unpredictable, and dangerous to both mother and child.

The court-appointed psychologist with significant expertise in custody matters stated that the father would make the better parent because the child had bonded with him. Even though a home study from social services showed the father to be a less than able parent, the psychologist testified that the threat to the child would be the same in either home, that Mrs. S. would be just as likely to expose her child to violence as was the father. The court-appointed psychologist stated that the husband would be the better parent because the wife had a history of relationships with abusive men.

In the end, the victim of abuse lost the argument, and the judge awarded custody to the father with supervised visitations for the mother. Although the appeals court overturned the judge's ruling, the mother could not afford the travel expense or the attorney's fees for another custody hearing.

Mrs. S.'s story illustrates the difficulty of being an expert witness on domestic violence in judicial proceedings. The definition of battered woman, the behaviors of battered women, and the explanations of their behavior all are factors in the debate over domestic violence. This debate intensifies when competing forms of knowledge attempt to understand a battered woman's experience in the legal arena. My own and others' experiences in court illustrate how these factors surface in the legal system.[1]

As an expert witness, I have worked on cases involving civil matters of custody and criminal trials on charges of homicide and attempted murder. A woman who is battered may encounter the legal system in different ways. By far, the most common courtroom experiences for battered women are divorce or custody proceedings. Also, a woman enters the court system in response to possible legal proceedings against her partner, such as a stay away order, temporary restraining order, or battery charge. The third and most spectacular way that a woman comes into contact with the court system is when she kills or attempts to kill her abuser.

Although violence in families is a common experience, the term "battered woman" did not enter the academic and popular discourse until the 1970s (Okun 1986). Both academic feminists and feminists in the community began to focus attention on women who were battered. In the past 20 years, there has been an outpouring of research about battered women from a variety of perspectives (Blackman 1989; Okun 1986; Pagelow 1992). These studies have examined women's self-esteem, severity of battering, children in homes where violence takes place, the cycles of violence — almost every aspect of domestic violence.

In many ways, the battered woman herself has been forgotten in the rush to discover this new area of research. As a consequence, a variety of disciplines are competing to define who is a battered woman and who is not. The definition of "battered woman" has wide-ranging implications for policy, funding, and legal decisions. Battered women, like many others who are powerless in our culture, are dependent upon others who have the power to define them in ways that may decide their future (Worrall 1990). In the case of a woman who is a victim of domestic violence, it is the law enforcement officials, judges, juries, prosecutors, defense attorneys, and experts who have the power to interpret her actions. Any of the players in the legal system and individuals from all of these groups are likely to have different views on domestic violence from their own experiences and training.

COMPETING VIEWS OF BATTERED WOMEN

Women Cause the Violence

Historically, battered women were seen by experts and society as either masochistic or passive (Dobash and Dobash 1979; Okun 1986). Battered women did not leave the situation, so they must have either been too passive to leave or enjoyed it too much. Also, women were seen as provoking or deserving the violence they received, that is, they were responsible for the violence inflicted upon them. This definition of battered women still is salient; the literature and the public discussion still explicitly and implicitly blame the woman (Okun 1986; Dobash and Dobash 1979, 1992).

Women Are the Victims of Domestic Violence

In the past two decades, another perspective has become popular: battered women as victims who are psychologically damaged by their victimization. Walker (1979, 1984, 1989) linked the concept of learned helplessness to her explanation of battered women's behavior and, through interviews with battered women, illustrated the violence as occurring within a three stage cycle based on the perpetrator's actions. Blackman (1986) reports that battered women believe that alternatives are not available to them. "They feel unable to stop the violence and believe there is no escape from the relationship" (Blackman 1986:229). Further, Blackman states that repeated instances of violence enable battered women to develop a continuum along which they can rate their ability to tolerate or survive attacks by their partners. Although Walker states that a battered woman must be seen within the context of the social situation, her analysis continues to concentrate on the individual.

Walker's term the "battered woman's syndrome" attempts to explain the violence that battered women experience and the psychological effects of such violence on the victims. It conceptualizes a battered woman as suffering from a reactive condition produced by the violence in which the woman lives and the history of the individual woman's upbringing. Battered woman's syndrome is used in criminal justice proceedings to explain the plight of battered women, and the term itself has appeared in state legislation allowing testimony of abuse in trials of women charged with killing their abusers.

This perspective challenges the masochistic view of women in violent intimate settings. Instead of the woman being asked how she provoked the violence, women are described as trapped by the violence and held hostage by their own perceptions. In Walker's perspective, the woman who is abused by her intimate partner is passive.

Violence as a Way of Life in the United States

Another perspective is that violence in families is pandemic, with any member of a family likely to be a victim or a perpetrator. Initially, studies concentrated on measuring the incidence of abuse. Straus and Gelles (1990) used a survey instrument with national samples to document the rate of family violence in the United States. From their perspective, violence is linked to structural factors such as violence in the society at large, generational transmission of violent norms, sexism, unemployment, and poverty. In a micro sense, they have examined in depth the social learning hypothesis that ties adult violence to witnessing violence or being a victim of violence as a child. This perspective has influenced the way in which social science has perceived and measured the concept of violence.

One of the more controversial findings in their work is the discovery of wife-to-husband violence and, subsequently, the concept of battered men. Both surveys revealed that wives were nearly as violent as their husbands in the home, with about the same rate of violence for women as for men in intimate relationships.

Women as Victims and Women as Agents

Another perspective identifies women as the primary victims in the intimate relationship dominated by violence and asks questions that attempt to classify what she thinks, what she does, and how institutions have responded to her requests for help (Dobash and Dobash 1979, 1992; Kurz 1989). Pagelow (1981) represents one of the first attempts from a sociological perspective to identify the social context of woman abuse. She looks at institutional responses, the resources of the woman (both external and internal), and the belief system of the woman. Pagelow hypothesizes that the more resources that a woman has, the more she does not believe in traditional ideology about gender roles, the more the institutions respond to her helpfully — the more likely she is to leave the situation. Conversely, the fewer resources that she has, the more that she believes in traditional ideology, the more that institutions do not respond to her — the more likely she is to stay. In other words, why women stay is a question that should be answered in a more complicated and structural manner than from the belief that she is masochistic or trapped and helpless.

Pagelow's work concerning institutions' reactions was the first of many studies that examined how institutions respond to women who are physically hurt (Kurz 1989). These studies, including qualitative interviews and content analyses of records, show that institutions often respond to violence in intimate settings by implying to the victim that it is her problem to solve. Physicians, for example, may treat the victim without asking if she needs help or may allow the batterer in the examining room with the patient. Police officers may take a man for a walk to "cool down" rather than arrest him, even in states that have mandatory arrest policies for domestic assault. These responses diminish the seriousness of the abuse and have the effect of showing the victim that it is her problem to solve.

Dobash and Dobash (1979, 1992) present the most critical challenge to the psychological and other sociological perspectives. In all their work, Dobash and Dobash have linked violence to the larger social and cultural relations of patriarchy. They show that violence in families reflects cultural arrangements that place men in a position of dominance both in public, and in the home and, more importantly, in a position to maintain this dominance. By asking the question why men hit their wives and not why women remain in abusive relationships, they are able to show how wives become the appropriate victims for men's violence.

Dobash and Dobash characterize battered women as active and courageous. They found that the women might be depressed and anxious but also were determined and brave. These women were continuously active in their attempts to find solutions to the violence. Dobash and Dobash found that abused women changed over time toward the relationship and the violence. After the first episode of violence, women were shocked and sought understanding about the violence. Instead of trapped and helpless, Dobash and Dobash characterized these women as "engaging in an active process we refer to as 'staying, leaving and returning'" (1992:231). This process is dynamic in that these women are evaluating and learning how to solve the problem throughout the period of abuse. They state that: "For most women, active pursuit of assistance is a continual aspect of their lives, ebbing and flowing with their experiences at the hands of violent men and of the institutions from which they seek assistance" (1992:232).

Women stay in relationships not because of their psychological characteristics or traits but because of the myriad of barriers they face as they attempt to leave. These barriers include cultural supports for remaining in the home, economic barriers to the ability to support themselves and their children, and lack of protection by the criminal justice system. Their attempts to leave are unsuccessful from a context of increasing violence and coercion, not from a perceived inability to "see the door."

CONVERGENCE

When a woman enters the courtroom, all the interpretive views just recounted enter the courtroom with her. Lawyers, judges, and juries need to form explanations about a particular woman and her experience. They draw on all forms of knowledge that exist, often contradicting themselves and each other. As a result of the competing forms of knowledge about battered women, a lack of agreement appears at every level of a legal proceeding.

All views have their problems in the courtroom (Gillespie 1989; Bowker 1984, 1989; Walker 1986; Crocker 1985; Schneider 1986; Maguigan 1991). Usually, the prosecution first attempts to dismiss the violence as nonexistent or not serious. This strategy is supplemented by one of two perspectives: she enjoyed or provoked the violence or she was as violent as her partner. The defense, on the other hand, opts for another version: she is suffering from a mental disorder, including battered woman's syndrome, or she was acting in self-defense. Depending on the facts of the case and the understandings of the attorneys, experts are chosen to represent one or more of these views to the judge and juries.

The prosecution's greatest strength is to play upon the prevailing stereotypes about women and battered women. Stereotypes about women on trial include that she is a bad mother, bad wife, and, to some degree, suspect as a woman (Jenkins and Davidson 1990). These stereotypes are compounded with beliefs about a battered woman, such as she provoked the violence, she is masochistic, and she could have left anytime. These stereotypes can lead to the characterization of a defendant as responsible for the abuse.

Adding to the stereotypes above are the newer characterizations from psychological perspectives that use battered woman's syndrome. Schneider (1986) and Crocker (1985) state that this new characterization does not describe all battered women. Such a stereotype about battered women's behavior threatens to create a separate standard of reasonableness for battered women. For example, some courts seem to treat battered woman's syndrome as a standard to which all battered women must conform rather than as evidence that illustrates the defendant's behavior and perception. As a result, a defendant may be considered a battered woman only if she never left her husband, never sought assistance, and never fought back (Crocker 1985). The use of the syndrome can create another stereotype that women must "fit."

My own perspective differs from these traditional descriptions of battered woman. Yet, my experience illustrates the difficulties with any perspective about battered women in the courtroom.

MY VOICE AS AN EXPERT:
AN INTERRUPTED NARRATIVE

Many experts are used in cases where abuse is claimed — psychologists, social workers, and, sometimes, even sociologists. Although psychologists have dominated in the legal arena by examining the personality and character of the defendant, other perspectives come into play as well. My own testimony is based on the social context of violence in which the defendant lived rather than on a psychological perspective and offers a different interpretation of the actions of women who are victims of violence.

My testimony is built on a specific analysis of a battered woman as both a victim and an agent. This perspective allows a woman's voice to be heard in a context of hopelessness rather than of helplessness. My testimony underscores the perpetrator's violence and the woman's attempt to develop the alternatives to the violence. It emphasizes the actions and behaviors of the woman rather than focusing on her pathology or state of mind. Schneider, in an admonition to lawyers, makes this statement about expert testimony: "Explanations of aspects of both victimization and agency make it possible for expert testimony to more accurately describe the complexity of battered women's experiences, respond to the hard defense problems presented in these cases, and allow for change by transcending static stereotypes. . . . Our work must simultaneously capture the reality of battered women's lives, translate this reality more fully and effectively to courts and push toward transforming this reality" (1986:195).

Within this framework that considers both victimization and agency, I attempt to help the defense understand that each case of a woman who is battered does not fall into a particular stereotype. There is not a battered woman's syndrome defense but a defense built upon the facts of the case and the interpretations of those facts.

THE PROCESS

One of the most important areas that I address with attorneys is the role the defendant will play in her own defense. Can she convincingly explain her own actions? If her actions are reasonable, why does an expert need to speak for her? Attorneys often decide whether the defendant will testify based on her demeanor, her affect, and how they feel she will stand up under cross-examination. In some cases, attorneys hope that I will be able to tell her story for her. Generally, I try to work only on cases in which the woman herself is prepared to tell her own story. My testimony places her story in a context, but it works best when she relates what happened to her in her own words.

My first interview with the accused woman concerns whether or not, from my perspective, she has been battered. In some cases, a history of violence is not relevant, and my testimony will not be important or valuable. However, in many cases, the violence is the focal point of the case. In those cases in which the violence occurs systematically over time and dominates a woman's life, my testimony may aid her defense.

From that first interview, I have developed a qualitative interview process that takes approximately 12 hours and covers the events leading up to the death of her intimate partner. The first part of the interview documents the history of the relationship; the second investigates the various types of control and violence in the relationship; the third focuses on her attempts to reach safety during the relationship; and the fourth part identifies whom she has told about the violence and their responses to the information. From this perspective, a defense may be developed that points to the reasonableness of her actions within a context of coercion and control.

Much like offering support for a research hypothesis, the belief that she acted reasonably is supported by a variety of sources, using a sociological framework. Building on the work of others (Pagelow 1992; Giles-Sims 1983; Dobash and Dobash 1979, 1992), I help to describe the social world of the defendant. To create a defense surrounding her actions and the response of others, four areas are developed:

First, the history of violence in the relationship is examined in detail to set the stage for her actions, define her as a victim, and counteract the prosecution's interpretation of the situation. The defense needs to show that her partner's efforts at coercion and control, including physical violence, dominated her life experience. To show the history of the violence, the defense can use her testimony, the testimony of others, and existing medical records.

A woman who is battered may not have told anyone directly, but there may be other indicators that will corroborate her story. What I found is that, in every case, no one person in the woman's social networks had complete information, but many knew of at least one incident of abuse. Her social network included coworkers, family, friends, and neighbors. Through the interview process with the woman, witnesses and other documents may come to light. For example, one woman's father came to get her after an attack by her husband. When he arrived, one of the perpetrator's family said that her husband had tried to kill her. In another case, the woman's sister testified that the perpetrator held a gun to his wife's head on one occasion while she was visiting. If the defendant was employed, she might have missed work because of her injuries or because her partner stalked her at work. Sometimes her hairdresser knows because she or he has worked around spots in the woman's scalp where the hair has been pulled or she was bruised.

The second part of the defense is to show that, no matter what she did, the violence continued. This portion traces her attempts to end the violence — her agency. A description of her actions shows that she did not enjoy the violence, she was not passive, and her actions did not stop the violence. Actions during the violence may have included playing dead, leaving, fighting back, or asking others for help. The types of help she may have sought are legal, medical, counseling, religious support, and social welfare.

This testimony may include documents from the police or medical emergency room records. More often, testimony will include her informal attempts at help. One of the ways that we have documented her attempts to leave is to trace all the places she lived during the relationship. Many women have moved away, only to have their partners find them and, subsequently, either move in with them or bring them back home. We also check records at the children's school, because a woman may have spoken about the abuse in relationship to her child's behavior. One woman told a day-care director that her husband beat her and that was the reason her son was acting out. Others have called or seen counselors in private and public settings.

The third part of the story is the incident itself. What did she see? What did the perpetrator say and do? For these women, there often are several incidents that are "rehearsals for death." For example, the perpetrator may have played Russian roulette with her on several occasions, or he may have strangled her until she passed out. After these incidents, many women come to believe that they will die at the hands of their partners (Browne 1987).

Finally, at trial, all the other witnesses with discrete observations of abuse testify first; then, the woman herself testifies; I prefer to testify last. If the research is carefully and thoroughly done, my testimony shows how her thoughts and actions fit the patterns of other battered women and substantiate a sociological perspective that reflects both her agency and her victimization.

This defense strategy allows for contrast in experiences and behaviors for women who are abused. It is a more inclusive perspective that can describe the complexity of a woman's life, rather than a more restrictive, psychological view. We do not attempt to prove that she suffers from battered woman's syndrome, only that she had reason to fear great bodily harm.

Ideally, this perspective should help contribute to a defense where the woman's actions can be understood. Problems with this defense can occur at every stage, however. Prosecutors and judges challenge the reliability and veracity of the witnesses, especially concerning the violence. The prosecution attorneys show that the woman was not battered, enjoyed the violence, or provoked the abuse and was not suffering from battered woman's syndrome. As the next section illustrates, the prosecution attempts not only to discredit the woman but also to discredit my testimony as an expert. The first challenge usually comes as an attack on my ability to report what the woman stated during the interviews.

YOUR HONOR, THIS IS HEARSAY

During direct testimony, each prosecutor has continually raised hearsay objections. In one trial, the prosecution objected every time I referred to what the defendant had told me. My testimony lasted over three hours, and the objections were a continuous interruption. Another interchange between lawyers illustrates this point:

DISTRICT ATTORNEY: Your honor, for the record, I would like to make my continuing objection to — excuse me. I would like to make my continuing objection that I did with Dr. ___ that the testimony that she gives is hearsay, that it is based on things that Mrs. ___ and/or husband told this lady after the crime and that it's irrelevant and self-serving and it is not germane to the issue of whether or not she was in imminent danger at the time of the commission of the crime. I would like to make that as a continuing objection so I won't have to interrupt her like I didn't have to interrupt Dr. ___ .

DEFENSE ATTORNEY: You didn't?

DISTRICT ATTORNEY: I don't think I interrupted him nearly as much as I could have.

DEFENSE ATTORNEY: May it please the Court, just for the record, I have been practicing law forty years. I have used psychiatrists and psychologists on many, many occasions and I can't recall but of one or two to testify that their testimony was not based on what somebody told them after the incident they were on trial for had occurred. This is exactly what we're doing here today. May it please the Court, I don't think there's any basis for his objection.

DISTRICT ATTORNEY: Your Honor, with due respect to my learned colleague's objection of my objection, I would like to have continuing objection rather than having to make one after each question. Could the Court accept that as a continuing objection?

The goal of the hearsay objection is to prevent testimony based on what the defendant told me from getting to the jury. At the heart of the prosecution's objection is the expert's interpretation of the woman's thoughts, feelings, and actions before and during the incident. If the defense is able to place her actions in a climate of fear that she reports, then the self-defense argument is strengthened. It is no surprise that prosecutors object strongly to this line of testimony.

In the quotation above, the defense attorney's response to the prosecution refers to a psychologist or psychiatrist. As the next section illustrates, comparing my testimony with that of a psychologist or psychiatrist is another avenue for the prosecution. If the hearsay objection is unsuccessful, the prosecution's next strategy is twofold: "Is she a battered woman?" and "Can my expertise define her condition?"

IS SHE BATTERED AND CAN
I MAKE THAT ASSESSMENT?

My testimony is challenged when the issue becomes "Is she a battered woman?" and not "Are her actions reasonable?" Maguigan (1991) and Crocker (1985) both state that, legally, the issue should be about the reasonableness of her actions, but often, judges, prosecutors, and defense attorneys must first agree that she has been battered. Agreement on her status as a victim of abuse often is thought to be a psychological diagnosis. This becomes an evidentiary nightmare in the courtroom for defense attorneys and expert witnesses.

DISTRICT ATTORNEY: Did you also evaluate her?

EXPERT: Yes, sir. I interviewed the defendant on three separate occasions for several hours a piece. And at the end of that time or even, actually — we had some criteria that we look at about battered women that we have developed over time and they are: One, is she afraid of him? And she was afraid of her husband; secondly, was she systematically abused by him? And she certainly was; and thirdly, did she change her behavior because of his violence? And she did, and we know that she did.

The criteria referenced in the quotation capture both her victimization and agency. These criteria are deceptively simple: did systematic abuse over time cause her behavior to change? This perspective does not measure the level of anxiety or depression but what she thought and did in reaction to the violence and the actions that she took to end the violence. However, the prevalence of psychology in the field of domestic violence and the legal arena has led to a set of definitions that are psychologically based. For example, Missouri law has the following definition of a "battered person's syndrome" that is typical of a psychological perspective:

"Battered person syndrome" means a group of concurrent psychological and behavioral characteristics resulting from repeated victimization by family violence or threat of family violence, including:
   a) an extreme level of anxiety or depression;
   b) repeated unsuccessful attempts to stop, decrease, or escape from actions or threats of family violence;
   c) extreme fearfulness of the family violence perpetrator and constant anticipation of future acts of violence;
   d) loss of belief in one's ability to take effective action for self-protection. (Mo. Stat. Ann. § 453, cited in Maguigan 1991)

The definition that I use supports a perspective that views her actions as reasonable when a person is in fear for her life. The psychological model describes a condition in which people act because of a set of psychological and behavioral characteristics. As I testify to her reasonableness using these criteria, the prosecution may try to impugn my testimony as not "fitting the psychological perspective."

DISTRICT ATTORNEY: Well, let me ask you this: You mean to tell me that if a psychologist — You're not a psychologist?

EXPERT: No, sir.

DISTRICT ATTORNEY: Are you a psychiatrist?

EXPERT: No, I'm a sociologist.

DISTRICT ATTORNEY: Let me ask you this, ma'am: In the course of your interview, did you conduct a psychological examination?

EXPERT: No, sir.

DISTRICT ATTORNEY: Any kind of examination pertaining to psychology?

EXPERT: No, sir, I'm a sociologist.

DISTRICT ATTORNEY: A mental examination?

EXPERT: What do you mean by that, sir?

DISTRICT ATTORNEY: I don't know, some kind of I.Q. test or anything like that, any type of examination like that?

EXPERT: No, sir.

A psychological perspective emphasizes testing of a particular individual condition. Testing seems to be important to lawyers on both sides and even to judges who want some objective, hands-on measure to define the parameters of the discussion. Although victims of domestic violence may suffer from post-traumatic stress disorder, this condition may not be important in the self-defense case. Many tests such as Minnesota Multiphasic Personality Inventory and the psychiatric tests often misdiagnose the battered women. Thus, the prosecution usually will try to use an attack based on the lack of psychological testing in interviews.

DISTRICT ATTORNEY: So the M.M.P.I. which had been performed on the defendant, would be of no use to you whatsoever?

EXPERT: Well, let me be more specific about that. The M.M.P.I. can't rule out the possibility that someone has been abused. It's not used as rule-out because of variation in scoring that happens.

DISTRICT ATTORNEY: Can it confirm that someone has been abused?

EXPERT: That is a good question. I am not sure how to answer that. Testing is often used more as rule-out than confirm. I am not certain about the rule-out possibility.

DISTRICT ATTORNEY: For a legal proceeding because that is the role you have here. An M.M.P.I. would not be useful to you in an assessment for testimony in a legal proceeding?

EXPERT: Not for the kind of work that I do. I think it's the kind of tool that might be useful for someone who is planning to treat somebody over time;

the psychologist who is planning to treat somebody over time to get all of those different measures.

In my testimony, I describe situations where her actions seem reasonable; testing and diagnosis are not part of my evaluation. So, the heart of my testimony is based on how I interpret, as an expert, the experience and the voice of the defendant. The reliance on my interpretation provides another opportunity for cross-examination.

IS THE DEFENDANT TELLING THE TRUTH AND CAN THE EXPERT KNOW THIS?

Much of any prosecution's cross-examination involves questioning the credibility of the defendant and my own credibility. This may result in a vigorous challenge to the defendant's truthfulness and my ability to recognize the truth. Several examples illustrate this process.

DISTRICT ATTORNEY: Let me ask you this, too: Now, when you all interviewed the defendant in jail, did you have a polygraph strapped to her, something like that, some kind of lie detector thing or something?

EXPERT: No, sir.

DISTRICT ATTORNEY: None at all?

EXPERT: No, sir.

DISTRICT ATTORNEY: Let me ask you this: So everything she told you, you assumed was correct; is that how the interview goes?

EXPERT: I don't ask her if she's a battered woman. She's not capable of making that — She can say she's a battered woman, but I don't ask her that. What I do ask her is a series of questions, three different sets of questions, and of a — and the kind of detail that you ask, you certainly — I would certainly think that she cannot fabricate the kind of detail that I asked her.

As part of the questioning to the truthfulness of the defendant, the expert comes under personal and professional attack. These attacks call into question not only the credibility of the witness but also the ethics of the expert. Several examples show how this works. The following example involves questioning the truth of the witness and my ability to judge the defendant's veracity.

DISTRICT ATTORNEY: Because she told you everything that was the truth?

EXPERT: Sir, I asked it in such detail and I repeated it at different points and different times, that if I gave this set of interviews to you — which I would be glad to do — you could see, you would see how hard it is to fabricate that kind of detail.

DISTRICT ATTORNEY: Did you ever do any work for the police department?

EXPERT: I've done police training, sir. I've trained young police officers about domestic violence.

DISTRICT ATTORNEY: Have you ever conducted interrogations of criminals or anything like that?

EXPERT: Ah —

DEFENDANT'S ATTORNEY: Your Honor, I would have to object to this. What is the relevancy?

DISTRICT ATTORNEY: This is a woman who can detect the truth. She's better than a polygraph machine. The police department would love to have her work for the police department.

Personal attacks on the expert witness are likely to continue. In this case, the prosecutor attempts to characterize the expert as biased:

DISTRICT ATTORNEY: Your honor, I think this lady is predisposed to help criminal female defendants who are charged with violent crimes against their husbands or their close friends and she's brought into this case as an expert witness on behalf of the defendant and I would like to know from the point of view of credibility whether she actually does sometimes find that people are deliberately using her services to perpetrate a fraud upon the court.

THE COURT: Why don't you ask her that question?

DEFENSE ATTORNEY: May it please the court, I object to the aspersion which he's casting on this lady that she could be prostituting herself on that witness stand. May it please the Court, all he asked her was the name of a person and she told him that because of the confidentiality she could not give it and now he is making all kinds of other aspersions.

DISTRICT ATTORNEY: Your Honor, I am not and I do not and I apologize if I have in any way insulted you. I am suggesting to this Court, and since you were here during Dr. ___ testimony, that this defendant is a very bright lady who only sought to have witnesses on this issue after she was in serious trouble and I'm questioning what she is doing and how she is doing it for the purposes of what she is presenting to this Court and so I am questioning that.

Another avenue to show the expert's bias toward the victim is to question the witness about men who are battered. The basis of this questioning is to show that men are battered, also, so that the deceased partner is viewed as a victim and also to imply that women are as violent as men.

EXPERT: There are men who get beaten by their wives, but they are not very many. They rarely call shelters.

DISTRICT ATTORNEY: How many are there?

EXPERT: It's — We have no idea, actually.

DISTRICT ATTORNEY: Have you ever interviewed a man?

EXPERT: No, sir. I have knowledge of people who have, but I have never myself.

DISTRICT ATTORNEY: Now, all of your work is done with women?

EXPERT: Yes

DISTRICT ATTORNEY: Okay. Battered men, a battered husband, what type of injuries would a battered husband sustain in this type of domestic violence?

EXPERT: Sir, I really don't know how to answer that since there's not much literature on that.

As a qualitative researcher, I report and interpret the voices of the people that I interview. The court (the judge) usually trusts that my knowledge has some basis; the prosecution's job is to discredit my knowledge base and to challenge my perception of battered women. The prosecution attempts to find gaps in my knowledge and research that will fray the defense's image of the defendant as battered.

SHE DOES NOT LOOK MUCH OR ACT MUCH LIKE A BATTERED WOMAN

With all the extant definitions of battered women, a key prosecution strategy is to pick one view and try to show that the defendant in this case is not a "real" battered woman. They attempt to use any possible stereotypes about battered women to question a defendant's authenticity.

DISTRICT ATTORNEY: The battered woman lives in a trailer out in the country and she has eight kids and she doesn't have a job and she doesn't have a car and her husband comes home and beats her. Isn't that really what we think about when we think about a battered woman, a woman that has no choice?

EXPERT: I think when you pick a woman to describe all battered women that sort of points out the kinds of myths and stereotypes that are available to who battered woman might be. It hasn't been my experience that you can fit it into that.

DISTRICT ATTORNEY: Don't you think if we allow a woman who has an expensive automobile, who has an education, who has access to the judges and to the courts of her community, a woman who has access to a large line of credit and a lot of money, who has a telephone, has family and has basically every opportunity to take any other course of action other than killing her husband, if we allow her to say that because her husband beat her up, committed a simple battery that she can kill him, that we are getting way out of bounds?

This interchange illustrates the difficulties of women who do not fit the cultural stereotypes about battered women. This defendant, a lawyer herself, had enormous problems convincing others that she was in need of help.

An insidious stereotype has emerged about a battered woman — she did not leave because she was too frightened and too trapped to do so. The predominant view is that battered women do not leave, even in the face of testimony that a particular woman left many times. As Dobash and Dobash (1979, 1992) point out, her leaving and staying are much more complicated — leaving a violent situation often is a process. Battered women often leave informally — running to their parents for the night, staying outside until their partners cool off, or calling a friend or neighbor. Yet, the stereotype persists that they have never left.

Belief in this stereotype functions to support another interpretation of the actions of women: that at the moment of the incident, leaving would make her safe. In other words, even if she actually has tried to leave before, the stereotype is of a hopeless, trapped woman who has never left or defended herself when she was hit before, and, therefore, she should have just walked out the door rather than killing her partner. Thus, at the moment when she killed him, she had a nonviolent option other than homicide.

Two illustrations show the contradictions that can arise where the belief persists that she does not leave because she is psychologically impaired. The belief that women fall into this stereotype is so pervasive that a woman's own lawyer may ignore the actual realities of the client's life. In my interviews with defense attorneys, I explicitly state that I do not speak about trapped or helpless women. Nonetheless, in a motion in limine to allow my testimony, one defense lawyer stated that I would testify to the following about battered women in general and his client in particular: "They live in quiet fear for years on end and become increasingly afraid for their own well-being; they have nowhere to go if their relationship could be ended; they suffer from learned helplessness; they continue to live with their abusers even though the beatings continue; and it is not unusual for them to remain in such a situation." Not only would I not testify to these criteria, this particular defendant had lived with her abuser only two and one-half years and during that time had formally left about five times and informally left more than a dozen times.

As this woman's case progressed, the subtext of the stereotype of battered women emerged. This same defendant was charged with second-degree murder for shooting her husband while he slept. At the conclusion of the state's case, the judge in conference stated that this was not second-degree murder but a manslaughter case. He would reduce the charge to manslaughter if the defendant agreed to plead guilty to this charge. The defendant agreed. At the sentencing hearing, the judge allowed the defense to put on their witnesses, whose testimony went to show that she was a battered woman. The judge grew increasingly impatient over the course of the hearing and stated that he knew she was a battered woman but that did not change how he perceived the charge of manslaughter.

In this case, the judge sentenced the defendant to 15 months in jail, not prison, with five years' probation. By accepting the reduced charge, the defense was unable to show that she acted in self-defense. She had, after all, pled guilty to a homicide charge. The mitigating circumstances of battering kept this woman from doing harder, longer prison time but did not keep her from temporarily losing her children or her job. The judge had understood that she had been a victim of domestic violence over time, but that did not change her guilty status. The judge's statement is worth quoting at length:

BY THE COURT: All right. The defendant pled guilty to manslaughter, killing her husband. The defendant is the mother of two children who lived in a domestic situation which was violent. The pre-sentence investigation had first recommended against probation, and then at the hearing, sentencing hearing, after certain facts were made known to the probation officer, they changed their recommendation to recommend probation. The guidelines in this particular matter accordingly, because of the defendant's lack of prior criminal history suggests a 60 to 90 month sentence. I have considered those guidelines and I'm going to deviate from them for many, many reasons. And all of them are mitigating factors. There's no question that life is sacred, and the Court has to consider that principle, or there is no need for us to continue having a criminal justice system in the community. The defendant had sought counseling. *There was . . . and I hate to use this "Battered Woman's Syndrome." I think it's a crutch in our modern-day world. . . . Why doesn't the offended party leave?* [emphasis mine] And, of course, this Court understands it's not always that easy, certainly from the pressure of our modern-day world and from our peers to keep marriage intact, and there are many, many times when there seems to be no alternatives.

A careful reading shows what the judge heard in the sentencing hearing and believed about battered women in light of my "expert testimony." First, he ascribed her condition to the battered woman's syndrome when there had been no such testimony, and second, he questioned why she remained in a violent situation when, in fact, she left numerous times. Yet, instead of the maximum of 40 years, which she could have received, she received 15 months of parish jail time.

In most cases where a woman has murdered or attempted to murder her husband, the best that the defense can do is to reduce the charges from second-degree murder to manslaughter. Then, during the sentencing hearings, the defendant can plead for little or no prison time. I testified in only one murder trial in which the woman was found not guilty of any charge. The courts seem prepared to say that she is battered but she also is guilty. Defendants and defense attorneys often make a difficult choice that is not about guilt or innocence but about the realities of the present-day legal context.

WOMAN ABUSE AND THE COURT

Even with experts and, in some cases, because of experts, defendants are having difficulty getting their stories to the juries. At present, expert testimony about domestic violence in some form is being allowed in evidence in most states (Maguigan 1991). In trials of battered women who have killed their abusive husbands, 40 percent of the battered women's convictions were reversed on trial errors. Only 16 percent of the reversals were because of errors dealing with expert testimony. The errors are usually that the trial courts had failed to apply to the women defendants longstanding principles developed in the context of a jurisdiction's ruling on appeals involving male appellants. Further, Maguigan (1991) found that, even with a reasonable battered woman definition, the application of the law works in such a way that precludes defendants' stories from getting to the jury.

Women who are victims of violence have encountered the court and legal system before, usually for protective orders, divorce, or custody arrangements. Nonetheless, when a woman takes action, she has to prove she was justified within a framework that did not believe her before and may not believe her this time.

Being an expert witness in the guilt phase of a murder trial is a frustrating and frightening experience. As a social scientist, I am acutely aware of my shortcomings in the legal system. My testimony can suggest only that the legal system reconsider the categories of homicide. To some degree, my testimony can indict the system by saying that woman abuse reflects behavior patterns not only of the woman and the perpetrator but also of the institutions that were unable to protect her.

It is not my testimony that challenges the court system; it is the lives of battered women that confront and confound it. Without a doubt, these women are victims, but they are also active participants in their own lives. They have lived in fear, but they also have worked consistently to save their own lives. At present, they cannot be heroes but, instead, are often guilty.

NOTES

1. I am indebted to Barbara Davidson for her help on this chapter. I am, however, responsible for any error in this text. The model that I use in expert testimony was developed with Davidson; we have, on occasion, testified at the same trial. Some of the quotes used in this chapter are trials in which she also testified; one quote used to illustrate a common experience is from a trial in which only she testified.

REFERENCES

Blackman, J. 1989. *Intimate Violence*. New York: Columbia University Press.

Blackman, J. 1986. Potential Uses for Expert Testimony: Ideas Toward the Representation of Battered Women Who Kill. *Women's Rights Law Reporter*, 9(3/4), 227–238.

Bowker, L. H. 1984. Coping with Wife Abuse: Personal and Social Networks. In A. R. Roberts (Ed.), *Battered Women and their Families: Intervention Treatment Programs* (pp. 169–191). New York: Springer Publishing.

Browne, A. 1987. *When Battered Women Kill*. New York: Free Press.

Crocker, P. L. 1985, Spring. The Meaning of Equality for Battered Women Who Kill Men in Self-Defense. *Harvard Women's Law Review, 8*, 121–153.

Dobash, R. E., & Dobash, R. P. 1992. *Women, Violence, and Social Change*. New York: Routledge.

Dobash, R. E., & Dobash, R. P. 1979. *Violence Against Wives: A Case Against the Patriarchy*. New York: The Free Press.

Giles-Sims, J. 1983. *Wife Battering: A System Theory Approach*. New York: Guilford Press.

Gillespie, C. K. 1989. *Justifiable Homicide*. Columbus: Ohio State University Press.

Jenkins, P., & Davidson, B. 1990. Battered Women in the Criminal Justice System: An Analysis of Gender Stereotypes. *Behavioral Sciences and the Law, 8*, 161–170.

Kurz, D. 1989. Social Science Perspectives on Wife Abuse: Current Debates and Future Directions. *Gender & Society, 3*, 489–505.

Maguigan, H. 1991. Battered Women and Self-Defense: Myths and Misconceptions in Current Reform Proposals. *University of Pennsylvania Law Review, 140*(2), 397–486.

Okun, L. 1986. *Woman Abuse: Facts Replacing Myths*. Albany: State University of New York Press.

Pagelow, M. D. 1992. Adult Victims of Domestic Violence: Battered Women. *Journal of Interpersonal Violence, 7*(1), 87–120.

Pagelow, M. D. 1981. *Woman-Battering: Victims and Their Experiences*. Beverly Hills, CA: Sage Publications.

Schneider, E. M. 1986. Describing and Changing: Women's Self-Defense Work and the Problem of Expert Testimony on Battering. *Women's Rights Law Reporter, 9*(3/4), 195–222.

Straus, M. A., & Gelles, R. J. 1990. *Physical Violence in American Families*. New Brunswick, NJ: Transaction Publishers.

Walker, L. E. 1989. *Terrifying Love: Why Battered Women Kill and How Society Responds*. New York: Harper & Row.

Walker, L. E. 1986. A Response to Elizabeth Schneider's Describing and Changing: A Woman's Self-Defense Work and the Problem of Expert Testimony on Battering. *Women's Rights Law Reporter, 9*(3/4), 223–225.

Walker, L. E. 1984. *The Battered Woman Syndrome*. New York: Springer.

Walker, L. E. 1979. *The Battered Woman*. New York: Harper & Row.

Worrall, A. 1990. *Offending Women: Female Lawbreakers and the Criminal Justice System*. New York: Routledge.

III

SOCIOLOGY, MEDICINE, AND PSYCHOLOGY: HINTS OF A PARADIGM SHIFT

7

Sociology and the New Religions: "Brainwashing," the Courts, and Religious Freedom

James T. Richardson

I am a veteran of what are often called the cult wars. Over 20 years ago, I began working with graduate students to try and understand the emergence of what have come to be called the new religions (e.g., Hare Krishna, Unification Church, and the Jesus Movement). I had no way of knowing at that time that, two decades later, I would be involved in a number of major legal and legislative battles over the role of new religions in society and in the lives of individuals, both in the United States and overseas, nor could I have guessed that my purely intellectual curiosity about how and why people choose to participate in these nascent religions would evolve into a career focused on legal issues and social policy relevant to the battle over the meaning of new religions. I also did not fathom that involvement in legal issues concerning new religions would contribute to my decision to earn a law degree later in my career (Richardson 1991b). I certainly did not grasp the level of public and professional controversy that was to develop over new religious phenomena.

This chapter discusses several issues in the cult wars that illustrate the importance of sociological and social-psychological knowledge in legal cases involving religious organization. Often at issue was the simple, but significant, question: Do the new religions use so-called brainwashing as a recruitment strategy? The issue has embroiled the American Sociological Association (ASA) and the American Psychological Association (APA) in internal controversies over expert testimony on the truthfulness of brainwashing claims. The National Council of Churches and several other religious and scientific organizations, including the Society for the Scientific Study of Religion (SSSR) and the Association for the Sociology of Religion (ASR), have joined in this major public policy debate. Cases involving this issue have reached the U.S. Supreme Court with the court making several important decisions relevant to the question. More recently, some of these professional organizations and individual scholars found themselves named as defendants in multimillion-dollar lawsuits in federal and state courts as a result of actions taken concerning one such case.

My story begins in a quite ordinary fashion: several graduate students and I were intellectually curious about why and how people join and participate in new religions.

BEGINNING OF A CONTROVERSY

When people participate in new religions, the question often asked is: Were they brainwashed or tricked through powerful and mysterious psychotechnology, or did they join of their own volition? Do they remain in the groups by personal choice, or are they under some sort of mind control? These controversial questions, which surfaced in the late 1960s and 1970s after public attention was focused on the phenomenon of new religions, have been the focal point of a number of legal cases and social policy debates.

Courts at every level have heard hundreds of cases of various types, most based on a public perception that cults brainwash naive youth. Political bodies, from city councils to state legislatures to the U.S. Congress and federal agencies, also have been involved in efforts to deal with the perceived cult menace. Claims by some former members (and their parents) that they were brainwashed and under mind control have fueled tort actions against several of the new religions. A few civil suits have resulted in multimillion-dollar damage awards to plaintiffs suing some of the newer religions (Anthony 1990; Richardson 1991a; Anthony & Robbins 1992). Claims in such suits by former members have been buttressed by a few social and behavioral scientists offering evidence that brainwashing was a legitimate problem.

Religious organizations that were sued for damages or attacked in legislative forums have defended themselves by claiming that members participate by choice and know what they are getting into before they join. Moreover, it has been pointed out that most new members leave the new religion group soon after joining, also of their own volition (Richardson 1985; Richardson 1993c). A few other social scientists and I who have been willing to offer rebuttal testimony in legal action and legislative hearings usually have stressed a more volitional model to explain participation. Our rebuttal testimony, however, usually was not effective with jurors or policy makers, many of whom seem to share a belief in cult brainwashing and think that the new religions should be controlled and punished.

Another variant of brainwashing cases involves criminal charges for kidnapping brought against deprogrammers. A deprogrammer is someone who rescues a participant and puts them through rigorous resocialization in an effort to return them to normal life. Deprogramming has become a new quasi-profession in the United States (and abroad), with thousands of deprogrammings carried out over the past two decades, usually involving participants who are of legal age (Bromley & Richardson 1983).

Defendants in these cases are likely to use the necessity or choice of evils arguments. The choice of evils defense argues that kidnapping someone from a so-called cult is a lesser evil than leaving them in the group, because, allegedly, they were initially brainwashed into joining and, thus, had lost their free will. It is, thus, necessary to break a law (kidnapping) in order to avoid a greater harm — leaving them in the hands of the evil brainwashing cult. The choice of evils defense usually is effective. Most such cases have resulted in acquittals of those charged, even in the face of significant rebuttal testimony, as well as constitutional defenses to such claims.[1]

There are important legal precedents, however, that challenge the brainwashing perspective. In a few recent cases, rulings by judges in pre-trial evidentiary hearings favored those opposing the use of brainwashing testimony. For instance, *United States v. Fishman* (1990), a criminal action, resulted in a strong ruling disallowing testimony for the defense from two prominent brainwashing theorists (see Anthony & Robbins 1992 on *Fishman*; Richardson 1991a and Shinn 1992 for mention of other such cases). The *Fishman* case served as an important precedent in other cases, including civil ones in which brainwashing testimony was limited or disallowed.[2] This chapter will document the difficulties of achieving such a result.

KNOWLEDGE ON NEW RELIGIONS

The involvement of a few sociologists and psychologists of religion in the so-called cult brainwashing cases in opposition to brainwashing theories was motivated in part by personal concerns about freedom of religion but mainly by questions about the quality of expert psychological and psychiatric testimony being offered in such cases. Charges of brainwashing ignore a large body of evidence published in major professional refereed journals in sociology, psychiatry, psychology, and religious studies, which concludes that participation in new religions is virtually always a volitional act of young people deciding to try, at least temporarily, different lifestyles, belief systems, and ethics (Barker 1984; Richardson 1985, 1993c, 1995a; Bromley & Richardson 1983). The research shows, as well, that participation in the new religions often serves an ameliorative purpose, enhancing a feeling of psychological well-being, and most people leave the groups (which are actually quite small) after relatively brief participation (Kilbourne & Richardson 1984; Galanter, Rabkin, Rabkin, & Deutsch 1979).

This body of scholarly research contradicts the idea of a magical and mysterious technique such as brainwashing or mind control that forces young people into joining the new groups. Rather, most scholarly research shows that ordinary social-psychological processes are at work in such affiliations (Solomon 1983; Richardson 1993c). The scholarly literature demonstrates overwhelmingly that most people who join the groups do so only temporarily, stay a relatively short time, and leave to try something different or return to their normal social location, if it remains available to them.

Research also shows that the idea of members being brainwashed into joining was being promoted by members of what some sociologists call the anti-cult movement (Shupe & Bromley 1980, 1994; Bromley & Shupe 1995; Solomon 1981; Wright 1984). Included in this growing international movement and attendant organizations are deprogrammers, a smattering of religious leaders, parents of some members, and a few key legitimators, such as one clinical psychologist who has testified about brainwashing in many cult cases (Richardson 1991a; Anthony 1990).

GENERAL HISTORY OF INVOLVEMENT

Allegations of brainwashing first appeared in mass media stories about the new religions and, within a short time, were used in legal actions against them. My initial concern was that brainwashing claims were being offered by a few social scientists and clinicians whose testimony ignored a growing body of evidence about the meaning and processes of participation in the new religions that supported the volitional model. This evidence took the form of papers presented at professional conferences and published in refereed professional journals, but it was seldom alluded to in media treatments or court cases dealing with the issue of the meaning of participation. My initial concern changed quickly into worry as it became obvious that the brainwashing claims were being attended to by the legal system and policy makers.

A pattern quickly developed in the legal arena, with advocates of the brainwashing theories winning in jury trials. It was disturbing to see juries award large damages to people who chose to participate in new religions, subsequently changed their minds, and redefined themselves as victims of cult brainwashing. It was also upsetting to see acquitted people who abducted those who voluntarily joined a new religion, allowing them to continue their practice of deprogramming.

My concern over these developments was compounded by the fact that a few social and behavioral scientists were, in my opinion, misrepresenting their disciplines by testifying in court in support of brainwashing claims. I decided, along with several colleagues in the sociology and psychology of religion, to respond to their interpretation of the practices of the new religions through a number of professional activities. We responded to requests to discuss the issues with representatives of some of the religious groups under attack. Some of us also had contact with other groups and individuals with an interest in the outcome of this issue, such as the American Civil Liberties Union and the National Council of Churches.

Several of the religious group leaders educated themselves about social science research on the new religions and tried to make use of it in legal proceedings. Eventually, some colleagues and I agreed to serve as consultants or as potential expert witnesses in several cases to rebut brainwashing-based testimony. This approach proved relatively ineffective, in part because the attorneys for the defense usually were uninformed about social science methods or research results and did not present them well in court.

These haphazard efforts had little effect on the outcome of the cases. Largely because of the popular appeal of simple brainwashing notions, a typical juror was prepared to believe that cults brainwashed unsuspecting and naive individuals. Another factor was the lack of courtroom experience among most of the participating social scientists. Frustrated, but unwilling to give up, we continued to talk among ourselves. We also met at professional meetings and exchanged papers and other communications relevant to the issue. We decided to seek the support of our professional academic organizations, including the SSSR, an interdisciplinary organization of some 1,700 members; the ASR, an organization of about 700 sociologists of religion; and Division 36 of the APA, a group of over 1,000 psychologists of religion.

We asked these professional organizations to assist us in limiting the affects of testimony from self-appointed brainwashing experts. The legal strategy we decided to use was the amicus curiae, or friend of the court, brief. Amicus briefs sponsored by professional organizations (and, at times, individual researchers) are a popular way for scholars to inform the legal system of important findings (Tremper 1987; Acker 1990; Roesch, Golding, Hans, & Reppucci 1991). Three amicus briefs were eventually written and filed in cases that will be discussed in more detail herein.

Also, short position statements were approved by some professional organizations that codified their collective stance on brainwashing. I participated in writing these statements, which argue that brainwashing testimony should not be accepted by courts because it was based on questionable assumptions and unsupported by most research in the area. The statements were written to be cited in future brainwashing cases. Some scholars began some research directly relevant to the issue of juror reaction to brainwashing testimony (DeWitt, Richardson, & Warner 1991; Pfieffer 1992; Richardson 1992b). Topics of interest included criteria and procedures appropriate to approving the use of social science testimony in cult cases, and the impacts of brainwashing evidence on jurors.

The issue of what standards should be applied when novel scientific theories are presented in court is a longstanding controversy within the U.S. legal system. The *Frye* test (1993) for expert evidence (see Chapter

1 in this volume) was the law in most courts during the legal cult wars. It encouraged efforts to challenge or stop brainwashing based testimony on the grounds that it was not generally accepted within the relevant disciplines doing research on new religions. Some success was achieved using *Frye*, either through having appeal courts overturn verdicts because the testimony on which they were based was questionable or by having trial courts disallow such testimony in the first place, given its questionable nature (Anthony 1990). The latter approach was based on pre-trial evidentiary hearings that focused on the issue of admissibility of brainwashing evidence. The following case illustrates the complex sociological and legal issues on cases involving the new religions.

THE *MOLKO/LEAL* CASE AGAINST
THE UNIFICATION CHURCH

The saga of *Molko/Leal* (1986) started innocently enough with the decision of two young people to try out an alternative lifestyle and belief system by joining the Unification Church (UC), popularly known as the Moonies. David Molko was a 27-year-old recent graduate of Temple University Law School in Pennsylvania. He passed the Pennsylvania bar exam in 1979. Undecided about his future, he went to California to examine career alternatives. While there, Molko encountered UC recruiters, who invited him to a dinner. At the dinner, he was asked to attend further sessions at a rural training center operated by the church. Molko agreed but would later claim that he was not told the true identity of the group until the twelfth day of this several-week-long process. Approximately 30 days after Molko first encountered members of the UC, he decided to become a member of this new religion.

UC recruiters may have encouraged Molko to become a member in part because of his legal training. They asked him to take the California bar exam, and agreed to pay a sizable enrollment fee for a review course to prepare for the exam. Molko took the course, traveling daily for several weeks from the recruitment camp to course meetings. He then took and passed the California bar exam, a test with the lowest pass rate in the country. Immediately after the exam, and just six months after joining the UC, Molko was kidnapped by deprogrammers retained by his parents. At first, Molko resisted the kidnapping and deprogramming, but after three days, he recanted his beliefs and affiliation with the UC.

Shortly after the deprogramming, Molko decided to sue the UC for torts of false imprisonment, fraud and deceit, and intentional infliction of emotional distress and for restitution of $6,000 he gave the church after he became a member. Molko was joined in the suit by Tracy Leal, who also had joined the UC in 1979.

Leal was 19 when she joined the UC. She admitted in deposition that she knew the group's identity prior to her decision to become a full member but claimed she was already under the spell of the UC by that time and could not make an informed decision about joining. Similar to Molko, Leal's parents hired a deprogrammer, and she was successfully deprogrammed in Los Angeles a few months after joining the new religion. At the urging of her father, a California attorney, she quickly joined Molko's suit.

Although the grounds for the suit were traditional torts such as intentional infliction of emotional distress and false imprisonment, the real issue was the claim that the two plaintiffs were brainwashed and subject to mind control prior to their decision to join the group. At first, few observers of the court took this suit seriously. Both parties were of legal age when they joined the UC, and each admitted that they knew what group they were joining before they made the decision and that no physical restraint was used to keep them in the group. The UC filed a summary judgment motion prior to the case going to trial. The group won a dismissal in 1993.

In response to the motion to dismiss, plaintiffs Molko and Leal filed depositions from psychiatrist Samuel Benson and psychologist Margaret Singer. Both experts had testified in the famous *Katz* (1977) case a few years previously in San Francisco in favor of allowing use of conservatorship laws to facilitate deprogramming several adult members of the UC. In that case, the California appeal court had over-ruled a lower court decision to allow such uses of the conservatorship laws, a ruling that quashed such efforts in California and also had a dramatic negative impact nationwide on applying conservatorship laws to members of new religions (Bromley 1983).

Singer has testified in over 40 cult cases around the country about the efficacy of brainwashing, and what she termed the "systematic ma-nipulation of social influence." Her testimony usually is quite effective with jurors, many of whom apparently shared a popular belief in brain-washing, and also appeared not to approve of new or exotic religions. Singer's testimony was instrumental in several multimillion-dollar verdicts for plaintiffs in suits similar to the *Molko/Leal* case.[3]

San Francisco Superior Court Judge Stuart Pollak, the trial court judge in *Molko/Leal*, decided not to allow such testimony presented to a jury. The judge granted the summary judgment motion by the UC and issued a rare written opinion of some 30 pages to make his point that there were constitutional prohibitions precluding the case going to trial. He also was very critical of the testimony of the two plaintiff's experts, stating that their opinions "are veiled value judgments concerning the entire outlook of the Unification Church." In a footnote to the quoted sentence, Pollak added: "Both doctors examined the Plaintiffs long after the events in question. They did not reach their opinion concerning the Plaintiff's state of mind based upon a contemporaneous examination independent of their views of Unification Church methods, but seem to have reasoned backwards from their disapproval of those methods to the conclusion that Plaintiffs were not thinking freely because they were persuaded by them" (unreported opinion of the Superior Court of California 1986).

Appealing the Dismissal

After such a resounding rejection, coupled with the earlier rejection of virtually the same testimony in the *Katz* case, plaintiffs Molko and Leal might have given up, but they persisted and filed an appeal with the California appeal court. A three judge panel of the appeal court made an even stronger statement about the case than did Pollak. In a lengthy opinion, the panel affirmed the trial court on all counts. It also held that a cross-complaint by the UC against the deprogrammers and Molko for violation of the civil right to exercise religious freedom by UC members was valid (the trial court had dismissed this cross-complaint for lack of standing to sue by the UC).

The ruling by the appeal court in 1986 agreed that constitutional protections precluded an evaluation of the beliefs and practices of the UC, as would be required in the *Molko/Leal* case. The court went much further and, with its ruling on the cross-complaint, indicated concern about the effects of forcible deprogramming on UC members, as was done with both Molko and Leal. Thus, the court seemed to take seriously the church's contentions that deprogramming violated the religious freedom of participants in new religions. The court also agreed with Pollak's assessment of the quality of the psychological and psychiatric testimony. The court noted that the testimony of the two experts for the plaintiffs even disagreed at crucial points with statements of the plaintiffs themselves. The appeal court, in discussing the fraud and deceit claim, found that: "If liability could be imposed in such circumstances, any disaffected adherent of a religion could bring suit alleging that he had been 'brainwashed' by the religious organization, and courts would become entangled in determining which adherents acted out of true faith and which were subject to 'mind control.' This result is clearly at odds with the First Amendment" (*Molko and Leal v. Unification Church* 1986).

Surprisingly, the plaintiffs appealed to the California Supreme Court. It was this appeal to the California Supreme Court that led to further discussion by scholars and religious groups.

Scholars Enter the Fray

A number of scholars were concerned about the appeal of *Molko/ Leal* to the California Supreme Court. Some scholars argued that the California Supreme Court, which had recently shifted in a conservative direction, would not support violating First Amendment protections in the area of religion. However, many observers were decidedly nervous about the prospect of the newly constituted conservative court ruling on the case. Other observers felt that the California Supreme Court's traditional leadership role in U.S. judicial circles made it imperative that the court have all relevant evidence prior to deciding the case. This was difficult because the case was at the court on appeal from a summary judgment motion; thus, little evidence was available, because there was no trial. Furthermore, a summary judgment required the court to consider the plaintiffs' case in the best possible light.

I participated in a series of meetings with a few sociologists and psychologists of religion and an attorney for the UC. Among the issues we considered was whether or not it was appropriate to file an amicus curiae brief with the California Supreme Court. I also was among those who participated in discussions with an officer of the 65,000 member APA. These deliberations were initiated by several scholars within Division 36 of the APA, a subgroup of nearly 1,400 research-oriented psychologists of religion. After reviewing a large amount of scholarly writing on the topics of recruitment and participation in new religions, APA legal counsel drafted an amicus curiae brief. The brief summarized relevant scholarship and undercut the brainwashing and mind control interpretation being offered by plaintiffs' experts. The brief assented that brainwashing based claims were not generally acceptable in the relevant disciplines and, therefore, should not be allowed as evidence. This assertion was based on the *Frye* rule (1923), an important criterion of general acceptance from a federal case on the use of scientific evidence in court.[4] This draft was read and commented on by several interested scholars, including myself.

The APA board of directors voted to sponsor the brief at its winter meeting in February 1987. The brief also was signed by several leading scholars in the fields of psychology and sociology of religion, including five past presidents of the 700 member ASR and several past presidents of the 1,700 member SSSR. Also signing the document were five past presidents of Division 36 of the APA, along with a number of other prominent scholars, including Martin Marty of the Divinity School, University of Chicago. Thus, the amicus brief was a unique and significant interdisciplinary statement opposing the use of brainwashing testimony in cult brainwashing cases.

In this brief, psychologist Singer's testimony was specifically criticized. A long-term member of the powerful clinical branch of the APA, she responded to the brief by organizing a protest among its membership.

This pressure, accompanied by rumors that many clinicians would withdraw from the APA if the brief was not disavowed, compelled the APA to withdraw its support for the brief. The withdrawal of the brief probably worked against upholding the lower court decisions in *Molko/Leal*, because it demonstrated that a controversy existed on major issues of the case. The California Supreme Court referred to this controversy in its decision and said that the matter should be resolved by a jury (Anthony & Robbins 1992).

The APA's official reason for withdrawing its sponsorship of the brief was that an ongoing task force already was examining issues relevant to the brief. A few years prior to the brief, Singer initiated an APA task force to examine the alleged deceptive practices of religious and therapeutic groups. At the time the amicus brief was submitted, Singer's task force was preparing a report relevant to the issues in the *Molko/Leal* case, a pendency cited by the APA as the reason for its withdrawal of sponsorship. When a draft of the task force's report finally was submitted to the APA, anonymous reviewers found it seriously flawed. The APA rejected the report, using particularly strong language.[5]

A number of religious groups also submitted amicus briefs in the *Molko/Leal* case because of their concern about the implications of the appeal for religious freedom. Briefs filed by the National Council of Churches, Americans United for Separation of Church and State, the American Baptist Church, and the Southern California Ecumenical Council focused on issues of religious freedom and discriminatory treatment of minority religions.

Ruling of the California Supreme Court

On October 17, 1988, the California Supreme Court issued a ruling reversing the California appeal court on counts of fraud, intentional infliction of emotional distress, and restitution (the false imprisonment claim had been withdrawn). The court completely ignored the APA amicus brief, which, because it initially was signed by individual scholars as well as the APA, technically was still before the court, even though APA had withdrawn as a sponsor. Rather, the court accepted the efficacy of the brainwashing perspective, even citing anticult publications that had not been submitted to normal rigorous review process used by professional journals. The court said, "We need not resolve the controversy: We need only conclude that the existence of such differing views compels the conclusion that Molko and Leal's theory indeed raises a factual question — viz., whether Molko and Leal were brainwashed — which, if not prohibited by other considerations, precludes a grant summary judgment for the church" (*Molko and Leal v. Unification Church* 1988).

Thus, the door was opened to the type of suits brought by Molko and Leal (see especially Anthony & Robbins 1992). Former members of religious groups not satisfied with what happened to them while in a group now could sue the group, especially if the plaintiffs allege deception in recruitment. Apparently, people who claim that they were brainwashed and under mind control are guaranteed a trial in California. Some observers also predicted that the use of brainwashing in civil actions involving religion would lead to an expansion of such diminished capacity-based civil actions outside of religion.

On to the U.S. Supreme Court

Concerned about the national implications of California's Supreme Court decision, a number of individuals and organizations suggested that the UC consider appealing the ruling of the California Supreme Court in *Molko/Leal* to the U.S. Supreme Court. We knew, of course, that the U.S. Supreme Court accepts for review only a minuscule percentage of cases submitted to it; moreover, this appeal would be from a ruling on a summary judgment motion (no trial had been held), diminishing further our already slim chances of winning a review. However, we thought it worthwhile to seek a review, in part because of a recent case (*United States v. Kosminski* 1988) with some important similarities, even though it did not involve participation in new religions.

The U.S. Supreme Court, in a 1988 opinion authored by O'Connor, had ruled in *Kosminski* that constitutional provisions against involuntary servitude could not be invoked without the presence of physical coercion. Because the issue of whether or not brainwashing can occur short of a physically coercive situation is an important area of disagreement among stakeholders in so-called cult recruiting cases, some of us thought the U.S. Supreme Court might take advantage of another opportunity to limit causes of action by articulating a physical coercion requirement for cases alleging damage from recruitment to religious groups. Other groups and individuals wanted the *Molko/Leal* ruling appealed because of concerns about the impact of the ruling on freedom of religion, particularly the freedom to proselytize (Richardson 1988).

Some scholars and religionists cautioned against seeking review at this point in the controversy because of the recent record of the U.S. Supreme Court in cases involving new and more exotic religions. The court has displayed an antipathy toward nontraditional religions while, at the same time, issuing rulings in a number of cases supportive of more traditional religious groups (Richardson 1988, 1995b; Bromley & Robbins 1992).

Nevertheless, the UC decided to seek review of the ruling of the California Supreme Court by the U.S. Supreme Court. Several scholars who worked on the original APA amicus brief agreed to make another effort to submit a statement of their views to the court. This discussion was facilitated by prior submission of yet another "scholars" amicus brief, which had been prepared and submitted in a different case then on appeal to the California appeal court, the case of *George v. International Society of Krishna Consciousness* (1989). The *George* amicus brief, which may have had a more positive impact, served as a model for the approach taken in the request for review submitted to the U.S. Supreme Court in *Molko/Leal*.

The *George* Case

George v. International Society of Krishna Consciousness was heard in California in the early 1980s and resulted in a jury award of close to $33 million (reduced by the judge to $9.7 million). The plaintiff was a young woman who participated in the group for nearly two years. Singer provided two days of testimony. On the witness stand, she invoked theories of brainwashing similar to those she used in the *Molko/Leal* and *Katz* cases (see Richardson 1991:59–64), in spite of the fact that *George* did not involve any allegations of deception of the underage recruit. A number of my colleagues and I were sufficiently concerned about Singer's testimony to write yet another amicus brief, which was sponsored by the SSSR.

The *George* case amicus brief may have influenced the outcome. The California appeal court threw out the overtly brainwashing based claims of the plaintiff. It did, however, allow other claims to stand, including some that indirectly related to brainwashing allegations. The plaintiff was awarded $2.7 million damages, plus accruing interest (a total of over $5 million). The California Supreme Court, on appeal, allowed the decision of the appeal court to stand but took the unusual step of disallowing its official publication.[6]

The U.S. Supreme Court was asked to grant review of the *George* case and issued a stay on executing the judgment. The Krishnas argued that the decision would force them to cease operations. Apparently, all the Krishna property in California and a number of other states had been legally obligated because of the judgment. The *George* case, along with one other involving brainwashing based testimony from Singer — *Wollershiem v. Scientology* (1989) — were eventually vacated by the U.S. Supreme Court. Both cases were remanded by the court for further consideration in light of a ruling concerning the legality of large punitive damages in a major insurance case. The *George* case has since been settled for an unknown amount, as was the *Wollershiem* case.

THE SECOND *MOLKO/LEAL* APPEAL BRIEF

The apparent partial success of the amicus brief in the *George* case was not known to us at the time a few others and I were deciding whether to work on an amicus brief for the U.S. Supreme Court appeal of *Molko/Leal*. Nevertheless, we entered the fray. A draft of the amicus brief to the U.S. Supreme Court in the *Molko/Leal* case was submitted to the SSSR Council, which eventually agreed to sponsor a revised version of the brief. It also was sent to a number of other scholars who signed on as individual sponsors. The list of individual sponsors included six past presidents and other officers of the ASR, two past presidents and a number of officers of the SSSR, four past presidents and other officers of Division 36 (Psychology of Religion) of the APA, along with a number of other scholars, including Martin Marty; Robert Ellwood, professor and director of the School of Religion, University of Southern California; and Bryan Wilson, an internationally known sociologist of religion from All Souls College, Oxford.

The thrust of the amicus brief sponsored by the SSSR and others in the *Molko/Leal* case was that self-selected experts should be precluded from testifying that recruitment methods in new religions approximate brainwashing and mind control. There was simply too much counterevidence in the research on new religions to support this perspective. The brief was based on the earlier-discussed *Frye* principle. The SSSR amicus brief to the U.S. Supreme Court (and earlier amicus briefs in *Molko/Leal* and *George*) claimed that the brainwashing theory applied to recruitment to new religions was not generally accepted, especially the theory's claim that brainwashing and mind control could be accomplished without physical coercion.

Other amicus briefs filed with the U.S. Supreme Court on the appeal of the *Molko/Leal* case focused on implications of the case for freedom of religion. These included briefs sponsored by the National Council of Churches, the Presbyterian Church (U.S.A.), the American Baptist Churches, and the Catholic League for Religious and Civil Rights.

During development of the SSSR amicus brief, I had conversations with the executive officer of the 10,000 member ASA. The executive officer was a sociologist of religion who was an individual signatory of the two earlier amicus briefs focusing on brainwashing allegations. The matter of possible ASA sponsorship was raised, and a decision was made within the ASA office to allow the organization to be listed as a cosponsor along with the SSSR and the individual signatories.

This decision turned out to be a fateful one. Submission of the brief on May 1, 1988, immediately involved the ASA in an internal conflict similar to the one that had enveloped the APA over submission of the initial amicus brief in *Molko/Leal*. One particular sociologist, Richard Ofshe, mounted a vigorous and continuing crusade to get the ASA off the brief. He threatened to sue the ASA for $500,000, which is what he claimed the ASA position would cost him in expert witness fees if it was not negated. Ofshe had been testifying in some of the cult brainwashing cases and had also developed a line of testimony that used a similar idea to assist people overcome their prior confessions when charged with criminal matters (see Anthony & Robbins 1995 for specifics on Ofshe's efforts in cult brainwashing cases).

Following several months of debate, the ASA council voted to withdraw its sponsorship of the brief, claiming that there was too much of a controversy for the ASA to take sides. The issue was already moot, however, because the U.S. Supreme Court refused to review the decision of the California Supreme Court in *Molko/Leal*, thus, paving the way for a trial on the issue. A trial was never held, however, because the case was settled out of court.

It is ironic that the major thrust of the amicus brief was demonstrated by the decision of the ASA to withdraw its sponsorship: that there was inadequate evidence to allow brainwashing based claims to be offered as expert testimony under evidence rules that require general acceptance. This same reasoning applies to the decision of the APA to withdraw from the earlier amicus brief. At this juncture in the cult wars, a new battle emerges.

Subsequent Developments

Singer and Ofshe were to testify for the defense in a federal case in California (*Fishman* 1990) involving mail fraud charges brought against a former member of one major new religious group who claimed he was brainwashed into violating the law (see Anthony & Robbins 1992, 1995; Richardson 1991a for discussions of this case). San Francisco Federal Judge Lowell Jensen ruled in 1990, in *Fishman*, that neither Singer nor Ofshe could testify on brainwashing and thought reform, because this testimony was not generally accepted in the scientific community. The judge used the controversy over the amicus briefs within the ASA and APA as evidence that no consensus exists on the brainwashing theories propounded by Singer and others in cult cases. He was informed about the substantive issues involved in brainwashing testimony by lengthy declarations on the issue of brainwashing testimony filed by sociologist Dick Anthony, consultant for the government in the case, and Perry London, a former dean of Educational Psychology at Rutgers University.

The *Fishman* ruling was encouraging for those opposed to brainwashing based testimony. A second decision also was reason for optimism. Prior to *Fishman*, Anthony had consulted in a brainwashing based civil case against Transcendental Meditation (TM), which was cited as precedent in the mail fraud case. The TM case was the first of several cases against the new religion filed by a number of former participants in district court in Washington, D.C. It illustrates the problem that social and behavioral scientists would face in arguing for the legitimacy of brainwashing in the aftermath of the APA and ASA amicus brief controversy. A jury awarded $137,000 damages (with no punitive damages) in 1988 to a plaintiff after hearing Singer testify, over strong defense protests based on the *Frye* principle that the testimony lacked general acceptance in the scientific community. The relatively small award was viewed as a victory by the defense, but they decided to appeal anyway, in an effort to get Singer's testimony thrown out.

On appeal, the D.C. Circuit Court of Appeals ordered a retrial in 1991 and suggested further examination of the issue of allowing expert brainwashing based testimony. The court suggested using a lower standard of acceptance — substantial acceptance — because this was a civil action and added that the plaintiff: "Has failed to provide *any* evidence that Dr. Singer's particular theory, namely that techniques of thought reform may be effective in the absence of physical threats or coercion, has a significant following in the scientific community, let alone general acceptance" (Kropinski 1988).

In March 1991, the trial court ruled that Singer, as well as Ofshe, who had by now joined the cases, could not testify to brainwashing and thought reform theories because they were not widely believed by the scientific community. Even allowing a weaker standard of admissibility, substantial acceptance as opposed to the *Frye*-based general acceptance rule, was not sufficient to save Singer and Ofshe's testimony. The district court did, however, allow discussion of participation in TM as a possible cause of mental disorders. Nevertheless, rulings in the TM cases represent an important victory for those opposing the notion that participation in new religions results from trickery and fraud. Two federal courts now have disallowed brainwashing based testimony, and one circuit court of appeals has issued a ruling calling such testimony into question. Battles continue in several cases on the issue, with "the jury still out" on whether the controversy over brainwashing testimony will lead to difficulties for such testimony in other cases. The controversy was to take another, quite significant, legal turn, however.

The Singer/Ofshe Lawsuit against Their Opponents

The two major proponents of brainwashing theories of participation in new religions filed lawsuits for large monetary damages against those who had, with some success, opposed their views in legal actions. Singer and Ofshe filed an action in federal court in New York in 1992 asking for some $30 million dollars in damages against the APA, the ASA, their officers and attorneys at the time of the *Molko/Leal* amicus brief development, and five other individuals, including three people who had participated most actively in developing the briefs and in promoting them within the two professional organizations. I was among the five named as defendants. My participation included serving as a rebuttal witness, helping draft the amicus briefs discussed herein, promoting the briefs within professional organizations, and, also, some writing that is quite critical of the Singer and Ofshe position (Kilbourne & Richardson 1984; Richardson 1986, 1991a, 1992a, 1993a, 1993b, 1993c, 1994, 1995a, 1995b).

The 90-page complaint filed in the suit was based on alleged violations of the federal racketeering statute, known by the acronym RICO. Allegedly, as we were discussing the problem of what to do about the testimony being offered by Singer and Ofshe, we were involved in a major conspiracy to ruin the plaintiffs' major source of livelihood. Every time a phone call was made or material mailed or faxed dealing with the general issue or the specific development of amicus briefs, this was alleged to be a violation of federal mail and wire fraud statutes by the defendants. The pattern of these acts allegedly constitutes the necessary illegal predicate acts to constitute a RICO conspiracy under federal law.

The defendants in the lawsuit filed lengthy motions to dismiss the complaint on a number of grounds. The argument of the defendants was based on the idea that a dispute among scientists cannot be transmuted into a violation of federal racketeering statutes. The major brief supporting the motion to dismiss went into considerable detail to point out that the RICO statute as it was written did not include using the statute for settling scholarly disputes. Also, the attorney Anthony and I used argued in a supplemental brief that involvement in developing possible amicus briefs for courts to consider has been a privileged activity in the U.S. legal system and that this privilege should continue.

The case took a year to decide. The decision was to dismiss the action "with prejudice" (which means it cannot be filed again in federal court). We were quite relieved, of course, but this was not the end of our difficulties. Early in 1994, plaintiffs Singer and Ofshe filed virtually the same action in state court in California, under state conspiracy and libel statutes. They dropped the attorneys for the two professional organizations as named defendants but retained as defendants the ASA and APA officers at the time of the actions taken to sponsor the two amicus briefs in the *Molko/Leal* case, along with the other individually named defendants, including myself. They also added Gordon Melton as a defendant, apparently because he, as director of the Institute for the Study of American Religion in Santa Barbara, had served as a rebuttal witness in some cases and had written a number of papers quite critical of brainwashing claims being offered by Singer and Ofshe.

After much difficulty in locating adequate legal council for the individually named defendants, who were not defended by their professional organizations,[7] motions to dismiss were filed with the court, along with some other relevant motions. On June 17, 1994, the case was dismissed, with the judge stating that First Amendment (freedom of speech) considerations allowed the type of activities engaged in by the defendants and precluded legal action such as the one before the court. He added that he did not even address the matter of whether development of amicus briefs is protected activity.[8]

Thus, this strange effort to use the courts to enforce a certain questionable perspective on participation in new religion may finally be over. If the court had not ruled as it did, then there would have been a remarkable precedent established for resolving scientific disputes in court and potential legal liability for those engaged in discussing controversial theories and research and publishing controversial opinions and research results. I should add that court costs for all defendants thus far in the second suit approximate $300,000.

Other Impacts of the Controversy

It is not known what long-lasting effects this controversy will have on the APA and the ASA, or other professional organizations less directly involved. The arguments for and against brainwashing in the new religions continue in the APA. Some members support the views of Singer, while others, especially many psychologists of religion, strongly disagree. The ASA had to deal with similar internal conflicts, with strong feelings on both sides of the issue.

Anticult organizations such as the Cult Awareness Network and the American Family Foundation continue to work diligently to promote their view that such groups are a threat to individual members and to the "American way of life" (Bromley & Shupe 1995:222). They continue to sponsor conferences and to publish materials supportive of the view that new religions are dangerous to the mental health of U.S. youth. They also are involved in high profile cases like the Branch Davidian tragedy in Waco, Texas, to promote their views of the significance of the cult menace (see Lewis 1994; Wright 1995).

Many religious groups and leaders continue to be deeply concerned about the implications of cult brainwashing cases for religious freedom in our society. This clearly is indicated by submission of amicus briefs from a number of traditional religious organizations and denominations in cult brainwashing or related cases (see Richardson 1984, 1992b). These more mainstream groups apparently have come to believe they could be the next target of attack in the courts, using brainwashing based theories (Anthony & Robbins 1995; Richardson 1995b).

In the background is the U.S. Supreme Court, biding its time before speaking directly on the issue of claims based on the controversial brainwashing theories. The direction the court may choose to take on the issue of a physical coercion requirement for brainwashing based torts will affect the role scholarly research and expert testimony will play in cases in the future as well as impact what freedom of religion will mean in the United States in years ahead. Some of those involved in the controversy predict that such a pronouncement may be forthcoming in the foreseeable future, perhaps deriving directly from a case involving brainwashing based claims made against one of the newer controversial religions.

The story of the new religions cannot be told accurately without solid work by sociologists and other social scientists. My own personal involvement in this debate is a lifelong career interest that even contributed to my obtaining a law degree. Not surprisingly, the knowledge that sociology brings to the study of new religions is critical to any legal considerations of their organization and actions. The question remains: Will sociology's account of recruitment and participation in the new religions assist the courts in reaching just decisions in the inevitable legal battles ahead?

NOTES

1. After thousands of such deprogrammings over the past 25 years (Bromley & Richardson 1983; Richardson 1995b; Bromley & Robbins 1992), the federal government has pressed charges only twice, with a conviction in one of the cases.

2. It should be noted that Anthony deserves considerable personal credit for development of the most thoroughgoing intellectual critique of brainwashing claims and of specific forms of such testimony. He consulted closely with the federal prosecutor in the *Fishman* case and served as a key consultant in other cases in which such testimony has been disallowed (Anthony 1990; Anthony & Robbins 1992; Richardson & Kilbourne 1983; Richardson 1991a, 1993c, 1995b).

3. Singer testified in a case against Scientology in Oregon that resulted in an initial $39 million verdict, although the trial judge eventually overturned that verdict and the case was not retried. She also was a major plaintiff's witness in another case against Scientology (*Wollershiem*) that resulted in a similar verdict and that eventually was settled for an unknown amount. She was the major witness in the *George* case against the Hare Krishna, which resulted in an initial $32 million verdict.

4. See Anthony and Robbins (1995) for discussion of this rule as it has applied to cult brainwashing cases, and see Richardson (1994) and Richardson, Ginsburg, Gatowski, and Dobbin (1995) for discussion of implications of a recent major change in this rule.

5. The Board of Social and Ethical Responsibility for Psychology found that "the report lacked the scientific rigor and evenhanded critical approach necessary for APA imprimatur" (letter from APA board to Singer 1988).

6. A decision to disallow official publication of a decision is a way of limiting its precedential impact. No "depublished" decision can be referred to in a court action in California without special permission of the court. In this particular case, depublishing the *George* appeal court decision avoided the obvious conflict between that decision and the ruling in *Molko/Leal*. The cases differed in significant ways, for example, deception was claimed in *Molko/Leal*, whereas it was not in *George*. See Richardson (1991a) and Anthony and Robbins (1995) for more on *George*.

7. The issue of how one defends against such a suit is a meaty one. When sued, one must defend or risk a default judgment. The fact that the two large professional organizations did not agree to defend individual defendants left us casting about for help. The tale of how this was accomplished is too complex to discuss here, but it clearly demonstrates that this is an issue of great significance.

8. This case was appealed by the plaintiffs, in part to obtain time to work out a settlement, given that they were responsible for attorney's fees for defendants in the case.

REFERENCES

Acker, J. 1990. Social Science in Supreme Court Criminal Cases and Briefs: The Actual and Potential Contribution of Social Scientists as Amici Curiae. *Law and Human Behavior*, 14, 25–42.

Anthony, D. 1990. Religious Movements and "Brainwashing" Litigation: Evaluating Key Testimony. In T. Robbins & D. Anthony (Eds.), *In Gods We Trust: New Patterns of Religious Pluralism in America*, 2d ed. New Brunswick, NJ: Transaction Press.

Anthony, D., & Robbins, T. 1995. Negligence, Coercion, and the Protection of Religious Belief. *Journal of Church and State*.

Anthony, D., & Robbins, T. 1992. Law, Social Science and the "Brainwashing" Exception to the First Amendment. *Behavioral Sciences and the Law*, 10(1), 5–29.

Barker, E. 1984. *The Making of a "Moonie": Choice or Brainwashing?* Oxford: Blackwell.

Bromley, D. 1983. Conservatorships and Deprogramming: Legal and Political Prospects. In D. Bromley & J. Richardson (Eds.), *The Brainwashing/ Deprogramming Controversy*. New York: Edwin Mellen Press.

Bromley, D., & Richardson, J. (Eds.). 1983. *The Brainwashing/Deprogramming Controversy*. New York: Edwin Mellen Press.

Bromley, D., & Robbins, T. 1992. The Role of Government in Regulating New and Nonconventional Religions. In J. Wood & D. Davis (Eds.), *The Role of Government in Monitoring and Regulating Religion in Public Life*. Waco, TX: Baylor University, Dawson Institute of Church-State Studies.

Bromley, D., & Shupe, A. 1995. Anti-Cultism in the United States: Origins, Ideology and Organizational Development. *Social Compass*, *42*(2), 221–236.

DeWitt, J., Richardson, J., & Warner, L. 1991. Novel Scientific Evidence and the Biased, Uninformed Juror. Paper presented at annual meeting of the American Association for the Advancement of Science, Washington, DC.

Galanter, M., Rabkin, R., Rabkin, J., & Deutsch, A. 1979. The "Moonies": A Psychological Study of Conversion and Membership in a Contemporary Religious Sect. *American Journal of Psychiatry*, *136*, 165–169.

Kilbourne, B., & Richardson, J. 1984. Psychotherapy and New Religions in a Pluralistic Society. *American Psychologist*, *39*, 237–251.

Lewis, J. (Ed.). 1994. *From the Ashes: Making Sense of Waco*. Lanham, MD: Rowman and Littlefield.

Pfieffer, J. 1992. The Psychological Framing of Cults: Schematic Representations and Cult Evaluations. *Journal of Applied Social Psychology*, *22*(7), 531–544.

Richardson, H. 1984. *Constitutional Issues in the Trial of Reverend Moon*. New York: Edwin Mellen Press.

Richardson, J. T. 1995a. Clinical and Psychological Assessment of Participants in New Religions. *International Journal of Psychology of Religion*, *5*(3), 145–170.

Richardson, J. T. 1995b. Legal Status of New Religions in America. *Social Compass*, *42*(2), 249–264.

Richardson, J. T. 1994. Dramatic Changes in American Expert Evidence Law: From *Frye* to *Daubert*, with Special Attention to Implications for Social and Behavioral Science Evidence. *Judicial Review*, *2*, 13–36.

Richardson, J. T. 1993a. Expert Testimony by Social Psychologists: Issues and Experiences. Paper presented at annual meeting of the Western Psychological Association, San Jose, California.

Richardson, J. T. 1993b. Religiosity as Deviance: The Use and Misuse of the DSM-III in Assessing Participants in New Religions. *Deviant Behavior*, *14*, 1–21.

Richardson, J. T. 1993c. A Social Psychological Critique of "Brainwashing" Claims About Recruitment to New Religions. In D. Bromley & J. Hadden (Eds.), *The Handbook on Cults in America*. Greenwich, CT: JAI Press.

Richardson, J. T. 1992a. Mental Health of Cult Consumers: Legal and Scientific Controversy. In J. Schumaker (Ed.), *Religion and Mental Health*. New York: Oxford University Press.

Richardson, J. T. 1992b. Public Opinion and the Tax Evasion Trial of Reverend Moon. *Behavioral Science and the Law*, *10*(1), 53–63.

Richardson, J. T. 1991a. Cult/Brainwashing Cases and the Freedom of Religion. *Journal of Church and State*, *33*, 55–74.

Richardson, J. T. 1991b. Reflexivity and Objectivity in the Study of Controversial New Religions. *Religion*, *21*, 305–318.

Richardson, J. T. 1988. Changing Times: Religion, Economics, and the Law in Contemporary America. *Sociological Analysis*, *49S*, 1–14.

Richardson, J. T. 1986. Consumer Protection and Deviant Religion. *Review of Religious Research, 28,* 168–179.

Richardson, J. T. 1985. The Active vs. Passive Convert: Paradigm Conflict in Conversion/Recruitment Research. *Journal for the Scientific Study of Religion, 24,* 163–179.

Richardson, J. T., Ginsburg, G., Gatowski, S., & Dobbin, S.. 1995. Problems of Applying *Daubert* to Psychological Syndrome Evidence. *Judicature, 79*(1), 1–9.

Roesch, R., Golding, S., Hans, V., & Reppucci, N. D. 1991. Social Science and the Courts: The Role of Amicus Briefs. *Law and Human Behavior, 15,* 1–11.

Shinn, L. 1992. Cult Controversies and the Courts: Some Ethical Issues in Academic Expert Testimony. *Sociological Analysis, 53,* 272–285.

Shupe, A., & Bromley, D. 1994. *Anti-Cult Movements in Cross Cultural Perspective.* New York: Garland.

Shupe, A., & Bromley, D. 1980. *The New Vigilantes: Deprogrammers, Anti-Cultists and the New Religions.* Beverly Hills, CA: Sage.

Solomon, T. 1983. Programming and Deprogramming the Moonies: Social Psychology Applied. In D. Bromley & J. Richardson (Eds.), *The Brainwashing/ Deprogramming Controversy.* New York: Edwin Mellen Press.

Solomon, T. 1981. Integrating the "Moonie" Experience: A Survey of Ex-Members of the Unification Church. In T. Robbins & D. Anthony (Eds.), *In Gods We Trust.* New Brunswick, NJ: Transaction Books.

Tremper, C. 1987. Organized Psychology's Efforts to Influence Judicial Policy-Making. *American Psychologist, 42,* 496–501.

Wright, S. 1984. Post-Involvement Attitudes of Voluntary Defectors from Controversial New Religious Movements. *Journal for the Scientific Study of Religion, 23,* 172–182.

Wright, S. 1995. *Armageddon in Waco.* Chicago: University of Chicago Press.

CASES CITED

Frey v. United States, 293 F.1013.1014 (D.C. Circuit 1923).

Katz v. Superior Court, 73 Cal. App. 3d 952, 141 Cal. Rptr. 234 (1977).

Molko and Leal v. Unification Church, 179 California Appeals 3d 450 (1986).

Molko and Leal v. Unification Church, 46 Cal. 3d 1092, 762 p.26 46 (1988).

United States v. Fishman, No. CR-88-0616-DLJ (Northern District of California 1990).

Wollersheim v. Scientology, (260 Cal. Rptr. 331, 1989), vacated 3 S. Ct. 1298 (1991).

United States v. Kosminski, 108 S. Ct. 2751 (1988).

George v. ISKCON, No. 27-65-75 Orange County Supp. Ct., altered in Cal. App. Ct. No. 0007153 (Cal. App. Ct. 4th Dist., 1989), vacated in 3 S. Ct. 1299 (1991).

8

Sociology, Medicine, and Chemical Dependency: Embedding Drugs and Alcohol in Sociocultural Contexts

Barry Kinsey

Sociologists who work on chemical dependency issues can offer valuable expertise in a wide range of civil and criminal litigation. Increasingly, the use or abuse of alcohol and other drugs complicates many of the critical issues in crime and punishment, personal and social liability, domestic law, and civil rights. Sociologists who are accepted as experts can observe and interpret problems of chemical dependency from a vantage point not customarily advanced in the courtroom. Perhaps of most importance, sociologists are in a position to critically evaluate the medical or disease model that influences the opinions of most clinical specialists in this field.

THE HEGEMONY OF THE DISEASE MODEL AND ITS CRITICS

Not surprisingly, traditional specialists in chemical dependency favor the medical or disease model. This is not hard to explain. The medicalization of substance abuse, its incorporation by the American Medical Association, American Public Health Association, and the American Psychiatric Association, insures that most people will perceive the problem as a type of disease. Like all perspectives, a disease model is both a way of seeing and a way of not seeing. In my opinion, sociology can assist attorneys and the courts in identifying aspects of substance abuse that typically are not recognized by the disease model.

A sociological review of the voluminous literature on chemical dependency, for example, found that definitions of the problem are influenced by political motives, ideology, personal interests, and professional training and not, as is popularly believed, solely on the basis of scientifically valid evidence (McNeece & Dinetto 1994:4). Consider the widely accepted idea that alcoholics can never drink in a controlled manner. This putative pattern of loss of control is important in cases in which relapse or probability of continued abuse is a critical issue for the court. There is, however, considerable debate over the validity of the loss of control idea, which is a cornerstone of the disease model. Interestingly, even a strong proponent of the disease model concluded that "it is . . . possible, for alcoholics to regain control over their lives" (Vaillant 1983). Presumably, this includes control over the use and abuse of chemical substances.

The disease model explains the origins of addictive behaviors, including alcoholism and chemical dependency, in genetic transmission. Scientific evidence on heredity and substance abuse is far from conclusive, however. There simply are insufficient data to make a clear distinction between environmental and genetic risks at this time (Peele 1988). Indeed, more weight currently is given to environmental or social causes than to genetic. A comprehensive review of genetic research by the National Institute on Alcohol and Alcohol Abuse concludes, "it is probably that environmental influences will be at least as important and possibly more important than genetic influences" (1992:7). McNeece and Dinetto (1994) support the NIAAA conclusion on the significance of environmental factors and add a number of more general critiques of the disease model, including proponents cannot demonstrate a clear etiology for addiction or predict its course of symptoms with any accuracy; the sequence of symptoms is highly variable, and there is no compelling evidence of an underlying biologic process that predisposes one to the disorder; and recovery from dependence bears no necessary relationship to abstinence, although such concurrence is frequently the case.

Moreover, as alluded to above, there are noticeable social and cultural differences in patterns of substance use, comportment while intoxicated, and meanings attached to various alcohol and other drug related behaviors. In their comprehensive, cross-cultural study, for example, MacAndrew and Edgerton concluded that, "the way people comport themselves while drunk is determined not by alcohol's toxic assault upon the seat of moral judgment, conscience, and the like, but by what their society makes of and imparts to them concerning the state of drunkenness" (1969:145). They found striking cross-cultural variations in intoxicated behaviors while also documenting variations from one social setting to another within the same community. Thus, alcohol and drug related behavior apparently is not the result of specific neurological effects but represents a complex interaction of physiology, psychology, and culture (McNeece & Dinetto 1994). These studies suggest that loss of control may be more a product of certain culturally induced expectations or norms than symptoms of an underlying disease. Affirmation of these observations also is found in the numbers of chemically dependent persons who apparently burn out, recover on their own, voluntarily reduce consumption to more socially approved levels, or report that the craving disappears under certain conditions, such as incarceration.

Finally, there is some evidence that the disease model may have outlived its usefulness and is not particularly helpful in addressing the problems of substance abuse. Although it is true that "medicalizing" chemical and alcohol abuse reduced some of the stigma, ignorance, and traditional prejudices associated with this problem, it also is true that medicalizing substance abuse promoted attitudes and behaviors with deleterious consequences for people. For example, recent research has demonstrated that alcohol abusers have much stronger expectations regarding the effects of alcohol than do social drinkers. They invest alcohol with tremendous power and readily accept the premise that, when they are drinking, they are out of control (Peele 1988). Thus, weight is added to the idea that, when disease is used in a metaphoric sense, it may create problems, especially when the metaphoric aspect is forgotten (McNeece & Dinetto 1994).

In summary, sociology asks a number of questions about chemical and alcohol dependency that go well beyond the traditional concerns of the disease model, complicating legal proceedings that include substance abuse.

SOCIOLOGY, SUBSTANCE ABUSE, AND THE COURTS

Not only are sociologists qualified to critique the historical, political, and social assumptions of the medical model, but also, at a more concrete level, sociology is likely to play an increasing role in litigation on alcohol and chemical related disability. Cases related to discrimination against the disabled, workmen's compensation, mandatory drug testing, and benefit limitations for treatment of chemical dependency invite a sociological perspective. With few exceptions, these cases are really conflicts over definitions of chemical dependency: Is it a disease? Is it learned behavior? How these cases are settled affects both the law and social policy.

Moreover, the question of volition often is crucial in criminal and civil cases. Most alcohol and drug abuse experts support the loss of control idea derived from the disease model. In my opinion, it is important that attorneys and policy makers are aware of critical perspectives on the medical model and alternative interpretations of substance abuse.

My areas of expertise include not only sociology but also behavioral pharmacology. Between these two vantage points, I enjoy a particularly advantageous position from which to observe and comment on events and circumstances pertinent to legal proceedings that consider the problem of substance abuse. However, my experience is not unique. Most sociologists develop areas of competency outside the specific methodological and conceptual boundaries of the discipline. Environmental sociologists, for example, often become quite knowledgeable about ecological systems and their human and environment interactions, and sociologists of religion frequently become comfortably conversant with complex theological systems. Thus, what I do in combining areas of expertise is an example of what most sociologists do.

The following discussion outlines a variety of legal cases in which my knowledge of sociology and behavioral pharmacology shaped, in some measure, civil and criminal proceedings.

CONTROLLING DRUGS AND ALCOHOL

Sociologists are particularly well-qualified to testify in legal disputes over the regulation or control of alcohol and drug sales, advertising, bars or taverns, nightclubs, and so forth. I was retained as an expert for a major city whose zoning ordinance prohibited location of bars within 300 feet of a residential neighborhood. The key issues were whether or not the regulation was reasonable and whether it could be justified on the basis of public policy or public safety. In this type of case, a sociologist can conduct neighborhood surveys, describe the range of problems (or opportunities) normally associated with various types of drinking establishments, and provide statistical data on public safety issues, including crime, traffic accidents, and related problems. Surveys were not necessary in this case, however, because the ordinance covering the more specific public safety issues (crime, traffic, and other problems) proved sufficient to deny the request for variance.

More significant than a zoning dispute are those cases in which injury or death is associated with drinking or drug use. Adolescents and young adults are at particularly high risk of abusing alcohol and chemicals. Not surprisingly, alcohol and other drug abuse is a major factor in adolescent and young adult suicide. I worked on one case to determine whether a teenager committed suicide or died in the course of alcohol-related activities. The question was volition. I examined the norms for drinking common to the deceased's peer group, noting the group's tendency to engage in drinking games and to combine the use of alcohol and drugs. I concluded that the death was unintentional and occurred in the context of a locally popular drinking game.

A second, similar case involved a spinal injury to a 16-year-old male in a shallow water diving accident. The mishap occurred when a group of high school students (ages 14–17) staged a party at a neighbor's pool. The neighbor was absent and unaware of the party. When asked to identify the goal of the party, most witnesses admitted they intended to get "wasted." The accident occurred after six or seven participants consumed approximately 118 ounces of rum in a 3 to 4 hour period. Immediately following the accident, no one sought medical assistance for the victim. Witnesses thought his symptoms were caused by intoxication rather than the result of injuries suffered in the dive. It was not until the following morning that the victim was taken to the emergency room. No blood alcohol tests were conducted at any time during this sequence of events.

I was asked to develop an opinion concerning the approximate level of intoxication of the victim at the time of the accident and the extent to which intoxication might have been a contributing factor in the accident. In the absence of actual blood alcohol tests, the level of intoxication was inferred from the estimated amount of alcohol consumed prior to the accident and from various descriptions of his behavior provided by witnesses. Drunken comportment or behavior is affected not only by the pharmacological effects of alcohol but also by social norms and expectations associated with various groups, individuals, and social settings. I am aware of recent trends in adolescent drinking norms and am familiar with the special language used by adolescents to describe drinking expectations, patterns, and individual conduct. Interviewing friends who observed the victim drinking prior to the accident strongly suggested that his behavior was consistent with blood alcohol estimates based upon the presumed level of consumption. Recalling their word, he was "wasted" at the time of the accident. I cited a review of the research literature on the role of intoxication in accidental injuries, including those related to shallow water diving, to support my opinion that alcohol was a significant factor in the mishap (Perrine & Bradley 1994).

Sociologists with expertise in statistics, research design, sampling, and related areas also are useful in many situations in which scientific evidence is in dispute. The current debate over whether or not certain drugs or medications used in clinical practice (fluoxetine hydrochloride [Prozac] or triazolam [Halcion], for example) are responsible for violent homicidal or suicidal episodes is an example of an area that could benefit from this type of expertise. Is the incidence of violence among patients taking these medications abnormally high when compared with appropriate control or comparison groups? Did the methods used to test the safety of these medications conform to generally accepted scientific norms? Are there alternative explanations for the individual's behavior that are credible in terms of his or her social history and current interpersonal relationships? Although the evidence for violence associated with therapeutic use of Prozac or Halcion is not convincing, there is reason to believe that this is not the case for cocaine, amphetamines, anabolic steroids, marijuana with very high tetrahydrocannabinol content, or high levels of alcohol intoxication. Thus, although there does not appear to be a Prozac defense at this time, sociologists may be useful when violent behavior has been associated with these drugs.

I worked on two other types of cases in which my training and experience in statistics, research design, and the effects of sociocultural variations on alcohol and drug related behavior proved useful. In the first type of case, alcohol or other drug use and abuse resulted in death or injury to others. In death and injury cases, I routinely am asked to form opinions concerning estimates of intoxication or blood alcohol levels and the effects of the level of intoxication on the person's actions. For example, a 45-year-old male was involved in a fatal accident at approximately 11:00 P.M. on a remote, rural highway. He was not brought to the hospital until 2:00 A.M. A blood alcohol test was done at 2:20 A.M. His blood alcohol level (BAL) was 0.19 percent. It was discovered in investigation that he was drinking at a bar approximately 20 miles from the scene of the accident until about 9:00 P.M. The accused claimed that he did not drink after leaving the bar, although an open bottle was found near his automobile. He was charged with driving under the influence and vehicular homicide.

In her statement to the police, the hostess of the bar testified that she served the accused five or six mixed drinks each containing 1.25 ounces of 90 proof bourbon. As an expert, I was asked by the prosecution to estimate the BAL of the accused at the time of the accident, determine whether or not the BAL obtained at 2:20 A.M. could have been the result of five or six drinks consumed at the bar, and evaluate the testimony of the accused that he had not continued to drink after leaving the bar, presumably from the bottle found at the scene.

Trained in statistics, probability theory, and the pharmacokinetics of alcohol, I was able to render opinions (estimates) related to probable blood alcohol curves and also evaluate the case in the broader context of sociocultural drinking norms and behaviors associated with specific subgroups in the population. The presence of alcohol near the vehicle and its likely consumption after the man left the bar were consistent with actual blood alcohol estimates, the defendant's past drinking history, and the drinking norms of his peers.

A sociology of BAL is not difficult to imagine. BALs are more than numerical coefficients of intake. They are influenced by such variables as gender, body type and weight, food consumption, time, type of beverage, prior drinking history, and many other factors. It is in this manner that sociology contextualizes addictive or abusive behaviors, locating them in more complicated webs of causal influence.

I have worked on a second type of case arising from a growing trend to hold individuals, organizations, and groups responsible for alcohol and drug related damages. Known broadly as "dram shop cases," these suits frequently involve a tavern, bar, or store owner and, in many instances, their employees. Like the case described above, sociology complicates the dram shop case in its insistence that the effects of alcohol or other drugs are only partly a product of dosage and cannot be evaluated independently of the sociocultural contexts in which they are used.

One case I worked on involved a 45-year-old male who was drinking at a bar for approximately four hours, from 8 to 12 P.M. According to witnesses, he was served approximately six rum and Cokes. There was evidence that, prior to going to the bar, somewhere between 3 and 5 P.M., he drank about six beers (3.2 percent alcohol) at a friend's house. He finished a relatively heavy meal at a local fast food restaurant at 6:30 P.M. and from there went to the bar.

Patrons at the bar testified that the defendant seemed happy and outgoing. In their opinion, he did not appear "drunk." Shortly after leaving the bar, he allegedly ran a stoplight, resulting in an accident that seriously injured two occupants in another vehicle. The injured persons sued both the defendant and the bar under the state's dram shop law, which makes owners of a public facility liable if they serve alcohol to a person they know or should know is intoxicated.

I was asked to render an opinion concerning whether a bartender had served alcohol to a person whom he should have known was intoxicated. In evaluating this situation, I reasoned that drunken comportment is affected by social, cultural, and individual factors. Thus, a person's overt behaviors are not always reliable indicators of actual levels of intoxication. My opinion was based not only upon estimates of his approximate blood alcohol curve and level but also upon whether or not his behavior or comportment (as perceived by others) was consistent with that of an "obviously intoxicated person" in the specific context in which it occurred. It was my opinion that the employees at the bar did not serve alcohol to an obviously intoxicated person as defined in the state's dram shop statutes.

Not surprisingly, there are a number of other issues related to public safety in which sociologists with expertise in chemical dependency can be very useful. One such situation was identified in an interesting analysis of the Los Angeles riots following the Rodney King verdict. In its report on the riots, the Office of Technology Assessment concluded that, "alcohol has been a little-noticed stitching on a vast urban quilt, connecting such seemingly distinct problems as crime, unemployment, black animus toward Koreans and community distrust. It is no coincidence that when the riots did erupt, both looters and arsonists made liquor stores a prime target" (Office of Technology Assessment 1993:57).

Should alcohol manufacturers, distributors, or sellers be held accountable for riots or other public disturbances in much the same way as now occurs in dram shop cases? For example, should distributors be liable for incidents, including riots, that occur after sales of alcohol such as kegs of beer that they know or should know will be consumed by minors? Is there any liability for predictable results of brazen advertising campaigns that use minority actors, athletes, or celebrities to pitch the more intoxicating malt liquors and fortified wines to high risk groups with the obvious message that the goal of drinking is to get drunk? Most alcohol and drug specialists focus on individual causation — some underlying personal vulnerability or pathology — as the primary etiological factor in alcohol and drug related deviance. Thus, they are not adequately trained or inclined to look at broader social and cultural factors that are crucial to these cases. Because they study social systems, communities, social organizations, intergroup conflicts, and similar areas, sociologists often are qualified to develop opinions regarding drinking and drug problems.

ALCOHOL, DRUGS, AND THE FAMILY

In addition to the two types of cases just outlined, sociologists with expertise in chemical dependency (including an understanding of the medical model) also are useful in legal disputes in which knowledge of social systems, interpersonal relationships, and the impact of alcohol and drug use in workplace, family, and community settings is important. This type of expertise is especially in demand in cases involving domestic disputes, including divorce, custody, visitation, and child welfare. The following is a rather simple case in which this type of expertise proved crucial to the outcome.

Sarah was a 28-year-old divorced female who had custody of three children, ages seven, five, and two. Her husband, joined by the paternal grandparents, initiated proceedings to obtain custody of the children, arguing that Sarah's dependency on prescription drugs represented a serious danger to the children's welfare. There was evidence that Sarah regularly used tranquilizers, sedatives, and synthetic opiates. Moreover, she apparently intentionally misrepresented herself to obtain prescriptions illegally. Finally, it was also alleged that she used her 2-year-old to obtain prescriptions for medications containing codeine.

I was asked to evaluate this pattern of drug use and render opinions regarding whether this pattern of drug use was indicative of chronic abuse, whether this drug use created unacceptable risks to the children, and what Sarah's prognosis is in light of her refusal to acknowledge a problem or seek assistance. This case was complicated by the fact that Sarah moved frequently and there was no way to tell whether the records that could be obtained reflected all the drugs that she used. This is not unusual, because abusers frequently try to avoid detection, and few states have adequate systems for monitoring prescriptions for controlled drugs. Thus, I had to base my opinion not only upon the objective evidence but also upon knowledge of the social and behavioral characteristics of abusers. My analysis went beyond observations of individual behavior and drew upon knowledge of alcohol and drug use and abuse patterns and how these vary within and among significant subsets of the abusing population.

My opinion that Sarah had a serious drug dependency problem was based not only upon actual prescriptions that exceeded medically acceptable use but also upon evidence that her behavior was consistent with these types of abusers, including frequent moves to avoid detection and the use of the youngest child to obtain codeine. It was my opinion that this pattern presented serious risks to the children that warranted immediate intervention by the court.

In addition to knowledge of sociocultural and interpersonal aspects of alcohol and drug use and problems associated with abuse, a sociologist often is called upon to use his or her knowledge of the literature related to risks to adults and children, effectiveness of treatment, potential for relapse, and the effects of parental abuse on children. I was asked, for example, to render an opinion in a case in which a father asked the court to approve unsupervised visitations with his 5-year-old daughter. The father admitted to a history of alcohol abuse and had completed two outpatient treatment programs, each followed by relapse in less than six months. After the last relapse, he had gone into residential treatment and supposedly had maintained five months' sobriety at the time of the court proceedings. All parties agreed that, when sober, the father was a responsible, capable parent; however, there was evidence of multiple cigarette burns on the furniture and major problems of neglect during drinking episodes.

Counselors from the alcohol treatment facility supported the father's request on the basis that he had gained control over his addiction (as evidenced by five months' sobriety). It was my opinion that relapse was a significant risk that created a potentially dangerous environment for the child. I based my decision, in part, on a body of literature that indicates that certain personality attributes and the nature of available social support systems are more reliable predictors of relapse than the nature of the treatment process (Harl 1987).

As this case illustrates, sociologists are prepared to look more broadly at social systems, interpersonal relationships, and social history in evaluating problems and issues related to abuse of alcohol and drugs. Thus, they sometimes can take the lead in complex cases that include a large number of issues, including some outside the usual areas of sociological expertise. For example, in the following case, I was asked to coordinate a range of information involving both my own opinions and those of other experts.

Jane was a 35-year-old female with a long history of alcohol abuse dating back to late adolescence. During the past ten years, her alcohol abuse was more controlled, with three short drinking episodes followed by treatment and relatively long periods of sobriety. She was abstinent for the past two years except for a relapse six months previously, which lasted three days. After the relapse, she voluntarily entered an inpatient treatment facility.

Her husband sued for custody of their 6-year-old son on the grounds that Jane's alcoholism (a disease) created an unhealthy, dangerous environment detrimental to the best interests of the child. Jane claimed that the father had shown very little interest in the child, as evidenced by infrequent contact (about one contact per year for the past three years) and failure to acknowledge important events such as birthdays. She believed that his primary motive was to avoid payment of approximately $10,000 in delinquent child support.

As the primary consultant, I was asked to review Jane's history, including her role as a mom, and develop an opinion concerning her "fitness" as a parent. I also was asked to assess whether a change in custody was in the best interest of the child. I found the second task troublesome. Although I could evaluate Jane's drinking history, drinking behavior, and potential for relapse, determining what was in the best interests of the child required additional information not available in Jane's social history and treatment records. Specifically, I needed an assessment of the child's adjustment to his current situation. One key question was what arrangements did the mother make for the care of the son when she was drinking. Another question was what were the effects a change of custody would have on the child at that time.

It was my initial view that such a change would be traumatic for the child and could be justified only if there were clear and compelling reasons to believe that Jane was unfit to be a mother. To get a better assessment of Jane's fitness as a parent, I asked a psychologist with training in alcohol abuse to take a comprehensive personality inventory of Jane, with special emphasis upon her potential for continued abuse and her ability to parent a young child. In addition, I interviewed a psychiatrist who was familiar with Jane's family and had supervised her treatment for a time. He was asked to assess the son's current social and emotional adjustment and the potential impact of a change in custody. This information was supplemented by interviews with school officials, neighbors, and other family members in order to get a more complete evaluation of the son's social and emotional well-being. I was particularly interested in such questions as: How was he doing in school? Did he have friends? How did he interact with peers? Was there evidence of neglect or abuse at any time, especially during periods when the mother was drinking?

Psychiatric evaluations and information obtained from teachers, neighbors, and counselors indicated that the son was doing well in school, seemed well-adjusted, and related well to peers. I combined the clinical evaluations of the psychologist and psychiatrist with my own sociological account of a single parent family culture. I looked specifically for patterns of constructive mother-son activities, family rituals (such as eating meals together), and activities that enhanced the child's self-esteem.

On the basis of these sociological and clinical data, I believed Jane to be a responsible parent with sufficient insight to recognize the indications of relapse. I also found that she made suitable arrangements for the son when she was in trouble. Thus, it was my opinion that Jane's history of alcohol abuse did not render her unfit as a parent, the potential harm to the child of a change in custody greatly exceeded that associated with the mother's drinking, and the best interests of the child would be protected by maintaining the status quo.

Jane's predicament suggests an important problem for attorneys and experts involved in cases of this type. Alcohol and drug abuse is traditionally defined as a lack of willpower, an inability to control oneself, or a disease that can be arrested but not "cured." Jane's husband tried to make the argument that her relapses indicated a "loss of control" and that she suffered from a disease that rendered her incapable of being a responsible parent. It is little wonder that women avoid treatment and the subsequent label that goes with public acknowledgment of an alcohol or drug problem. They are seen as either persons of little moral worth or persons with an incurable disease. There is evidence, in fact, that women are so afraid of losing custody of their children that they avoid treatment for addiction. Sociologists who take a broader view of these issues can be of considerable value to attorneys as they attempt to deal with these biases in the legal system.

ALCOHOL, DRUGS, AND DEFENSE STRATEGIES

Earlier, I emphasized that the courts are facing increasingly complex questions regarding volition and individual responsibility or culpability as traditionally defined in criminal law and social policies. I increasingly am asked to render opinions in a wide range of cases involving questions of how alcohol and drug use affects mental states, motives, relationships, risks, or criminal culpability. For example, I was asked for an opinion about whether chronic alcohol abuse on the part of an alleged abuser would weaken or support a battered wife syndrome defense to homicide.

It is a basic principle of U.S. law that there must be a criminal state of mind or mens rea that coincides with some overt act or acts, actus reus (Reid 1992). In addition, most criminal acts must include some type of criminal blameworthiness or culpability. In more and more cases, intoxication is being used as a defense (often an affirmative defense) to show lack of ability to form the necessary intent, diminished capacity, or as mitigating factors in the degree of culpability.

These defenses often are used when it can be established that a mental condition of the defendant, though not sufficient to establish insanity, insured that the defendant was unable to achieve the requisite intent at the time of the crime (American Law Institute 1962). Although many states do not follow the model penal code, most have provisions that allow for an affirmative defense that involves alcohol use. The rationale is simple: by reason of intoxication at the time of the deleterious act, the defendant lacked substantial capacity either to appreciate its criminality or to conform his conduct to the requirements of the law. Thus, the question of volition and how chemical abuse is framed can have a major impact on questions of guilt, innocence, treatment, and punishment.

In addition to the question of whether persons can control their use of substances is the more perplexing and problematic question of whether, and to what degree, they can control their behavior when under the influence. These are two distinct issues but often are confused in actual cases in which questions of criminal intent, volition, and responsibility associated with use of alcohol or drugs are important. The following are typical of the types of cases based in some measure on substances, volition, and legal culpability.

In the first case, two young males, ages 18 and 20, attempted to rob a convenience store and, in the process, shot and killed the store clerk. They were charged with first-degree or capital murder; the defense claimed that the two offenders had not formed the requisite criminal intent because they had been "speeding" for three or four days prior to the event, leading to a condition referred to as amphetamine (stimulant) psychosis. The defense argued that the shooting was not premeditated but resulted from an aggressive movement by the victim into the "personal space" of one of the offenders, which triggered a violent, aggressive response. I was asked by the defense attorney to provide opinions concerning the following questions: What are the symptoms and behavioral patterns associated with stimulant-induced paranoid reactions sometimes referred to as amphetamine or cocaine psychosis? Were the violent reactions of the offenders to a perceived threat — an aggressive movement into personal space — consistent with behaviors typically observed in these conditions? Could persons in this drug induced condition form the requisite criminal intent as defined in the state's capital murder statutes?

In order to develop opinions concerning these questions, it is necessary to know the pharmacological effects of stimulants and whether specific behaviors are likely to be the product of cultural norms or expectations rather than chemical changes in the brain. The fact that these symptoms are found in a wide range of subjects, environments, and situations suggested that the prevailing literature in pharmacology and clinical psychology is essentially correct in identifying this as a drug induced disorder; the disorder could have and probably did result from the pattern of abuse alleged by the defense; violent reactions to perceived threats, especially invasions of personal space without permission, are common responses by persons with this condition; and it is up to the court to determine whether their mental condition and actions met the legal definitions of first-degree murder. After being informed of these opinions, the prosecuting attorney negotiated a plea bargain in which the defendants accepted a life sentence to avoid a trial and possible death sentence. I was informed that the prosecutor did not want to risk a precedent in which a drug induced mental disorder could be used as a defense in a first-degree murder trial.

In another case, a defendant was charged with aggravated assault, which, under the laws of the state, required that the assault be preplanned, intended, or premeditated. The defendant was drinking in a bar when he had an argument with another patron. He was asked to leave, which he did, but he continued to drink in another location. Two hours later, he returned to the bar, where, apparently without further provocation, he assaulted his protagonist. The defendant claimed to have no memory of any events that occurred after he left the bar and was in an alcohol induced blackout (amnesia) from that time until about 10 A.M. the next morning. When the prosecutor found out that I was scheduled to testify about the nature of alcohol induced amnesia, he agreed to reduce the charge to simple assault. I found this interesting, because I do not personally believe that alcohol induced amnesia (blackout) prevents a person from forming the intent as required by the law in question.

In the past two years I have consulted in cases in which very high levels of intoxication have been associated with violence. In one case, a young male (age 20) supposedly had gone into a rage and murdered several members of his family. Extensive evaluation of the case could produce no apparent motive or previous acts of violence, and this episode seemed totally inconsistent with the accused's character and prior history. He had consumed a large amount of alcohol (BAL over 0.20 percent) and the public defender wanted to know if this level of intoxication could have been the primary reason for this violent episode. The defendant's lawyer was looking for possible mitigating factors and possible answers to a truly perplexing situation. The crime appeared to be totally inconsistent with her client's personality, social history, and past behaviors. As she explained it to me, "If it could happen to him, it could happen to anyone."

The accused had a history of alcohol use but no previous episodes of an alcohol induced rage disorder. There was little I could do in this case, so I referred the attorney to a body of literature that shows that intoxication might be a direct cause of violence, even potentially lethal violence, in situations in which there is both a high level of intoxication and perceived interpersonal threat (MTI 1990). This is especially true in situations in which there are strong cultural norms or expectations that support the use of violence in association with alcohol and drug use (Vatz and Weinberg 1989).

CONCLUDING COMMENTS

In this chapter, I have emphasized that sociologists with expertise in chemical dependency are becoming increasingly relevant to a broad range of criminal and civil law. Sociologists bring specific talents in research, cross-cultural and intracultural variations, social organization and systems analysis, and a wide range of perspectives not typically found in traditional clinical paradigms of chemical dependency. In order to be effective, sociologists not only must have these traditional skills but also should know about behavioral pharmacology, patterns of alcohol and drug use and abuse, and the various theoretical perspectives on the etiology of chemical dependency, especially the medical or disease model.

Most contemporary litigation is occurring in an environment of great confusion, distrust, and conflict among psychiatry, medicine, behavioral science, and the law. The field has tended to be dominated by specific groups or specialists, each tending to use the evidence that supports its own attitudes, traditions, and interests. In this environment, a sociological perspective can be a useful vantage point from which to negotiate dangerous and difficult gaps in science, law, and public policy. In its capacity to expand the range of issues typically considered by the courts, sociology pushes the law toward a more inclusive version of justice, one that includes but goes beyond psychology and medicine.

REFERENCES

American Law Institute. 1962. *Model Penal Code*. Washington, DC: ALI Publishing.
Harl, E. 1987. *The Role of Personality, Social Support, Life Stressors, and Emotional Functioning on Outcome Following Treatment for Chemical Dependency*. Unpublished doctoral dissertation, University of Tulsa, Oklahoma.
MacAndrew, C., & Edgerton, R. B. 1969. *Drunken Comportment*. Chicago: Aldine Press.
McNeece, C., & Dinetto, D. 1994. *Chemical Dependency: A Systems Approach*. Englewood Cliffs, NJ: Prentice-Hall.
MTI. 1990. Cruel Spirits: Alcohol and Violence. [videotape] New York: Simon and Schuster.
National Institute on Alcohol and Alcohol Abuse. 1992. Genetics. *Alcohol Alert, 18*, 328.
Peele, S. 1988. *Visions of Addiction*. Lexington, MA: Aldine Press.
Perrine, M., & Bradley, A. 1994. When Alcohol and Water Don't Mix: Driving Under the Influence. *Journal of Studies on Alcohol, 55*(5), 517–524.
Reid, S. 1992. *Criminal Law*, 2d ed. New York: Macmillan.
U.S. Congress, Office of Technology Assessment. 1993. *Biological Components of Substance Abuse and Addiction*. OTA-BP-BBS 117, Washington, DC: Government Printing Office.
Vaillant, G. 1983. *The Natural History of Alcoholism: Causes, Patterns, and Paths to Recovery*. Cambridge, MA: Harvard University Press.
Vatz, R., & Weinberg, L. 1989, September. Confusion Over Alcoholism: Psychiatry, Medicine, and the Law. *USA Today Magazine*, pp. 68–71.

9

The Sociologist, Gangs, and Battered Women: Representing the Discipline in the Courts

Lee H. Bowker

Some of us became sociologists because we wanted to change the world. Somewhat naively perhaps, we thought that, by writing and teaching sociology, we could make the world a better place to live. After all, the promise of change at least is implicit in our discipline. Few of us are fortunate enough to see our written work change some aspect of the world, however modestly. Likewise, few of us see our students contribute to the solution of social problems.

I continue to be frustrated by the wide gap between teaching and research on the one hand and meaningful social change on the other. I am pleased to report on one arena in which sociology is making a difference: the courts. If it is now commonplace to refer to the pervasive influence of the courts on modern life, it is also worth noting the increasing use of sociology in the courts. Expert witnessing is increasingly a venue for sociology to say something that might change the life circumstances of people faced with poverty, abuse, homelessness, and contaminated environments, among other contemporary issues. Sociologists who are good teachers and either contribute to or know the literature also are likely to make good expert witnesses.

I represent sociology in civil and criminal proceedings. If I am frustrated by the discipline in the academy, I am pleased by its potential to affect the thinking and decisions in the legal arena. Sociology challenges the courts to consider the limits of police science, psychology, and medicine in the explanation of motive, intention, and behavior. A sociologist pushes the boundaries of a court's deliberations to include more complicated webs of explanation. If sociology makes a court's job more difficult, in my opinion, it is likely to make a court's decision more just.

To illustrate how sociology complicates the reasoning of the courts while increasing the chances that a more just decision is made, I will describe in some detail my participation in two unrelated court proceedings: gang membership and sentencing and women who are victims of battering. Following a felony arrest and conviction, California courts are likely to enhance a sentence if it determines that the felon is a member of a gang. It is not difficult to see how sociology can contribute to deliberations over appropriate criteria for group membership. Challenging the limits of the physical evidence strategy favored by police investigators, sociologists encourage the courts to consider other, more nebulous, but no less real, social and cultural evidence of gang membership.

Women who are battered and injure or kill their abusers in self-defense face a particularly difficult time defending themselves in court. One difficulty that battered women face when they commit a violent act is the traditional privilege accorded psychology in explaining the origins of their fear. By locating an abused woman within a psychological frame of reference, it is possible to ignore the systemic complexity of the violence in her life. Indeed, as we will see, in the absence of a sociological frame of reference, the tendency is to blame the victim.

CALIFORNIA'S STREET TERRORISM
ENFORCEMENT ACT AND ITS APPLICATION

I turn first to gang membership and sentencing. California's Street Terrorism Act created Penal Code § 186.22 (Hall and Waxman 1994). This code states that an individual convicted of a felony who also belongs to a friendship group defined as a gang in 188.22 (e) may receive a felony sentence enhancement of up to three additional years of imprisonment beyond the sentence judged appropriate for the crime (pp. 5–6). In 188.22 (a), participation is equated with crime so long as the individual "promotes, furthers or assists" in any felony committed by (any) members of a gang. It is possible to meet the requirements for the gang enhancement penalty in one of three ways: when the original felony is shown to be for the benefit of the gang, when the felony is committed at the direction of the gang, or when it is committed in association with (any) members of the gang. A friendship group becomes a gang if it is shown that some combination of members committed, attempted to commit, or solicited two felonies from a long list of crimes, and that one of these felonies occurred after September 26, 1988. Eligible felonies are not limited to violent crimes but also include auto theft and all felony drug offenses.

California's Street Terrorism Act is defined in such a manner that a large proportion of the crimes committed by adolescents and young adults in low income, urban neighborhoods could be interpreted as predicate acts for a gang enhancement. Prosecutors now wield a powerful tool to motivate confessions in return for having the gang enhancement dropped. Of course, this same tool also can be used to produce false confessions from innocent young people whose overworked public defenders advise them to "make a deal" rather than risk a conviction and a lengthy term of incarceration.

Police officers responding to the Street Terrorism Act developed a new specialty that combines elements from the traditional social work role of the community group worker with lessons from the canon of law enforcement.

Constructing this new specialty was aided by closed-circuit televising of courses on gangs throughout California under the sponsorship of the Peace Officer's Standard and Training Division. In addition, new organizations were formed, including the Northern California Gang Investigators Association, the Asian Gang Investigators Association, and the North Valley Gang Investigators Association. These organizations hold regular meetings that supplement county-wide interagency gang suppression meetings. Inspired by these social and educational activities, a new gang investigators subculture developed over the past several years in northern California.

What does it mean when 186.22 (a) targets a person for "active participation" in a criminal street gang? Ironically, the law provides limited guidance on how active participants in a group defined as a criminal gang are to be identified and differentiated from other friends and acquaintances. Thus, gang investigators responsible for discovering "active participation" must rely on simple, observable indicators. Among the indicators of gang membership relied on by investigators are distinctive clothing, tattoos, graffiti, photographs of members together, the observed flashing of hand signs, and the possession of gang paraphernalia. Gang investigators are apt to use physical evidence of gang membership instead of carefully investigating the less concrete aspects of group dynamics such as common definitions of the situation or the empirical delineation of patterns of association.

In the absence of sociological imagination, California's Street Terrorism Act is subject to considerable misuse. Consider the following scenario as an example of what could happen in the application of the act.

Twelve boys and young men ages 12 to 23 are neighborhood friends. Living in close proximity for several years, they enjoy one another's company. Two years ago, two of the young people pled guilty to stealing an uncle's car. They served only limited jail time as a sanction, followed by community supervision. A short time ago, ten of the young people got into a discussion about how to avenge an attack on one of them by a young man from another neighborhood. Four of them decided that a drive-by shooting would be adequate vengeance. They thought they would be satisfied by just shooting at the young man's house rather than directly at him or any of his relatives. They carried out the act, were apprehended shortly thereafter, and were charged with Penal Code § 246, "Shooting at an Inhabited Dwelling," plus several enhancements, one of which was for gang membership (Hall and Waxman

1994). In the prosecutorial definition of the situation, culpability spread first from the shooter to the driver of the car and the two friends who sat passively in the backseat and then to the other six friends who participated in the discussion that preceded the shooting (labeled as "planning" by police officers as well as the prosecutor's staff).

Sociological knowledge could be an essential part of this case. Consider the following questions:

Was the neighborhood friendship group sufficiently organized to be labeled a gang?

If a gang did exist, how was it organized?

What characteristics, activities, and entrance rituals differentiated gang members from gang associates and other friends in the neighborhood?

What were the beliefs, symbols, and other cultural as well as structural elements that characterized the gang?

Were the two car thieves associated closely enough with the group two years ago to be considered gang members?

Were the four young people who carried out the drive-by shooting really gang members on the day they committed the act?

Were the six "planners" who did not participate in the shooting really gang members that day?

These questions are not likely to be asked or answered using current criminal justice system terminology, nor are they adequately addressed in the Street Terrorism Act. I would contend that sociological testimony is as necessary to gang enhancement prosecutions as psychological testimony is to the determination of an individual's fitness to stand trial based on an evaluation of his mental health.

I recently worked on a gang enhancement case at the invitation of the court. I was asked to join the defense team rather than to assist the prosecution, whose expert was the gang investigator from the local police department. A joint hearing for three of the defendants was held on June 6 and 7, 1994. Each defendant had his own lawyer. One of the lawyers argued, to no avail, that the freedom of association is guaranteed by the U.S. Constitution. In the absence of specific proof of a gang's existence, the gang enhancement regulation is inappropriate. This argument carried no weight with the court, but the court did indicate concern about whether a pattern of criminal conduct existed among gang members. The judge asked for evidence of conviction, to which the prosecutor answered, "Statute simply says a crime. There does not need [to] be a conviction." The judge queried, "How do you have a crime without a conviction?," to which the prosecutor responded "That crime has occurred. You can bring someone in to testify that something has happened" (Hurley 1994, Exhibit C:14). The judge accepted this incredible explanation, and the hearing continued. It subsequently was discontinued when two of the defense lawyers argued successfully that they needed to have an expert witness in order to provide an adequate defense against the gang enhancement charge. I joined the defense team shortly thereafter.

My duties on the defense team included interviewing one of the defendants in prison and conducting telephone interviews with relatives, a female friend, and her parents. I also reviewed all of the police and court records relating to the case and the sociological literature on delinquent gangs. I found a source (Sanders 1994) that presented information on San Diego gangs that supported defense arguments. The report I submitted to defense counsel was used as a bargaining point to persuade the prosecution to drop the gang enhancement charge. In the meantime, defense counsel submitted a Petition for Writ of Prohibition against the Superior Court of Shasta County asking that the gang enhancement charge be dropped. He argued persuasively that, "There is nothing but speculation in the court record to support the assumption that the petitioner has anything more than a casual acquaintance or association with any gang members," and "There has been no evidence offered regarding the petitioner's active or willful participation in a street gang, nor that the petitioner had knowledge of a gang's pattern of criminal activity or that there was a sufficient pattern of criminal activity" (Hurley 1994:13,16,17). Based on the court's own records, these assertions were beyond dispute. Yet, the prohibition petition was rejected without comment by the court.

Progress in the case depended more on defense counsel's negotiating with the prosecution to modify the charges than on legal actions filed with the court. This is where a sociologist's verbal or written report can prove useful as a bargaining chip. When a defense lawyer can threaten to go to trial with a sociologist to challenge the unsupported sociological judgments made by a police gang investigator, the prosecution may reconsider its bargaining position. In this particular case, defense counsel was able to convince the prosecution to drop the gang enhancement charge as part of a plea bargain. I was saved from having to testify in a trial and, instead, wrote a defense sentencing report arguing against incarceration in an adult prison and showing how the defendant's participation with alleged gang members sprang from normal nondelinquent friendships, not from involvement in criminal activity. I was able to show that the defendant had many prosocial influences in his background and that he was an excellent candidate for rehabilitation. As of this writing, sentencing has not yet occurred, so it is not clear whether the defense team will be successful in obtaining benefits for the defendant beyond the removal of the gang enhancement charge and modifications of other charges that defense counsel successfully secured.

More important to this chapter, however, is the observation that sociology constructs and defines group membership and group dynamics in a more complicated manner than the traditional physical evidence criteria of law enforcement officials. Perhaps, as this case illustrates, a more complex deliberation may result in a more just decision.

REDEFINING THE BATTERED WOMAN SYNDROME IN SOCIOLOGICAL TERMS

If sociologists can challenge the state's naive criteria for gang membership in sentencing enhancement cases, it also can challenge the hegemony of psychology in cases involving abused women.

The battered woman syndrome (BWS) is an example of a concept that originally was developed within the discipline of psychology and now is being redefined in sociological terms. The BWS concept was first publicized by the psychologist Lenore Walker in her book *The Battered Woman* (1979). The publication of a psychological explication of the BWS concept was widely welcomed by feminists and other victims' advocates in practice communities ranging from psychotherapists to defense lawyers. This line of analysis has been continued within the discipline of psychology through the publication of books such as *The Battered Woman Syndrome* (Walker 1984), *Domestic Violence on Trial* (Sonkin 1987), *Terrifying Love* (Walker 1987), *When Battered Women Kill* (Browne 1987), *The Domestic Assault of Women* (Dutton 1988), and *Empowering and Healing the Battered Woman* (Dutton 1992). Sociological treatments of BWS began with the book *Violence Against Wives* (Dobash and Dobash 1979), followed by books such as *Woman-Battering* (Pagelow 1981), *Beating Wife-Beating* (Bowker 1983), *Wife Battering* (Giles-Sims 1983), *Ending the Violence* (Bowker 1986), *Battered Women as Survivors* (Gondolf with Fisher 1988), and *Women, Violence and Social Change* (Dobash and Dobash 1992).

Competing disciplinary approaches to the battered woman syndrome were brought together in a volume on *Current Controversies on Family Violence* (Gelles and Loseke 1993). Representing sociology, I argued that "A Battered Woman's Problems are Social, Not Psychological" (Bowker 1993) and Walker answered with "The Battered Woman Syndrome is a Psychological Consequence of Abuse" (1993). Walker continues to see BWS as "part of a recognized pattern of symptoms called post-traumatic stress disorder" (1993:133), a conception that is narrower than her original formulation of BWS (Walker 1979).

My approach in the 1993 debate was quite different from Walker's. I argued that BWS "is really a shorthand term for a variety of conditions that hold battered women captive in violent marriages, conditions that exist in the social system more than in the personalities of battered women" (1993:154). Walker's equation of BWS with learned helplessness implies that an abused woman who is not helpless cannot use the BWS defense in court, thus, denying her an important defense strategy.

I found in my work, however, that battered women are not helpless but, instead, constantly engage in personal antiviolence strategies and extrafamilial help-seeking activities until the violence ceases (Bowker 1984, 1987; Bowker and Maurer 1985, 1986, 1987; Donato and Bowker 1984). This perspective allows me to provide BWS support for battered women who are active as well as passive. The psychological reductionism inherent in Walker's perspective can be turned around by prosecutors to blame the abuse victim for the violence in her life. It also is used to successfully argue that battered women are too mentally ill to be awarded custody of their children in divorce proceedings.

An example of the disadvantages of a psychological profile of BWS is found in comments made by a psychologist who acted as an expert witness in a homicide case tried in 1994 in Tuolumne County, California. He described the woman as suffering from low self-esteem, poor judgment in choosing male partners, malignant drug abuse, mood disorder, deep depression, and low self-confidence. He also offered the opinion that the victim might have made up everything she told him, which indicates that he did not study the investigator's reports or other evidence that supported her testimony. He concluded that BWS victims do not recover emotionally after several years of freedom from the batterer, unless they have had psychological treatment. The idea that BWS cripples a victim for years after her escape from abuse runs counter to all of my research on battered women over the past 15 years.

For expert witnesses to use sociological insights to aid BWS victims in court, there must be published literature that is supportive of these insights. For example, when I was asked to write a commentary on a colleague's article in *Sociological Imagination* (Bowker 1994), I took the occasion to publish my dominance theory of woman battering. This is a set of 35 propositions that interprets woman battering and its cessation in a broadly interdisciplinary context. For example, proposition 17 reads: "The primary dynamics involved in the development of the battered woman syndrome typically include: (a) an extreme power imbalance between the aggressor and his victim, (b) the mixing of psychological and physical abuse so as to undermine the victim's self-confidence, (c) intermittent positive reinforcement (often romantic or at least apologetic) that pleases and confuses the victim, and (d) unpredictable and inconsistent violence, sometimes mixing instrumental and expressive elements, which deprives the victim of any possibility of dealing rationally with the violence" (Bowker 1994:55). With this theory now in the literature, I can cite it in court as part of the generally accepted knowledge about battered women.

INFLUENCING THE DECISION MAKERS

In spite of the fact that ideas on BWS are now in the literature, authorities who will make decisions on various issues in a case are unlikely to know about the sociological literature on domestic violence prior to the start of the trial. An expert witness is at a distinct disadvantage in attempting to pioneer a new approach with a skeptical judge and jury. It is better to influence them before the trial begins, as both the prosecutor and the defense attempted to do in front of a national television audience in O. J. Simpson's double murder trial. Sociologists increase the possibility of influencing the courts every time they write a journal article, a piece in the popular press, or, especially, a book. Publications such as *The Journal of Psychiatry and Law* are full of articles by expert witnesses from various disciplines who are using this strategy to increase their influence in future civil disputes and criminal prosecutions.

Another way to influence decision makers before they are enmeshed in the details of a specific case is to become involved in training them. Police officers, judges, prosecutors, and defense lawyers all participate regularly in training conferences, some of which are mandated by law. I was privileged to be a presenter at one such session for the California Board of Prison Terms in 1994. The board provided me with seven questions around which to organize my training presentation. The questions were reasonable and to the point, such as How does an expert diagnose someone as suffering from the battered woman syndrome? and Why does the woman stay in an abusive relationship? The board's curiosity was piqued by my presentation, and they asked me to prepare a training document based on the session. I did so, enlarging my answers to the seven questions and adding an appendix that outlined my dominance theory of woman battering in quantitative and qualitative terms. My goal in preparing this document was to influence board members to make appropriate custody determinations regarding battered women in the California penal system. I wanted them to eschew a psychological perspective and adopt a sociological framework for understanding BWS.

Recalling Parson's (1977) action system model, I specified six dimensions of oppression that abusive men use to increase and perpetuate dominance over their sexual partners. These dimensions are cultural, social, economic, psychological, physical, and sexual.

Cultural System Abuse

I look for myths and symbols that are used to oppress and demean the battering victim. Terms such as "bitch" and "whore" are common symbols that come to mind and are found in a high percentage of battering cases. Many myths are also voiced by the batterers as excuses for their behavior. One common myth is "women are emotional, irrational, and stupid." The constant repetition of these cultural elements is used to reinforce the man's control over his victim and is a major part of psychological system victimization, which is discussed below.

Social System Abuse

Batterers generally isolate their victims from friends, relatives, and other sources of help in the community. They force their wives to miss appointments. They make it uncomfortable for visitors to come to the home. They may control or remove the telephone from the home. They may move their family away from extended family, particularly the wife's relatives, who might provide her with an escape from the abusive relationship.

Economic System Abuse

Batterers typically control more than their share of the money in a marriage or live-in relationship. It is not unusual to find that they have so completely controlled the money in the family that the woman has to save pennies over a lengthy period in order to escape. The batterer may have the car and the house in his name alone, rather than in both names. Another detail commonly seen is that batterers whose wives receive welfare or pension checks will go with them to cash the check to make sure that they have no chance to spend the money on their own.

Psychological System Abuse

The terror of living in an abusive relationship is likely to increase when an abuser tortures pets, makes violent threats against the victim and her family, tells her she will never see her children again if she leaves him, destroys valued property (such as heirlooms from the victim's family), and gestures to remind the victim of the physical punishment that she will receive should she resist him.

Physical System Abuse

This is what most untutored lay people and, unfortunately, criminal justice decision makers think of as being wife beating or woman abuse. It includes all kinds of battering, nonsexual torture, and, ultimately, femicide.

Sexual System Abuse

Marital rape is very highly correlated with battering. It includes not only forced oral, anal, and genital intercourse but also forced exhibitionism, forced prostitution, sex with animals, sex with others, and sexual torture.

When I take a case, I interview the possible BWS victim (and others as appropriate), read all of the criminal records on the case, and consult with the victim's lawyer and investigator on the case and with any woman's advocate who might be involved with the BWS victim. I then make two profile comparisons. The first compares the profile of the woman's abuse with BWS profiles established in my own research and other scientific findings. The first profile is based on the six system levels of abuse as defined above. The second comparison is between the profile of selected observable effects of her battering by the aggressor with effects profiles that have been developed by researchers in the field.

Batterers may use several systems to dominate a victim. Two or three system levels also are used interchangeably. In fact, it is the involvement of multiple system levels of abuse that makes the BWS such a compelling method of behavior control. Like the prisoner of war syndrome and the Stockholm syndrome, the BWS involves amazingly high levels of control and domination through multiple manipulative techniques (Dutton 1988).

In most of the BWS cases with which I am familiar, the batterers have developed extensive control mechanisms at all six system levels. Elements of cultural, psychological, and physical abuse are always present; social, economic, and sexual abuse are present in 80 to 90 percent of the cases. Looking at it another way, evidence of all six system levels of abuse is found in 80 percent of the cases, while at least four of the systems are found in the remaining 20 percent of the cases. It is worth noting that the physical system abuse is not always grossly manifested. It may be so subtle as to be missed by professionals who are untrained in BWS assessment.

The second profile I generate is the effects of victimization. Here, I compare evidence of a specific case of battering with the effects literature on battering to determine whether or not the defendant fits the profile of a battered woman. An exhaustive list of the effects of battered woman syndrome is beyond the scope of this chapter, so I will limit myself to just six examples of the many elements one considers in this profile comparison.

1. Psychological domination normally leads to immobilization and low self-esteem, in which the woman will report an inability to make decisions because of fear that her decision will be the wrong one. Victims of the BWS typically think that the batterer is right. They think that they love the batterer and that the batterer loves them, despite his many beatings.

2. The victim never wins arguments with the batterer and even may be afraid to argue at all.

3. The victim has no resources at hand and may live in poverty, even if she is wealthy.

4. The victim tries very hard to please the batterer. Minute details of the temperature of food, its placement on the plate, and the timing of its serving become topics of vast importance for the BWS victim. If there is

little evidence that the battered woman tried very hard to please the batterer in many different ways, one must be most doubtful about the existence of the BWS.

5. The battered woman believes that the batterer is essentially omnipotent. She thinks that she never could kill him and is sure that she could not live without him. Because of this, a battered woman who has seriously injured her abuser in the course of protecting herself often will not believe that he is in danger of dying. Some men have bled to death while the women they abused talked to them as if they were not even seriously hurt. Other battered women refuse to believe that their abuser is dead even after having seen his lifeless body.

6. The victim takes the batterer's definitions and perceptions of the world as her own. She is strongly bonded to him and lives through him via the traumatic bond.

All of the elements that constitute the profile of battering effects must consist of data that are in some way objectively observable. One cannot provide an accurate BWS determination based on psychological testing or feminist theory alone. Evidence of many sorts is needed to establish BWS, even though batterers typically destroy evidence and are extremely secretive about their battering.

In short, two profiles are necessary, and their mutual reinforcement is critical to a successful defense. Not only must the defense demonstrate system level abuse, but also it must show evidence that the abuse produces visible, tangible effects. The comparatively narrow range of abuse systems (physical and sexual) typically used by psychologists has the unwanted result of limiting the search for effects to a much smaller arena than imagined by sociologists.

In the appendix of my training document for the California Board of Prison Terms, I translated the theoretical and practical material in the body of the document into a simple system for the quantitative representation of BWS determinations. I collapsed the abuse characteristics and effects ratings into a single severity factor for each system level of abuse. I also collapsed the psychological and cultural system levels into a single system, because there is so much overlap between the two when they are applied to real people as opposed to people in theory. Each system level of abuse is expressed on a linear scale of zero (no abuse) to ten (the most severe abuse imaginable), which can be represented on a bar graph. The resulting visual enhancement has a quantitative dimension that is an effective means of communicating with judges, attorneys, and jurors.

JOINING THE DEFENSE TEAM

Successful battered women's defense teams routinely require at least four specialties: defense lawyer, investigator, counselor, and sociologist. The opportunity for the sociologist to learn something from the other specialists is complemented by the addition of a sociological perspective to the complicated issues of abuse. The task of the sociologist is to determine the plausibility of the BWS defense.

I will never forget interviewing a girl who was separated from her mother for most of a year by the criminal justice system. She was the prosecution's star witness against her (battered) mother, who was charged with murdering her stepfather. Although later released on bail pending the beginning of the trial, the mother initially was jailed and her daughter was packed off to live with her biological father in another state. When she finally was reunited with her mother, grandmother, and other relatives for a few days during her Thanksgiving school holiday, I arranged to interview her and invited her mother's counselor and attorney to join me.

Our four-hour session succeeded in our learning about the abuse the girl had seen her mother take from the stepfather, the ways in which he manipulated her to side with him against her mother, and the depth of the girl's resentment toward her mother for killing the stepfather, who paid so much attention to her.

The psychologist and the lawyer who worked with me were both women. I was the only man in the room. The girl's mother had retired to another part of the office suite so her daughter would feel free to speak her mind. The three professionals all asked questions, provided encouragement and support, and gave appropriate feedback throughout the evening. We simultaneously covered the same material from three different disciplinary perspectives, our questions differing as to the aspect of each subject that was most relevant to therapeutic healing (the psychologist), building an airtight legal defense (the lawyer), and developing the facts needed for a BWS determination (the sociologist).

I have discussed several contributions a sociologist could make to battered women and their defense teams. In summary, I can identify 15 specific tasks appropriate for sociologists who are thinking about working on cases involving women who are victims of abuse.

1. Testimony in criminal court — trials and sentencing hearings
2. Testimony in civil court
3. Interviewing clients and writing reports on their cases (average length, 20 pages)
4. Writing reports in support of clemency petitions for incarcerated victims
5. Consulting with lawyers to prepare them for trials
6. Educating clients on the process of domination through battering and other dominance-enhancing techniques as well as the effects of this dominance-enhancing abuse on themselves and their children
7. Drafting sentencing reports and treatment (rehabilitation) plans
8. Directing investigations to develop evidence

9. Analyzing legal documents and other evidence
10. Linking clients to help sources and monitoring quality of services they receive
11. Acting as an advocate for the client with defense lawyers, criminal justice system decision makers, and community agencies
12. Reassuring and educating the relatives of the victim
13. Conferring heroine status on successful self-defenders and influencing others to adopt a more positive definition of victims who have successfully asserted their right to freedom from violence
14. Aiding victims in obtaining restraining orders
15. Protecting children against an abusing parent by supporting safe custody arrangements

CONCLUSION: ADVOCACY VERSUS ACCURACY IN EXPERT WITNESSING

The sociologist is a scientist and is, therefore, expected to strive for accuracy in measurement and prediction as well as in identifying causal influences. If that sociologist also is committed to social justice, then what happens to the alleged neutral objectivity of the scientist? Can social science coexist with social justice advocacy when the scientist is asked to examine oppressed people such as abused adolescents, welfare clients, ghetto dwellers, or battered women who have killed their abusers?

I believe that committed advocacy and "neutral" accuracy are at opposite ends of a continuum that also can be used to array four basic activities of expert witnesses in criminal and civil cases: data collection, theory development, expert testimony, and interaction with the defendant and the legal defense team. Data collection must be as accurate as possible. Theory development is the process of making sense of the data in a sociological framework. There is a certain subjectivity in this theoretical operation, because there are many possible theories that will be consistent with the available data in a criminal or civil case. Choosing the best theory is not just a matter of the best fit; it also contains an element of advocacy in the tradition of action in support of social justice. Expert witness testimony, both written and oral, has stronger advocacy elements than the theoretical work that precedes it, but it is still scientific and scholarly.

It is in interaction with the defendant, the defense lawyer, the investigator on the case, and assorted relatives that advocacy becomes dominant. The sociologist who also is committed to social justice may choose to withdraw from a case if the data and their theoretical interpretations are hostile to the interests of social justice. Alternatively, a report to the defense attorney can become the terminal activity in a consultation, for example, advising against a BWS defense for a woman who has killed her oppressive but nonviolent husband. If sociologists are to retain their reputations as scientists, they must be willing to make findings of "no battered woman syndrome," "insufficient evidence of child abuse," or "lack of mitigating merit in the social situation of the defendant" where the facts so warrant. The alternative of advocacy running wild undermines the basis for the sociologist's expertise.

As a sociologist, I attempt to balance the tension between my role as a scholar and my role as an advocate for justice. This tension is not resolved at any one point, but involves a continual evaluation of my thinking and, consequently, my participation. From those accused of alleged gang membership to victims of abuse, a sociological perspective may be critical for a fair and just outcome in the courts. Our challenge as sociologists may be to increase our relevance and influence in the legal arena.

REFERENCES

Bowker, L. H. 1994. Existing Community-Based Alternatives Will Not Deter Serious Woman Batterers. *Sociological Imagination, 31*, 50–62.

Bowker, L. H. 1993. A Battered Woman's Problems are Social Not Psychological. In R. J. Gelles & D. R. Loseke (Eds.). *Current Controversies on Family Violence* (pp. 154–165). Beverly Hills, CA: Sage.

Bowker, L. H. 1987. Battered Women as Consumers of Legal Services: Reports from a National Survey. *Response to the Victimization of Women and Children, 10,* 10–17.

Bowker, L. H. 1986. *Ending the Violence*. Holmes Beach, FL: Learning Publications.

Bowker, L. H. 1984. Battered Wives and the Police: A National Study of Usage and Effectiveness. *Police Studies, 7,* 84–93.

Bowker, L. H. 1983. *Beating Wife-Beating*. Lexington, MA: D.C. Heath.

Bowker, L. H., & Maurer, L. 1987. The Medical Treatment of Battered Wives. *Women and Health, 12,* 25–45.

Bowker, L. H., & Maurer, L. 1986. The Effectiveness of Counseling Services Utilized by Battered Women. *Women and Therapy, 5,* 65–82.

Bowker, L. H., & Maurer, L. 1985. The Importance of Sheltering in the Lives of Battered Wives. *Response to the Victimization of Women and Children, 7,* 2–11.

Browne, A. 1987. *When Battered Women Kill*. New York: Free Press.

Dobash, R. E., & Dobash, R. 1992. *Women, Violence and Social Change*. London: Routledge.

Dobash, R. E., & Dobash, R. 1979. *Violence Against Wives*. New York: Free Press.

Donato, K. M., & Bowker, L. H. 1984. Understanding the Helpseeking Behavior of Battered Women: A Comparison of Traditional Services and Women's Groups. *International Journal of Women's Studies, 7,* 99–109.

Dutton, D. G. 1988. *The Domestic Assault of Women*. Boston, MA: Allyn and Bacon.

Dutton, M. A. 1992. *Empowering and Healing the Battered Woman*. New York: Springer.

Gelles, R. J., & Loseke, D. R. 1993. *Current Controversies on Family Violence*. Beverly Hills, CA: Sage.

Giles-Sims, J. 1983. *Wife Battering*. New York: Guilford Press.

Gondolf, E. W., with Fisher, E. R. 1988. *Battered Women as Survivors*. Lexington, MA: D. C. Heath.

Hall, H. J., & Waxman, R. N. 1994. *California Juvenile Court Practice: Delinquent Minors*, Vol. 1. Berkeley, CA: Continuing Education of the Bar.

Hurley, J. 1994. Petition for Writ of Prohibition (P.C. 991a). Redding: Court of Appeal of the State of California, Third Appellate District.

Pagelow, M. D. 1981. *Woman-Battering*. Beverly Hills, CA: Sage.

Parsons, T. 1977. *Social Systems and the Evolution of Action Theory*. New York: Free Press.

Sanders, W. B. 1994. *Gangbangs and Drive-bys*. New York: Aldine De Gruyter.

Sonkin, D. J. 1987. *Domestic Violence on Trial*. New York: Springer.

Tuolumne County Superior Court. 1994. Transcript of Criminal Case Number CR0518. Sonora, CA.

Walker, L.E.A. 1993. The Battered Woman Syndrome is a Psychological Consequence of Abuse. In R. J. Gelles & D. R. Loseke (Eds.), *Current Controversies on Family Violence* (pp. 133–153). Beverly Hills, CA: Sage.

Walker, L.E.A. 1987. *Terrifying Love*. New York: Harper & Row.

Walker, L.E.A. 1984. *The Battered Woman Syndrome*. New York: Springer.

Walker, L.E.A. 1979. *The Battered Woman*. New York: Harper & Row.

IV

DEFINING THE LIMITS OF
MORAL ACCOUNTABILITY

10

Sociology and Negligent Security: Premise Liability and Crime Prediction

Lydia Voigt and William E. Thornton, Jr.

Criminological research methods and theories are growing in demand by policy and decision makers, as well as by courts of law. Indeed, the call for criminologists as expert witnesses is not confined to criminal court. Increasingly, criminologists are invited as expert witnesses by the civil court, particularly in premise security liability or third-party liability suits.

Through the vehicle of civil law, premise security liability is the civil liability of property owners to provide reasonable and adequate security to customers and other invited patrons onto their premises. When a property owner fails to provide a reasonably safe environment to patrons and, as a result, an invited individual suffers a criminal victimization such as a rape, armed robbery, or assault by a third party, the property owner may be liable under civil jurisdiction for losses the patron incurs. Relatives of patrons who are murdered on premises are, likewise, subject to civil remedy associated with the loss of a loved one. Losses may include costs associated with physical injury, psychological trauma leading to inability to enjoy life or earn a living, and future income foregone as a result of victimization.

To a large extent, the standards necessary to trigger the charge of negligent security on the part of public and private establishments are subject to legal debate and vary from jurisdiction to jurisdiction. The controversy usually focuses on several key questions that generally must be answered when inadequate security is alleged against a property owner or manager in a civil action. Does the owner or occupier of the property owe a legal duty of care to the plaintiff? Was the interpersonal crime foreseeable on the premises? Did the owner or occupier of the property fail to conform to a "reasonable standard of care"? Was the negligence the *proximate* cause of the assaultive crime upon the plaintiff? Was the plaintiff damaged or otherwise injured as a result of that breach of duty? (McGoey 1990:19).

Experts often are called upon to help clarify the issues and to provide defensible guidelines for making decisions or judgments pertaining to questions of "foreseeable crime," "reasonable standard of care," and "adequate security." Attorneys employ a wide variety of experts to both collect data for their cases and render advice and opinions regarding the grounds for the case. Given that no uniform standard of criminal foreseeability to guide courts exists, the "definition of the situation" proffered by criminologist experts at each stage in a premise liability case — beginning from initial conception and moving to deposition to settlement or trial — has a tremendous influence on whether a case is lost, settled, or won. Perhaps in no other area of law is it possible for criminologists to define and set the parameters of legal decisions as well as to establish precedence as in the realm of premise liability.

This chapter illustrates, through case examples, how our training in criminology and sociology has been instrumental in influencing the overall development of cases as well as outcomes of specific cases. Much of what we bring to our clients, chiefly attorneys, in terms of methodological and analytical skills comes from our training as academic sociologists and criminologists.[1] As premise liability consultants and expert witnesses, we have participated in more than 100 cases, both plaintiff and defense, and have been declared criminological experts by numerous courts in several states. Our consulting practice has brought us in competition with many experts coming from varied backgrounds. Rarely have these other experts brought to clients the panorama of analytical, methodological, and theoretical skills necessary to fully conceptualize, investigate, and develop a case. Indeed, we argue that the very "stuff" of criminology as a discipline strongly lends itself to this particular area of litigation.

This chapter introduces our "crime foreseeability model," which we developed utilizing many years of experience in premise liability litigation. The model demonstrates the practical applicability of research methods, theories, and the use of sociological and criminological imagination. Our discussion begins with a review of the history of third-party criminal liability suits and current developments in civil procedure as they relate to premise security litigation.

HISTORY OF PREMISE SECURITY LIABILITY

Until recently, most victims of interpersonal violent crimes did not realize that there was another legal avenue available to them for both increased crime protection and financial remedy for their losses. The first major award for an inadequate security claim involved a $2.7 million dollar judgment for entertainer Connie Francis, who was raped in a Howard Johnson Motor Lodge in upstate New York in 1974. Her assailant gained entry through a faulty sliding glass door. Francis alleged inadequate security and presented evidence of past similar offenses being committed against motel guests during the few years prior to her victimization (*Gannilli v. Howard Johnson's Motor Lodge, Inc.* 1976).

Over the years, there has been a growing trend to expand liability from third-party criminal actions to include such diverse businesses or entities as hotels and motels, shopping centers, parking lots, apartment complexes, hospitals, fast-food establishments, bars, casinos, convenience stores, restaurants, airports, train and bus depots, and educational institutions. More recently, municipalities that operate such facilities as public parks, amusement parks, and museums have been held to higher standards of security than in the past and, hence, are subject to civil liability for inadequate security. Even public schools are not immune to civil liability suits from parents who have children hurt by the criminal actions of third parties who intrude on school premises. There is no doubt that the threat of inadequate security suits has motivated owners, managers, and administrators of public and private establishments to be more cognizant of potential criminal dangers to patrons and to respond by making their facilities safer (Wright 1994; Holl and Newton 1992).

In the past decade, premise liability tort filings have increased more than 260 percent, with the average settlement being in excess of $545,000 and the average jury award being $3.35 million (Bates and Dunnell 1993). A study of 267 premise security cases reported in *The Law Reporter,* published by the Association of Trial Lawyers of America, found that the crimes that cause the vast majority of premise liability suits are found in four main categories: rape and sexual assault (44.5 percent), assault and battery (24.9 percent), wrongful death (18.5 percent), and robbery (8.7 percent). The types of businesses most often involved in inadequate security torts are residential properties (37.6 percent), hotels and motels (24.2 percent), and retail establishments (8.4 percent). Others include restaurants, bars, and casinos (6.7 percent)[2]; office buildings (5.1 percent); colleges (3.9 percent); and common carriers (e.g., buses, trains, airplanes) (11.3 percent). Apartment units, parking lots, and garages account for more than 40 percent of the specific locations where crimes are committed against invited patrons (Bates and Dunnell 1993).

One reason that rapes result in the highest percentage of premise liability claims is the nature of the violence perpetrated against the victim. In addition to the physical harm that usually ensues with a rape, deep emotional trauma often is associated with the attack. More recently, the fear of contracting AIDS further exacerbates the fear of the victim long after the initial rape. Wrongful deaths in which the victim dies as a result of the negligence of a third party usually result in the highest awards, based upon considerations of lost future earnings and loss of consortium claims by spouses (Bates and Dunnell 1993).

COMPETING APPROACHES TO CRIME FORESEEABILITY

Three competing schools of thought regarding the criteria necessary to establish crime foreseeability can be found in tort law decisions, chiefly at the state level, regarding premise liability. The first is the impending assault doctrine. Some courts have maintained that a business owner has a duty to exercise reasonable care to protect patrons only from the criminal acts of third parties that he or she knows are about to occur (i.e., the impending assault). If a business owner had knowledge of a crime to be perpetrated against a customer, he or she would be under a legal obligation to either warn or attempt to prevent the impending assault. As a minimum caution, the owner is under obligation to at least warn patrons of potential dangers. Courts have generally maintained, however, that rarely are business owners in the position to actually know that a customer or patron was the target of an impending attack. For example, criminal victimization of acquaintances or relatives that spill over into the commercial areas generally are considered unforeseen unless the manager or proprietor has been put on prior notice.

CASE ILLUSTRATION:
IMPENDING ASSAULT

A case that occurred a few years ago involved a woman who was assaulted in a strip shopping center parking lot by a man. Upon investigation, we found that the perpetrator was an ex-employee of the company where the woman worked. He recently had been fired by the victim, who was a personnel manager of the company. The man had been stalking her for several days prior to the attack. The court held that the attack upon the woman in the parking lot could not have been foreseen by the shopping center management. The center's management had no prior knowledge of the conflict between the two individuals and, therefore, could not have warned the woman of the impending attack.

Other courts accept the notion that a crime is unforeseeable unless the owner or manager knows that there have been a "high" number of similar offenses that occurred on the premises (the prior similar crimes rule). Thus, if a plaintiff is a victim of rape in a business' restroom, and it can be proven that other women have been raped in the restroom in the past, the crime in question could be argued as foreseeable on the part of the business owner. Conversely, pending no prior similar crimes at a site in question, it may be argued by some that the crime was unforeseeable. Recent decisions have called into question exclusive use of the prior similar crimes rule on the grounds that the victims of crime are victimized twice if they are attacked in a facility for the first time. Initially they suffer from the criminal attack, and then they are unable to recover in lawsuits because they were the first victim. The prior similar crimes rule has been likened to the legal maxim, "Every dog is entitled to one free bite." Issues raised against the exclusive use of the prior similar crimes rule have resulted in widening the variables under consideration. In essence, knowledge of a canine's dangerous propensities can be established *before* the first bite.

More recently, courts have examined a greater variety of circumstances in crime foreseeability (the totality of circumstances rule), arguing that, in addition to prior similar crimes, the general circumstances surrounding a criminal incident must also come into play (e.g., other patterns of criminality at a site and crime in adjoining areas, frequency of pedestrian and vehicular traffic, demographic conditions, and security measures such as ingress and egress devices, monitoring technology, architectural design, and guards).[3] The totality of circumstances rule seems to offer a better reasoned basis for determining crime foreseeability because it suggests a multivariate analysis of crime — something sociologists and criminologists have been doing for a long time. Much of the discipline of criminology, including crime measurement, crime etiology, crime prevention, and crime control, supports the components of the totality of circumstances rule.

THE CRIME FORESEEABILITY MODEL

Although not every case demands an in-depth investigation of all variables, most cases will require several stages of development. The crime foreseeability model that we propose is based on a checklist of data and information necessary for a systematic and comprehensive case development. It includes standard methods of criminology for collecting data and a rich body of theories to render an opinion on crime foreseeability and security adequacy for a client (plaintiff or defendant). The model introduced here ensures the orderly (i.e., scientifically sound) collection of data and theoretically adequate analysis of data. Our comprehensive and systematic approach to the discovery of information and to the defensibility of evidence is composed of the following areas of investigation:

Analysis of prior similar and other interpersonal crimes
Analysis of incident reports and supplemental crime data
Analysis of other types of crimes at the site
Analysis of the level of security at the site
    Physical security factors
    Security plan and philosophy
Review of any relevant security standards
Analysis of social, economic, and demographic characteristics
Nature and profile of the offender
Nature and profile of the victim

ANALYSIS OF PRIOR SIMILAR AND
OTHER INTERPERSONAL CRIMES

Irrespective of the legal debate (e.g., *Siebert v. Vic Regnier Builders, Inc.* [1993]) regarding the problems associated with the exclusive use of prior similar crimes rule, our model necessitates the acquisition of this information. It is important to conduct a complete crime analysis of same-type crimes utilizing police statistics (e.g., offenses reported to local police) for the specific geographical locale (e.g., police district, zone, or subzone) where a case is located.[4] This information is not used exclusively but represents only the first step in a more comprehensive approach.

For example, if a case that is being investigated involves the rape of a woman in the parking lot of a shopping center, we begin with an examination of the occurrence of other rapes at the site and in the surrounding area. An arbitrarily designated geographical area with specific boundaries can be used for this purpose. However, police district and zone maps are considered standard for the display of this information, especially because official crime data are collected in relation to such districts. Specific crime rates then can be generated for the area in question as well as for an entire city.

In addition, crime analysis almost always should include a rate analysis of the major Uniform Crime Reporting (UCR) index offenses (i.e., murder, rape, robbery, aggravated assault, burglary, larceny theft, motor vehicle theft, and arson). It is impossible to speak of "low" or "high" crime areas without some means of comparison (Thornton, McKinnon-Fowler, and Kent 1991).

Through a general crime statistical analysis, it may be possible to show that the rate of violent crime at a site is substantially higher (or lower) than that for surrounding areas or, possibly, for an entire city. Thus, whether or not prior rapes had occurred on the premise, the relative dangerousness of the site and the relative adequacy of security can be established. Based on our experience as premise liability consultants, we have found that armed robbery is one of the best indicators of an area's or city's general level of "dangerousness." Armed robbery, unlike other crimes of violence, usually involves strangers rather than acquaintances or relatives.

Utilizing official statistics, we rank armed robberies by police districts and zones and subzones for several years, statistically weigh these, and create an index that can be used for comparative purposes. This index can be further decomposed by controlling for population size, types and numbers of commercial establishments versus residential facilities, and so on. For instance, the robbery rates per 100,000 population at a shopping center and in the surrounding area (e.g., number of customers per day or number of cars in the mall parking area divided by the number of incidents of robbery) could be computed. If, for example, the robbery rate is lower at a shopping center where a rape occurred than in the surrounding area, it would be difficult to argue inadequate security. Computing per capita crime rates for both the specific crime in question as well as other index crimes, especially armed robbery, for "defendant" premises and for the surrounding community cannot be overvalued. This places a particular victimization in a broader crime and security context.

CASE ILLUSTRATION:
FAST-FOOD RESTAURANT

An example of a defendant case in which we served as consultants illustrates the need for a thorough analysis of prior similar crimes in conjunction with a more general crime analysis. We were retained by an attorney representing a Mexican fast-food restaurant that recently had gone out of business. The plaintiffs in the case were the parents of a young man who had been murdered in a parking lot adjacent to the restaurant. The young man and his girlfriend parked in the lot (about 50 feet away), walked to the restaurant to eat, and, upon returning to their car, were victimized. Although the owners of the business did not own the adjacent parking lot, over the years, customers often parked in the lot because of its convenience to the restaurant. Management had made no effort to discourage parking in the lot, which was located next to an abandoned mechanic's shop. Upon investigation, our analysis of prior similar crimes at the restaurant revealed two other murders in the parking lot adjacent to the business. We also uncovered several armed and simple robberies of patrons and cashiers working in the restaurant. The management of the business had no security measures in place, in spite of the relatively large number of past interpersonal criminal offenses. Many of the crimes had occurred at night, and the lighting in the parking lot was inadequate. The general area surrounding the business likewise was ranked high in both the volume and the rate of violent offenses in comparison with other police districts in the city.

Our opinion to the attorney was that, given past crime events on the site, the general dangerousness of the surrounding area, and the absence of even minimal security measures, the deceased victim's parents had a very strong case against the Mexican restaurant. The owners of the business had not, in our opinion, responded in a responsible manner to protect customers, given the past crime trends on and off the site. There was a high probability that a crime such as the one that occurred could have been foreseen. Our advice to the attorney was to settle the case early. The case was, indeed, settled for the defendant. We later found out that the owners had decided to close this particular restaurant because they were having difficulty hiring employees, who were frightened by the past reputation of the business as being a dangerous place to work.

ANALYSIS OF INCIDENT REPORTS AND
SUPPLEMENTAL CRIME DATA

As part of the crime analysis for specific crimes on and off a site, more detailed information can be obtained by acquiring the official incident reports available from law enforcement agencies. If the case is closed and does not involve juvenile offenders or victims, such reports are public record and can be obtained easily for a fee; some police departments allow researchers to view such reports on microfiche at no charge. If the case is still active, a subpoena duces tecum must be obtained in order to access this data. Included in these reports are detailed information regarding the victim and the offender and the circumstances surrounding the crime event. In addition to these reports, more information may be gleaned about the crime and the crime scene from depositions and other materials that invariably accompany a civil action for third-party criminal liability and may be requested from the attorneys representing the case.

Often, the experts must conduct interviews and develop other supplemental information using standard social science methodologies. For instance, if an official incident report appears incomplete or somehow confusing, the expert may attempt to check out certain details or facts by going on location and interviewing individuals in residences or businesses where the incident took place. The expert also may conduct interviews to confirm or refute certain perceptions of dangerousness ("fear of crime") or opinions regarding the adequacy of security on the premise. If this information is intended to be used as evidence in court, all the rigors of the scientific method come into play. Increasingly, courts place emphasis on "scientifically derived information," that is, challenging expert testimony on scientific grounds.

CASE ILLUSTRATION:
A CITY PARK'S SAFETY AND SECURITY

In a past case, we served on the plaintiff's side against a city park commission for not providing reasonable security for a man who was shot and robbed in a park restroom. Part of our task was to establish that enough past crimes had occurred in the park (40 acres) (and periphery of the park) to merit increased security for the protection of park patrons. Park security (which, in this case, amounted to two untrained groundskeepers) claimed that they maintained very few records of crimes that occurred in the park. The security director, an accountant, suspiciously testified that files regarding past criminal activity in the park could not be found, although he was sure there was little criminal activity in the park. We, therefore, requested from the crime analysis section of the police department a printout of all offenses that occurred in the park and the police zone and subzone in which the park was located for a period of five years prior to the incident.

Based on interviews with residents living on the periphery of the park and on interviews with a systematic sample of park patrons, common knowledge indicated that many crimes occurred in the park. We consequently expected that our official police statistics would confirm the relatively high crime rate for the park (and adjoining areas). We were surprised to find only a few officially documented crimes from the reports (a computer printout with a police item number, address, date, time, and type of crime occurring). For instance, the crime statistics for the area uncovered eight serious inter-personal crimes in the park during the same year of the crime in question. Something was wrong. Subsequent investigation (including a door-to-door survey of the residents in the adjacent area and an analysis of the more detailed police incident reports) revealed that, when a park crime was reported, the victim or bystander usually proceeded to the nearest phone (e.g., pay phone booths across the street from the park) or to a home on the boundary of the park. Consequently, the address where the call was placed — rather than the location of the criminal act (i.e., the park) — was registered on the official police report. As a result, the crime appears to have taken place *outside* the park. In fact, this was the case with the crime in question. This practice, we found, was quite common and reflected a definite flaw in the police reporting system.

Only by requesting a more detailed incident (and supplemental) report (i.e., the officer's field interrogation report and subsequent follow-up) could we pinpoint specific crimes that occurred within the boundaries of the park. Consideration of incident reports, however, still failed to account for the discrepancies between official reports and the common perceptions of this area as having a high crime rate.

In an effort to augment the official statistics, we did a content analysis (for the same years) of the local newspaper and discovered a few additional crimes reported to have occurred in the park that did not show up in the official statistics. We concentrated on those crimes that we could definitely document (i.e., those that occurred within the boundaries of the park), and then we examined more closely those "official" crimes that occurred on the boundaries of the park and adjacent neighborhoods. A comparison of crime patterns occurring in this particular police district (or, more precisely, the geographical subzone of the district) with those occurring in other districts of the city did suggest that this section of the city experienced a relatively higher number of victimizations. Especially in relation to its size, population, and square miles, the park was the site of a disproportionately high number of crimes. We also uncovered a survey conducted by the city a few years earlier that drew a similar conclusion. The survey included a fear of crime inventory in which the citizens in the area indicated that they were seriously concerned about crime and their protection.

Our opinion to our client, and the subsequent opinion in court, was that, given the overall crime patterns and lack of security in the park, it was logical to infer that this type of crime was reasonably foreseeable. Furthermore, we also offered an analysis of the location and architectural design of the restrooms in the park that was based on an area of criminology known as "crime control through environmental design" (Harries 1974; Jeffrey 1977; Kaplan, O'Kane, Lavrakas, and Pesce 1978; Rubenstein, Murray, Motoyama, and Rouse 1980; Crowe 1991). The judgment for the case ruled in favor of our client, and he was awarded in excess of $2 million. The judgment, however, later was overturned at the appeals level, reverting back to the exclusive prior similar crimes rule.

ANALYSIS OF OTHER TYPES OF CRIMES AT A SITE

In addition to the examination of prior similar and other interpersonal crimes at a site (and in the surrounding area), a crime analysis also must examine other types of crimes, such as property offenses, that may have occurred on a premise. Although property crimes such as auto burglaries or auto thefts usually are not good predictors of crimes against the person at a site, the prevalence of large numbers of auto burglaries, even in the absence of prior similar violent crimes, may be used to suggest that opportunities for more serious crimes against customers or other invited guests may occur. Certain types of property crimes, such as shoplifting in a store, may have no relationship to either other property crimes or interpersonal crimes occurring in a parking lot against patrons. In general, even a large number of minor property crimes are not substantially similar enough to predict future stranger violence in many situations. At least some empirical research has suggested that property crime statistics are not valid indicators of future crimes of violence. For instance, an analysis of UCR data indicated that one aggravated assault can be expected in 1,000 motor vehicle thefts and that one murder can ensue from 45,000 motor vehicle thefts (*Security Law Newsletter* 1990). Courts usually do not accept the expert opinion that minor property crimes at a site are good predictors of violent crimes.

It is worth noting that comparing crime trends, even property crimes, from one site, such as a shopping mall parking lot, with those at another comparable site in the same vicinity can be used to point to possible security problems. If one shopping center parking lot, for example, has roving security guards and, as a result, has a minimal amount of auto burglaries or auto thefts, and another shopping center in the same vicinity has no guards but a large number of property crimes, an argument can be made for the relative inadequacies of security at the latter site. Thus, although the numbers of minor property crimes may not be valid indicators of future crimes of violence, they can indicate the relative adequacy of security and, thus, be useful from that perspective.

THE LEVEL OF SECURITY AT A SITE

Levels of security at a site can range from minor precautions (e.g., written warnings, signs, fencing) to major precautions (e.g., contract or proprietary security personnel, elaborate security lighting, full perimeter security fencing, electronic monitoring systems, intrusion detection devices). The nature of the third-party criminal event and the past crime trends, if any, on the premises and in the surrounding area generally dictate the level of security necessary at a particular site.

Standard investigation of a case usually requires a security evaluation or assessment, in which a number of key factors must be examined. Such an assessment includes an intensive physical examination of the premises in order to determine the current state of security, to locate or assess weaknesses, and to make recommendations for "hardening" the facility in order to prevent future criminal intrusions. Obviously, in a defense case, the investigator tries to emphasize existing security measures and points to their general adequacy. In a plaintiff case, weaknesses in security at a facility become the focal point, and recommendations of security improvement measures that may have prevented a third-party criminal offense are stressed.

Although each site or facility is unique in terms of the actual risks it is designed to control and its subsequent vulnerabilities, two general areas of crime prevention methodology may be addressed in premise liability cases as being necessary for a reasonable standard of care to protect customers and other invited guests: environmental design and physical security factors and security plan or security philosophy.

ENVIRONMENTAL DESIGN AND PHYSICAL SECURITY FACTORS

A number of physical environmental variables have long been associated with crime deterrence or crime displacement. Under Crime Prevention Through Environmental Design the architectural design, placement of buildings, parking lots, and movement generators (e.g., walkways, overpasses, corridors, and halls) at a site can affect the opportunities for criminal events to occur. Crime Prevention Through Environmental Design chiefly attempts to achieve crime prevention by modifying the physical features of the target setting. For example, it offers methods for designing or redesigning commercial and residential buildings, other commercial areas, parks, or even entire neighborhoods in order to reduce crime. These methods may be as sophisticated as Oscar Newman's (1973) design directive for public housing developments or as simple as locating an automatic teller machine so that it lends itself to natural observation.

Another body of theoretical works that provides a rich supply of theory and research evidence that experts may use to "support" conclusions regarding environmental and social conditions associated with high and low crime trends is routine activities theory (Cohen and Felson 1979; Felson 1987). The routine activity approach to crime rate analysis suggests that, by guiding the natural flow of individuals and activities so that offenders and targets rarely meet in the absence of natural, informal controls (e.g., public observation), crime temptation and victimization may be reduced.

SECURITY PLAN AND SECURITY PHILOSOPHY

Many premise liability cases hinge on the presence or absence of a master security plan at the establishment. Such a plan should address such things as the establishment's or management's philosophy toward security, allocation of resources for security, the name or type of security employment (is there a security director with a clear line of authority and accountability?), the name of the security plan, training of security personnel (is the training of security guards adhering to state licensing requirements or industry?), clear direction for security personnel, maintenance of records of problems and criminal events (e.g., incident reports), integration of security hardware into a secure plan, integration of local law enforcement into the master plan, coordination of security codes, and periodic review of the security program.

A security plan, of course, must be carried out on a daily basis if it is to be of any use to a particular establishment. Failure to implement security procedures, even if they exist on paper, can be just as bad from a liability stance in some states as having no security plan at all. Usually, the first step in judging the adequacy of a security plan is to do a security assessment of a site, including an analysis of the types of criminal events that occur at a site and in the surrounding area. We have used the illustration below in several different cases that required comparative data regarding levels of security in relation to crime patterns and citizens' perceptions of fear of crime.

CASE ILLUSTRATION:
SECURITY ASSESSMENT OF PUBLIC HOUSING DEVELOPMENTS

Surveys sponsored by the Department of Housing and Urban Development as well as several national conferences on public housing show that the quality of life of public housing residents is reduced more by crime and fear of crime than by any other social problem. Crime analysis studies conducted by Brill and associates (1972, 1973, 1974, 1975, 1978) show that crime rates in various public housing complexes are five to ten times higher than the national average. More recent studies, many undertaken by the Department of Housing and Urban Development, place the rate at a much higher level (Robinson 1985). Studies of residents who live in public housing uniformly report that 60 to 70 percent of respondents indicate that it is very dangerous to go out of their apartments at night. Several studies undertaken of New Orleans public housing residents over the years indicate similar findings (e.g., Criminal Victimization Surveys in New Orleans 1977; Neighborhood Profile Series in New Orleans 1980; Thornton and Voigt 1986). Victimization in public halls, elevators, and other common areas particularly are cited as being dangerous. Parents especially fear for the safety of their children and have no assurances that they can play safely on the grounds of the developments, even during daylight hours. Thornton and Voigt (1984–86) found that the children in public housing developments often have a view of the world much different than that of middle-class children living in private residential areas. Children who live in public housing, as early as three or four years old, see the world as a dangerous place, one in which survival is highly questionable and dependent on street skills rather than school skills.

Given this backdrop, we were retained by a large public housing authority to examine specifically those types of crimes committed in ten public housing developments with a combined tenant population of about 100,000; conduct a residential survey of crime and ways to combat crime in the developments; review existing security measures, including an environmental assessment of each complex; and provide the data necessary to develop a comprehensive security plan for the public housing developments (Thornton and McKinnon 1992).

Our crime analysis utilized official data spanning a 5-year period for each housing complex. Major UCR index crime categories were employed, with special attention given to drug-related homicides and other interpersonal crimes of violence, such as rape and armed robbery, that occurred in the public housing boundaries. A separate analysis of crimes in surrounding neighborhoods of the developments was also completed. A property and violent crime index was calculated for each site for every year that data were collected.

Our tenant survey revealed that structural and physical security appeared to be the overwhelming concern of tenants. Everyone felt that limited access to the developments would be a key factor in eliminating the outside influences that terrorized the residents and their children. Some of the suggestions made by residents included cutting off streets to limit access, constructing attractive, contemporary fencing in and around the development, enhancing lighting, and redesigning the configuration of the buildings. Along with modifications to the area surrounding the perimeter of the development, residents suggested a need to modify the buildings themselves. Residents stated many times that a large proportion of the illegal activities occurring in the developments are conducted in the hallways of buildings. There was general agreement that these hallways should be eliminated and replaced by exterior stairs.

Our audit of existing security and vulnerabilities was aided greatly by tenant input and included a site-by-site checklist and detailed analysis of such things as location of buildings in relation to one another; ingress and egress patterns of buildings, sites, and parking lots; existing lighting; existing police patrols; maintenance records of buildings and grounds; location of public transit stops; pedestrian and traffic flows onto sites; surrounding neighborhood crime magnets; and existing housing authority security in place — patrols, past incident reports, personnel, and so on.

Our recommendations for a comprehensive security plan for the developments included several categories: physical environmental recommendations, social environmental recommendations, drug control and prevention recommendations, law enforcement and security recommendations; and housing authority management recommendations.

Under physical environmental factors, recommendations were made regarding type and placement of outdoor lighting, ways of controlling penetrability of sites, ways of enhancing territoriality of tenants by installing barriers, defining and enhancing private space boundaries for housing units, and clustering multifamily dwellings with well-defined common areas such as courtyards and playgrounds. We also recommended reducing tenant density by moving or tearing down abandoned buildings, which served as havens for drug users.

Under social environmental factors, the recommendations involved the enhancement of tenant cohesiveness and leadership in relation to apartment management; the development of more community service activities, especially for juveniles (e.g., expansion of afterschool and weeknight activities for the children); and domestic crisis and family support centers.[5]

Under drug control and prevention, the recommendations concerned greater law enforcement efforts to target "upper level" drug dealers in and near public housing. Likewise, we recommended that drug prevention programs be established or enhanced for public housing residents.

Under law enforcement and security, the recommendations focused on a plan to coordinate the housing authority and the metropolitan police in an effort to establish cooperative approaches to crime prevention and crime control. More specifically, the recommendation addressed the need for dedicated law enforcement to be assigned to specific housing developments rather than utilizing periodic patrols that just drive through the developments occasionally. It also was recommended that existing housing authority security be enlarged with better trained and better deployed personnel according to a comprehensive security plan.

Security plans and assessments such as this one are not uncommon. People residing in housing developments not only are more aware of their crime problems but also are more likely today to demand that their rights to live in safe environments be regarded by public authorities. Residents of public housing developments who are victimized by crime are increasingly bringing successful liability suits against municipal authorities. This trend is consistent with the greater likelihood that many businesses and public entities will develop comprehensive crime control and prevention plans and programs as part of their routine operations and management (e.g., universities, schools, hospitals). The growing need for professional crime and security evaluations offers significant opportunities for practicing criminologists.

REVIEW OF INDUSTRY STANDARDS OF SECURITY

Over the past few years, business-specific regulations have been proffered by various professional organizations (e.g., National Association of Chain Restaurants, National Association of Convenience Stores, International Council of Shopping Centers, Property Management Association, American Bankers Association, International Association for Healthcare Security and Safety). In addition to regulations regarding the operation of a particular business or franchise, minimum security standards are often set in place as a model to guide business owners.

For example, crime prevention studies of ways to reduce convenience store robberies suggest that designing stores to enhance visibility from the street, eliminating concealed access, closing stores between midnight and 6 A.M., and utilizing more than one sales clerk can be successful in reducing robberies (Weapons Against Crime 1994; Hunter and Jeffery 1992). In addition, the National Association of Convenience Stores provides training for store owners and managers in robbery deterrence through various seminars and other publications (National Association of Convenience Stores 1987). Convenience store owners who have a crime perpetrated against a customer or salesperson and who have not familiarized themselves with crime prevention strategies used in their particular industry run the risk of being held to a higher level of accountability than store owners who avail themselves of all possible knowledge and ways to reduce the probability of a crime occurring at their place of business. It is the responsibility of the crime expert to be knowledgeable of the standards in the industry.

The development of standards providing minimal guidelines for security is relatively new. Therefore, assessments of the effectiveness of these standards are greatly needed and frequently become the focal point of civil lawsuits. These recent developments offer criminologists working on such impact or outcome assessments groundbreaking opportunities to study the corresponding effects of security policies and plans and to contribute to the development of security standards in the future.

Public schools, for example, are not immune from civil liability and litigation as the result of crime and violence. The problem of school crime and violence is serious. At least 40 percent of the robberies and assaults on teenagers occur in schools (Rapp, Carrington, and Nicholson 1992:2–3). Victims of school violence have responded to school crime by demanding that schools provide an orderly and safe environment or compensate victims for their injuries. School systems largely remain under local control with respect to the operation of schools on a day-to-day basis. Some minimum standards for securing the safety of students and faculty have evolved over the years, with many coming from research and guidelines set by the National School Safety Center located at Pepperdine University (*School Safety Check Book* 1990).

Various approaches to security measures have been attempted in order to curb public school crime and violence. Most schools use relatively unobtrusive measures to control the problem; however, stricter, more traditional security measures also are used to control school violence. The less intrusive security measures include limited ingress point into a facility; the use of visible student, faculty, and visitor identification cards; monitoring of ingress and egress points into a facility; the use of signs informing visitors to check in at the main office; supervision of student restrooms, especially in primary and elementary schools; putting greater distance between the school and public transportation (e.g., moving bus stops farther away from school grounds); the implementation of a security plan at the school involving all personnel and students in creating a safe environment; the involvement of parents in the school security and safety plan; the establishment of a neighborhood school watch program, involving residents in neighborhoods near the school; a well-organized and carefully monitored department of safety and security for the municipal school district and office; the creation of conflict resolution programs in the school; and the establishment of an incident and tracking system in the school to identify problems and potentially dangerous students (or staff and faculty).

In some cases, more intrusive security measures have been implemented (especially in high crime schools located in high crime areas). Such measures include surveillance cameras placed in "hot spots" (e.g., halls, cafeterias, playgrounds, open spaces surrounding the school); metal detectors at ingress points in the school; school security personnel making regular rounds in the school; and periodic searches of student lockers for "reasonable cause" cases, and so on.

The development of standards providing minimal guidelines for security is relatively new. Therefore, assessments of the effectiveness of these standards frequently become the focal point of civil lawsuits. These developments offer criminologists working on such impact or outcome assessments groundbreaking opportunities to study the corresponding effects of security policies and plans and to contribute to the development of security standards in the future.

Schools were never intended to be minijails, nor were they designed to be urban or suburban "fortresses" walled off from their communities. We have found that the more traditional security measures, when applied to an educational setting, often alter the very atmosphere of the school, creating an environment not conducive to learning. In cases involving security at public schools, we usually help defense attorneys develop arguments and justifications for less intrusive, more informal, and more community oriented security measures.

CASE ILLUSTRATION:
SECURITY ASSESSMENT OF A PUBLIC ELEMENTARY SCHOOL

As consultants retained by a law firm representing a metropolitan school board, we were asked to assess security at an elementary school where an alleged incident of sexual battery occurred between two learning disabled adolescents; one was a student at the school, the other had been a student at the school. The police did not file formal charges because of the lack of evidence in the case; there was a reasonable suspicion that the alleged sexual act was one of mutual consent. The mother of the 14 year old, however, filed a premise liability suit against the school, alleging that the school created a dangerous environment for her son.

The neighborhood school was relatively small, with fewer than 500 students, and had a reputation for its caring and concerned faculty and administrators. It was located in what might be described as a lower income, working-class community with a moderate degree of criminal activity as evidenced by an examination of property and violent crime trends over a 5-year period prior to the incident in question.

According to our security assessment, the school met the minimum standards provided by the National School Safety Center. It was a well-maintained facility with a ten-foot chain-link fence enclosing the full perimeter of the site. However, we found that there were several unmonitored ingress points to the school. The restroom where the incident occurred was near an open and unmonitored gate on a side street adjacent to the school.

Our review of internal incident reports maintained by the school revealed no prior sexual incidents between students, and aside from a few behavioral problems with some students, no serious offenses had ever been reported at the school. Official police reports for the area revealed the same. Aside from two burglaries that occurred after school hours, no official crimes had been reported.

Our opinion in the matter was that, given the lack of prior incidents at the school, given the high level of supervision that was evidenced by teachers and staff, and given the lack of evidence of an actual sexual assault having occurred, the offense in question was not reasonably foreseeable by the school. However, our security assessment of the school indicated that several changes were warranted in order to better control strangers' access to school grounds. Although there were numerous signs around the campus indicating that visitors must check in with the main office, several ingress points into the school made it difficult to prevent nonschool personnel from entering the school. We recommended, in particular, that the open gate near the restroom in question either be locked (which would not violate fire codes) or be monitored. Likewise, we recommended that the number of access points in the school be reduced to only those that could be monitored or watched by school personnel. We also recommended that a formal plan be instituted by the school to ensure regular checks on restrooms during the school day; no such plan had been formally in place. As part of a larger range plan, we recommended developing greater community ties and giving more attention to community-oriented security approaches. The case never went to trial; it was settled out of court. Our recommendations, however, were accepted and have been implemented.

ANALYSIS OF SOCIAL, ECONOMIC, AND DEMOGRAPHIC CHARACTERISTICS

A thorough analysis of the social, economic, and demographic characteristics of an area are of utmost importance in any crime foreseeability study.[6] Through hundreds of crime prevention studies, criminologists have found correlations between certain types of demographic data and street-type crimes. Census data are very useful for this type of analysis (Voigt, Thornton, Barille, and Seaman 1994).

Census maps allow the researcher to analyze even neighborhood block level data. It is possible to obtain detailed information about a particular area, including average household income, percent of rentals versus home ownership, number of abandoned or substandard houses, number and type of multidwelling units (e.g., apartment complexes), government subsidized houses, ethnic dispersions, and the like. Other data sources that supply regional data can be found in most locales (e.g., neighborhood profile studies, chamber of commerce, and marketing studies). Geomapping software (utilizing digital geographical files and various attribute data) to plot crime data on census maps in relation to specific social demographic variables is also available. Such software allows researchers to engage in innovative types of crime analysis. For example, "hot spots" can be targeted in terms of specific types of interpersonal and property crimes by geographical areas as small as city blocks. It also is possible to plot, depending on available data, offending patterns to determine the "routine activities" of offenders (Felson 1987; McIver 1981; Cohen, Felson, and Land 1980). These data are invaluable in trying to determine the "career patterns" of certain types of offenders within specific geographical locales. This new computer technology is revolutionizing the uses of census and crime data, not only by criminologists but also by urban planners, developers, law enforcement personnel, and courts.

Although each crime site must be analyzed on its own merits, criminologists for a long time have found that several demographic factors are empirically correlated with crime trends. Generally, the interdispersement of residential properties with commercial properties is associated with greater criminal opportunities, leading to the victimization of people and property. For example, residential complexes located on direct routes to bars, convenience stores, fast-food restaurants, and, especially, liquor stores usually suffer from higher rates of interpersonal crime (e.g., rapes and armed robberies) and property crime (e.g., burglaries and auto thefts) than complexes located in exclusively residential areas. Again, as mentioned earlier, the presence of public pathways substantially adds to criminal opportunities. Even the location of public transit stops such as bus stops can have an impact on criminal opportunities at a site (see, e.g., Institute of Transportation Engineers 1985). Also, the presence of public schools in inner city residential neighborhoods often is strongly correlated with property crimes. Neighborhoods that have larger proportions of owner-occupied dwellings usually experience lower crime rates than neighborhoods characterized by rental properties, mixed land use, and public housing (e.g., Section 8 or other types of government subsidized housing). These types of factor-related trends suggest that the practical application of sociological crime theories and empirical research evidence is great. Expert analysis of sociodemographic factors may be easily supported by an extensive body of theory and research (Stark 1987; Shaw and McKay 1969; Chilton 1964; Bordua 1958; Lander 1954).

THE NATURE AND PROFILE OF THE OFFENDER

Generally, little is known about offenders. As most experts who study crime know, the clearance rates for certain types of crimes are extremely low. For example, according to latest UCR data, the national clearance rate for the crime of robbery was 24 percent, and the clearance rate for aggravated rape was 50 percent (regional clearance rates for rape are substantially lower). Crimes such as murder have somewhat higher clearance rates, about 65 percent nationally; however, because more than 50 percent of murder victims are either related to or acquainted with their assailants, this higher figure is not surprising (Uniform Crime Report 1993).

Despite the generally low clearance rates, some offenders are actually arrested and convicted for the crimes that they commit against invited guests and patrons to public or private establishments. Interviewing an apprehended offender can, in some instances, be of use to the crime expert in a civil liability suit. If an offender indicates, for example, that he/she selected a victim at a particular site because it appeared that security was weak, this information can be damaging for the defendant (Brill 1990). Obtaining a profile of the offender (or, at least, a prior offense history — arrests and convictions) may be of use in security negligence cases for several reasons.

Simply counting prior murders at a site such as an apartment complex without examining what David Luckenbill (1980) refers to as the "murder transaction" (the relationship between the offender and the victim) often can result in a "false" count of murder (p. 276). If several stranger-opportunity murders have occurred in an apartment complex with no apparent concern on the part of management to provide minimum security measures, the past number of such offenses becomes extremely important from a crime foreseeability standpoint (Thornton et al. 1991).

On the other hand, domestic or acquaintance-related assaults, rapes, and even homicides may fall outside the parameters of crime foreseeability in third-party liability suits. For example, a disgruntled boyfriend who stalks his girlfriend to a place of business and then assaults her would probably not be in the same crime foreseeability category as a patron who is assaulted by a stranger in the same place of business. Both crimes violate the same criminal codes, and the offenders can be charged and arrested with the same violent crime. From a civil liability standpoint, however, it is not reasonable under most situations to hold the business owner responsible for the domestic assault (recall the impending assault doctrine). He or she, given no warning, could not reasonably foresee that such an offense might occur at the place of business.

Recent research on workplace violence indicates that employers are increasingly legally obligated to protect employees, especially women, who have been *repeatedly* threatened or harassed on the job by ex-spouses or ex-boyfriends (or by other employees). Documented repetitive behavior in the form of threats, stalking, surveillance, and the like can signal to the employer that potential assault or worse is possible at some point in the future (Thornton, Voigt, and Wallace 1994).

Certain types of particularly heinous or dangerous offenders who have severe character disorders or mental illnesses (e.g., antisocial personality, conduct disorders, or psychoses) or who otherwise commit bizarre, one-of-a-kind types of offenses (e.g., rampage or mass murders) present threats to public or private establishments that cannot *reasonably* be predicted or deterred by usual security methods.[7] It would not have been possible, for example, for McDonald's management in San Ysidro, California, to have predicted that James Huberty would murder 21 people at their place of business in 1984. In fact, *Lopez v. McDonald's* (1987) summary judgment was upheld for the defendants on the basis that mass murder is not foreseeable, there was no duty to prevent unforeseeable events on the part of McDonald's, and any breach of duty in failing to employ armed guards was not a proximate cause of injuries and death to customers.

CASE ILLUSTRATION:
FORESEEABILITY OF CRIME BY MENTALLY ILL OFFENDERS

In this case, we were retained by the attorneys for the defendant, who was the manager of a multiple apartment complex for a large elderly population. The granddaughter of an elderly woman, while visiting her, was dragged from the complex parking lot into a back woods bordering the complex. The young woman was raped and murdered. The plaintiffs (the woman's family) alleged that security was inadequate for what they believed to be a relatively high crime area. They believed that the crime should have been foreseen by the management and that measures should have been taken to prevent the crime.

In our crime analysis, we found that the complex, including the surrounding area, was a relatively low crime area. We also uncovered that the management, irrespective of the relatively low crime levels, did evolve a solid security plan. A security guard was hired to patrol both inside the complex and outside in the parking lot. Trees and shrubs in an adjacent lot had been cut down in order to increase visibility. Lighting was installed in the parking lot. A back fence was not there at the time of the offense but was erected immediately after the crime occurred. Whether the back fence could have prevented the crime in question is, of course, debatable.

Upon investigation, we found that the offender in this case had been apprehended. The offender himself was also a guest of one of the tenants of the apartment complex. It was further uncovered that the offender had an extensive history of a mental disorder (antisocial personality disorder) of which violent outbursts were symptomatic. He had been charged with murder (of a young mother), attempted murder (of a 3- and a 6-year-old), and two prior rapes, for which he was unable to stand trial and was judged mentally incompetent and committed to a state mental hospital, where he stayed for ten years. He also attempted to kill one of the orderlies in the hospital where he was committed. The man was released by a psychiatrist and judged to be not dangerous just one week prior to the rape-murder incident.

The victimization of the young woman was certainly tragic. Given the circumstances of the case, however, the crime could not have been foreseen or reasonably prevented by the management of the apartment complex. The case was settled and never went to trial.

THE NATURE AND PROFILE OF THE VICTIM

Criminologists only recently have developed an interest in the victims of crime. Typologies of victims normally have one or two fundamental bases or variables, specifically the relative responsibility of the victim for the crime (i.e., to what degree is the victim culpable for the actions of the offender) and the relative vulnerability of the victim to crime (i.e., what social conditions or environments lead to more or less risk of crime for the person). Using these two variables (responsibility and risk), criminologists attempt to explain the dynamic and varied relationship between the criminal and the victim (Voigt et al. 1994:101–103).

Complete innocence is the most commonly accepted category of victimization. It includes people who did nothing that conceivably could have elicited criminal action. They have no culpability for the crime. Unintentional facilitation is unwittingly, carelessly, or negligently making it easier for a crime to occur, such as leaving car keys in the ignition of a car or leaving a door to an apartment unlocked. If carelessness increases the likelihood of crime and there is a reasonable presumption that the crime could have been prevented, does the victim bear some small social, if not legal, responsibility for the crime? Some say yes; considering that nearly 50 percent of burglaries take place without any forcible entry, the victims, if even unintentionally, establish themselves as easy marks.

Victim precipitation, on the other hand, occurs when a person willfully initiates the encounter with the eventual offender, directly enticing, challenging, insulting, provoking, or even initially assaulting the person. Victim precipitation is most common in homicides and aggravated assaults. It is estimated, for example, that about 20 percent of homicides involve prior provocation from the victim (Wolfgang 1958; Bordounis 1974).

CASE ILLUSTRATION:
DOES THE USE OF MACE CONSTITUTE VICTIM PRECIPITATION?
The attorneys for the plaintiff retained us as consultants for this case. The case involved a multiple list of defendants, including a hotel, a city park, a private security company, and a travel magazine, to name just a few.

A woman accompanied her husband on a business conference trip. While the husband attended the conference, the woman used the time for sight-seeing. She noted a travel magazine advertisement for a well-known park in the area. After checking with the hotel concierge regarding the relative safety and general directions to the park, she hailed a taxi cab and by 10:30 A.M. was dropped off at the park, where she planned to take pictures. She had received no warning from anyone in the hotel — nothing regarding the relative safety of the park was cited in any of the magazines or brochures advertising the park.

This particular city park was regarded as a very high crime rate area. The park borders on a public housing development that also experiences among the highest crime rates in the city. The park was patrolled by only two security officers, who worked for a private security company that was contracted by the city to secure the park. Evidence suggested that the two guards were asleep in an adjacent building at the time of the incident.

While the woman was exploring the park, a youth attempted to rob her using a gun. When she reached into her purse to hand over her wallet, she pulled out a Mace ejector and sprayed the assailant in the face. Startled by the Mace, the youth pulled the trigger and shot the woman in the head, killing her. He fled into the adjoining housing development, screaming that he did not mean to do it and why did the woman spray him! He hid until he finally was convinced by family members to give himself up.

The attorneys for one of the defendants alleged that, had the woman not used the Mace, she might have been alive. This argument, however, was not successful. The case was very complex and long. The litigants in the case settled with the victim's family for an undisclosed amount of money.

The case included a wide range of experts and was mainly argued using the totality of circumstances approach. More specific data on crimes perpe-trated against out-of-town tourists were utilized in the case. The consultants were asked to conduct literature reviews and original research studies on the correlation between the use of Mace and homicide. No conclusive evidence was obtained. No scientific research had been done on this topic. According to the "common wisdom" of police officers (based on interviews at select police departments in major cities), Mace seems to offer a false sense of defense or safety and may, indeed, be more of a hazard than a help. Its use could not be considered, by any stretch of the imagination, as an act of victim precipitation. This information was useful in deflating the arguments of the opposing sides.

A SOCIOLOGICAL IMAGINATION:
SOME CONCLUDING REMARKS

Premise liability often is difficult to evaluate. It always involves an act or event, its relationship to a particular space, and the degree to which the owner or manager of the space and the victim are, in part, responsible for the unfortunate occurrence. The ironic and debunking nature of sociological thought is aptly suited to this type of case.

A sociologist and criminologist imagines a world where a single act or event is embedded in a complex array of spatial, temporal, historical, and interpersonal contingencies and conditions. It is a world where causality and liability are not readily discernable but might reveal themselves through informed speculation, a willingness to dig for seemingly unrelated patterns and occurrences, and a little luck. Black and white, good and bad, and other binary styles of reasoning rarely work in this world. It is, more often than not, a gray world where no one is simply liable or innocent, but shades of both. It is, in short, a sociological world.

We close on a practical note. It frequently is observed that expert witnesses use the good ideas of other sociologists and criminologists found in papers, books, and journal articles to develop and argue their opinions. It has been our experience, however, that expert witnesses often are able to contribute to their disciplines.

Criminologists, who work as experts, often have access to potential research data that otherwise would be impossible to obtain. The results of research conducted in connection with developing a case (e.g., analysis of police reports, supplemental surveys, content analysis of documents, evaluations, outcome assessments) offer a rich source of theoretically and methodologically significant information. The work of many "experts" has not enjoyed the status of legitimacy accorded traditional academic research and, therefore, largely has been ignored on the assumption that applied research does not represent a high level of commitment to "theory and methods." Given the increased pressure placed by courts (especially since the U.S. Supreme Court decision *Daubert v. Merrell Dow Pharmaceuticals, Inc.* [1993]) for experts to scientifically justify their positions, we feel this charge is unfounded. We suspect that the collected works of practicing criminologists is both extensive and significant in terms of its contribution to the field of criminology, and it is not easily separated from more traditional "pure" research activities.

NOTES

1.   We both have a doctorate in sociology with a concentration in criminology and research methods.

2.   In Las Vegas, 70 percent of all premise liability cases are casino related.

3.   The case *Isaacs v. Huntington Memorial Hospital* (1985) serves as the fountainhead of the totality of circumstances rule of crime foreseeability. The plaintiff, a doctor, was shot in the physician's parking lot at a major hospital in what was considered a "high" crime area. At the nearby emergency room parking lot, large numbers of interpersonal crimes had occurred, and security guards patrolled the parking area. The emergency room was open around the clock and attracted a parade of drunks, drug addicts, and assorted criminal types. Isaacs was shot by an assailant

near his car in the physician's parking lot. The court rejected any type of prior similar crimes argument because it would, in their opinion, discourage landowners from improving their security until the first victim had been attacked (Tom on Torts 1993:357).

4. Local police data are not to be confused with data from uniform crime reports (UCR). Although local police data provide the basis for the UCR, it is more comprehensive and more detailed, offering specific information such as the exact time, and the district and address of the occurrence. In addition, a wider range of crimes are recorded, not just index crimes. Definitions or codes associated with crimes are based on local and state codes, not the general or standard codes used by the UCR.

5. In our report, we put a lot of emphasis on the prevention of domestic violence. Morally, we feel this is an important area of crime that must be addressed. We feel it is important to include even in evaluations that target nondomestic crimes. It is important to keep in mind that domestic violence impacts the general perceptions of dangerousness held by residents of housing developments and by the public at large, who often cannot distinguish between stranger- or domestic-related crimes. The prevention of domestic violence can have significant effects on overall perceptions of crime and safety.

6. The importance of the demographics of a community or neighborhood cannot be underestimated from a security standpoint. We have conducted social-demographic and crime analyses of areas for developers during their planning stages. If it is found that there are a large number of urban crime risk factors at a proposed location for a business, either stricter security measures must be incorporated into the plan or the business may be relocated in a safer environment.

7. We are not saying that there is a relationship between mental illness or disorder and criminality per se. We realize, of course, that the two concepts are largely unrelated (e.g., Monahan and Steadman 1984). There is, however, evidence to suggest a relationship between certain types of mental disorder (e.g., sociopathy or psychopathy, child conduct disorder DSM-III-R, Axis II, Cluster B, 301.70) and predisposition to violence. Such individuals have a higher base rate of violence than "normals" (e.g., Hare 1983; Hall 1987) and are overrepresented in the commission of much violent interpersonal crime including sadistic rapes, murders (particularly serial murders or murder rampages) and other unpredictable, impulsive crimes (Robins 1966; Lewis 1989; Holmes and DeBurger 1988; Voigt et al. 1994). Thus, although mental illness and crime are largely unrelated, what makes matters difficult is that they are not completely unrelated.

REFERENCES

Bates, N. D., & Dunnell, S. J. 1993. *Major Developments in Premises Security Liability*. Framingham, MA: Liability Consultants.

Bordua, D. 1958. Juvenile Delinquency and "Anomie": An Attempt at Replication. *Social Problems, 6*, 230–238.

Bordounis, J. 1974. A Class Reaction to Homicide. *Criminology, 11*, 525–540.

Brill, W. H. 1990, November 2. Criminal Profiling in Premises Liability Rape Cases. *Trial Diplomacy, 13*, 1–5.

Brill, W. H. 1973. *Security in Public Housing: Deterrence of Crime In and Around Residences*. Washington, DC: Department of Housing and Urban Development.

Brill, W. H. 1972. Innovation in the Design and Management of Public Housing: A Case Study of Applied Research. Paper presented at the Environmental Design Research Conference, University of California, Santa Monica, CA.

Brill, W. H., & Associates, 1978. *Phipps Plaza South Safety and Security Analysis and Recommendations*. Annapolis, MD: Department of Housing and Urban Development.

Brill, W. H., & Associates. 1975. *Housing Management Technical Memorandum #1, Safety and Security*. Washington, DC: Department of Housing and Urban Development.

Brill, W. H., & Associates. 1974. *A Crisis Intervention Program for Scott/Carver Homes*. Washington, DC: Department of Housing and Urban Development.

Chilton, R. 1964. Continuities in Delinquency Area Research: A Comparison of Studies for Baltimore, Detroit, and Indianapolis. *American Sociological Review*, *29*, 71–83.

Cohen, L. E., & Felson, M. 1979. Social Change and Crime Rate Trends: A Routine Activity Approach. *American Sociological Review*, *44*, 588–608.

Cohen, L. E., Felson, M., & Land, K. 1980. Property Crime Rates in the United States: A Macrodynamic Analysis 1947–77 with Exant Forecasts for the Mid-1980s. *American Journal of Sociology*, *86*, 90–118.

Criminal Victimization Survey in New Orleans. 1977. Washington, DC: U.S. Department of Justice.

Crowe, T. 1991. *Crime Prevention Through Environmental Design*. Boston, MA: Butterworth-Heinemann.

Felson, M. 1987. Routine Activities and Crime Prevention in the Developing Metropolis. *Criminology*, *25*(4):911–932.

Hare, R. D. 1983. Diagnosis of Anti-Social Personality Disorder in Two Prison Populations. *American Journal of Psychiatry*, *140*(7), 887–890.

Harries, K. 1974. *The Geography of Crime and Justice*. New York: McGraw Hill.

Holl, J. P., & Newton, C.E. 1992, August. Landowners Responsibility for Violent Acts of Others. *Trial*, pp. 36–43.

Holmes, R., & DeBurger, J. 1988. *Serial Murders*. Beverly Hills, CA: Sage.

Hunter, R. D., & Jeffery, C.R. 1992. Preventing Convenience Store Robbery Through Environmental Design. In R. V. Clarke (Ed.), *Situational Crime Prevention* (pp. 194–204). New York: Harrow and Heston.

Institute of Transportation Engineers. 1985. Proper Location of Bus Stops. Publication RP-003. (available from 525 School Street, S.W., Suite 410, Washington, DC).

Kaplan, H., O'Kane, K., Lavrakas, P., & Pesce, E. 1978. *Crime Prevention Through Environmental Design*. Portland, OR: Westinghouse Electric Co.

Lander, B. 1954. *Towards an Understanding of Juvenile Delinquency*. New York: Columbia University Press.

Lewis, D. D. 1989. Adult Antisocial Behavior and Criminality. In H. I Kaplan and B. Sadock (Eds.), *Comprehensive Textbook of Psychiatry*, vol. 2 (pp. 1400–1405). Baltimore, MD: Williams and Wilkins.

Luckenbill, D. F. 1980. Criminal Homicide as a Situated Transaction. In D. H. Kelly (Ed.), *Criminal Behavior* (pp. 275–290). New York: St. Martins Press.

McGoey, C. F. 1990. *Security — Adequate or Not: The Complete Guide to Premise Liability Litigation*. Oakland, CA: Aegis Books.

McIver, J. 1981. Criminal Mobility: A Review of Empirical Studies. In S. Hakim and G. Rengert (Eds.), *Crime Spillover* (pp. 20–47). Beverly Hills, CA: Sage.

Monahan, J., & Steadman, H. J. 1984. *Crisis and Mental Disorder* (pp. 1–5). Washington, DC: U.S. Department of Justice.

National Association of Convenience Stores. 1987. *Robbery Deterrence Manual*. Alexandria, VA: National Association of Convenience Stores.

Neighborhood Profiles Series. 1980. New Orleans, LA: Office of Analysis and Planning.

Newman, O. 1973. *Architectural Design for Crime Prevention*. New York: New York University, Institute of Planning and Housing.

Rapp, J., Carrington, F., & Nicholson, G. 1992. *School Crime and Violence: Victims' Rights*. Malibu, CA: National School Safety Center.

Robins, L. N. 1966. *Deviant Children Grown Up: A Sociological Psychiatric Study of Sociopathic Personality*. Baltimore, MD: Williams and Wilkins.

Robinson, M. 1985. Case Studies of Effective Management Practices Within Public Housing Agencies. Washington, DC: Department of Housing and Urban Development.

Rubenstein, H., Murray, C., Motoyama, T., & Rouse, W. 1980. The Link Between Crime and The Built Environment. Washington, DC: U.S. Department of Justice.

School Safety Check Book. 1990. Malibu, CA: Pepperdine University, National School Safety Center.

Security Law Newsletter, 10(4), April 1990, p. 47.

Shaw, C. R., & Mckay, H. 1969. *Juvenile Delinquency in Urban Areas*. Chicago, IL: University of Chicago Press.

Stark, R. 1987. A Theory of the Ecology of Crime. *Criminology, 25*(4), 893–910.

Thornton, W., & McKinnon, E. 1992. *Security Needs Assessment and Crime Analysis: New Orleans Housing Developments*. Final report for the New Orleans Housing Authority of New Orleans and C.J. Brown Property Management Company. New Orleans, LA: Housing Authority of New Orleans.

Thornton, W., McKinnon-Fowler, E., & Kent, D. 1991, April. Stalking Security Statistics. *Security Management, 35*(4), 54–58.

Thornton, W., & Voigt, L. 1992. *Delinquency and Justice*, 3rd ed. New York: McGraw Hill.

Thornton, W., & Voigt, L. 1984–86. *Non-Probability Survey and Case Studies of Children Raised in Public Housing Developments*. Unpublished paper. Loyola University, New Orleans, Louisiana.

Thornton, W., Voigt, L., & Wallace, S. 1994. Lethal Workplace in the U.S. Postal Service. Paper read at a meeting of the Academy of Criminal Justice Sciences, Chicago, IL.

Tom on Torts. 1993, December. *American Trial Lawyer Association Reporter, 36*(16), 356–360.

Uniform Crime Reports for the United States, 1992. 1993. Washington, DC: U.S. Department of Justice, Federal Bureau of Investigation.

Voigt, L., Thornton, W., Barille, L., & Seaman, J. 1994. *Criminology and Justice*. New York: McGraw Hill.

Weapons Against Crime. 1994, April. National Association of Convenience Stores, *13*(4), 8–10.

Wolfgang, M. E. 1958. *Patterns of Criminal Homicide*. New York: Wiley.

Wright, W. R. 1994, February. America's Litigation Explosion and the Liability of Owners and Operators of Off-Street Parking Facilities. *Parking: The Magazine of the Parking Industry*, pp. 39–42.

CASES CITED

Daubert v. Merrell Dow Pharmaceuticals, Inc., U.S. S. Ct., No. 92-102, 1993 WL 224478 (1993).

Gannilli v. Howard Johnson's Motor Lodge, Inc., 419 F. Supp. 1210, 1212 (E.D.N.Y. 1976).

Isaacs v. Huntington Memorial Hospital, 38 Cal. 3d 112, 211 Cal. Rptr. 356, 695 P.2d 653 (1985).

Lopez v. McDonald's, 193 Cal., App. 3d 495, 23, Cal. Rept. 436 (1987).
Siebert v. Vic Regnier Builders, Inc., 856 P.2d 1332 (Kansas 1993).

11

Obscenity and Child Pornography: Sociology in Defense of Sexually Oriented Materials

Philip Holley

One of the places where sociology is often uninvited, if not unwelcome, is the courtroom. Yet, when the sociologist is asked to contribute to cases involving obscenity and child pornography, such contributions can be and often are quite significant. This chapter addresses the role of the sociologist as expert in criminal cases involving allegations of obscenity and child pornography. Referenced in this chapter are five such cases in which I have participated. Four were obscenity cases; the other was a child pornography case.

OBSCENITY AS A MORAL CRUSADE

The prosecution of obscenity is associated with various moral or "sex" panics (Heins 1993; Zurcher and Kirkpatrick 1976). For example, certain highly publicized contemporary efforts to prosecute both creators and retailers of rap music that emphasizes sex and violence can be understood in this context (Heins 1993). Prosecution of sexually oriented written and visual materials operates similarly, well-illustrated by the views of Phyllis Schlafly. She worries about minds and spirits being polluted by "pictures of violence and perversions" and the need to protect children and families from the "$8 billion-a-year pornography industry" (1987:11). The 1986 report of the Attorney General's Commission on Pornography, although fundamentally lacking in scientific objectivity, included recommendations pertaining to citizen action against pornography (Nobile and Nadler 1986). Social activists of all political persuasions, along with zealous police and prosecutors, represent the backbone of efforts to rid society of pornography (Heins 1993).

Two types of enforcement efforts directed at sexually oriented materials typify the actions of police and prosecutors. First, they have sent letters threatening retailers with arrest unless they removed specified materials from their establishments (Heins 1993; Zurcher and Kirkpatrick 1976). Such threats are generally considered improper rather than categorically illegal, although retailers, lacking sufficient resources for an adequate defense, frequently comply with the demands. A second strategy is to arrest and prosecute employees or owners of retail establishments or museum directors for commercial distribution or display of obscene materials or child pornography. Those who produce and possess such materials are also arrested and prosecuted (Heins 1993). It is with these types of actions that a moral panic can mobilize into a moral crusade (Ben-Yehuda 1985).

Sociologists who represent defendants in pornography and obscenity cases must tack between the law and community standards. Does this material violate the public's ideas of decency and morality, or does it fall within a range of accepted content? Sociologists, I would suggest, are particularly well-suited to determine the relationship of sexually oriented materials to community norms of sensual propriety.

SUMMARY OF CASES

Between 1985 and 1990, I worked with attorneys in four different law firms on five criminal cases involving allegations of obscenity and child pornography in Oklahoma. I testified at a pre-trial hearing challenging the constitutionality of federal statutes (*Sexual Exploitation of Children* 1989) prohibiting the visual depiction of material commonly referred to as child pornography. In this case, nude photographs of two young girls were alleged to have been taken by the defendant. My participation was part of a defense strategy to convince the court that the statute was overbroad and vague and, therefore, unconstitutional.

The other four cases involved charges of obscenity. In three of the cases, managers or employees of retail establishments were charged under Oklahoma statutes with the distribution of obscene materials, specifically videotapes and magazines (*Obscenity, Oklahoma Statutes*, 1991). The final case involved a citizen defendant charged with possession of obscene magazines.

In two of the four cases, I conducted surveys in two different communities, reporting the results in two criminal trials. Although I was prepared to testify in two other cases, using the results of one of the surveys, plea agreements were reached prior to the trials. In one case, an agreement was reached minutes before the trial was scheduled to begin.

My participation addressed the fundamental issue of whether the videotapes or magazines in question violated community standards regarding erotic or pornographic materials. The legal justification for this approach is the *Miller* test (*Miller v. California* 1973), a law that says if a community's standards can be identified and the materials in question do not violate these standards, the defendant cannot be found guilty.

OBSCENITY, THE *MILLER* TEST, AND CHILD PORNOGRAPHY

Oklahoma statutes criminalize the creation, sale, purchase, distribution, exhibition, and possession of "any obscene or indecent writing, paper, book, picture, photograph, motion picture, figure or form of any description" (*Obscenity, Oklahoma Statutes* 1991). The Oklahoma statute defines obscene material as "depictions or descriptions of sexual conduct which are patently offensive, and . . . taken as a whole has the dominant theme an appeal to the prurient interest, as found by the average person applying contemporary community standards, and . . . taken as a whole lacks serious literary, artistic, educational, political or scientific purpose or value" (*Obscenity, Oklahoma Statutes* 1991).

State statutes such as the one in Oklahoma are modeled after the three part test set out in *Miller v. California* (1973). Because *Miller* is the prevailing Supreme Court decision relating to obscenity, states make only minor changes in its wording (Copp and Wendell 1983). The test set out in *Miller* requires that all three elements be met in order to find a work to be obscene.

Miller was decided as a response to problems with *Roth v. United States* (1957). *Roth* is the first significant U.S. Supreme Court ruling fundamentally challenging English case law dating from 1868 (Copp and Wendell 1983). There were five key parts to *Roth's* determination of obscenity (Feinberg 1983:118):

1. The work is judged on the "dominant theme" in the entirety of the work.
2. The effect of the work on the "average person" must be examined.
3. "Contemporary community standards" must be applied.
4. The work must be "utterly without redeeming social importance."
5. The work must "appeal to the prurient interest."

According to Heins, the requirement that the work be "utterly without redeeming social value" or importance made it possible to more easily defend suspect sexually oriented materials, along with bringing about numerous obscenity conviction reversals (1993:21). In spite of hopes that *Roth* would settle the questions pertaining to the nature of materials not protected by the First Amendment, the case resolved none of the questions. *Miller* should be viewed in this historical context.

Feinberg asserts that the intent of *Miller* was to "permit more aggressive prosecution of pornographers" (1983:130). Additionally, and consistent with a moral crusade, Heins states that "instead of doing away with obscenity laws, the Supreme Court made criminal convictions *easier* to obtain by loosening the three-part obscenity test" (1993:22). Obscenity cases were more readily prosecuted under *Miller*, although they account for a very small percentage of criminal cases (Maguire and Pastore 1994:528; Maguire, Pastore, and Flanagan 1993:520).

According to Heins (1993), two fundamental changes took place in *Miller*. First, instead of proving that a work of art or literature was "utterly without redeeming social value," prosecutors now had to prove only that the material "lacked serious literary, artistic, political or scientific value" (Heins 1993:22). Second, under *Roth*, the community standards that were applied were national standards; under *Miller*, state or local standards prevail (Heins 1993).

In summary, it is important to note that the *Miller* decision retained the "obscenity exception to the First Amendment" earlier set down by *Roth* (Heins 1993:20). Despite Heins's accusations of elitism in the utilization of expert witnesses in obscenity cases, however, the emphasis on local or state standards made it possible, if not essential, for sociologists to be called as experts for the defense. To the extent that sociologists have or can access empirical data regarding community standards and attitudes toward sexually oriented materials, sociologists are particularly suited to contribute to obscenity cases.

CHILD PORNOGRAPHY

Child pornography represents a specific class of sexually oriented materials unprotected by the First Amendment and regulated by federal statutes entitled, *Sexual Exploitation of Children* (1989). *New York v. Ferber* (1982) removed child pornography from the *Miller* test. The statute criminalizes the production, transportation, receipt, and distribution of visual depictions of "a minor engaging in sexually explicit conduct" (*Sexual Exploitation of Children* 1989). Sexually explicit conduct is defined as "actual or simulated sexual intercourse, bestiality, masturbation, sadistic or masochistic abuse, or lascivious exhibition of the genitals or pubic area" (*Sexual Exploitation of Children* 1989).

Although there is no *Miller* test, and, therefore, no consideration of community standards, sociologists and other scientists may participate in constitutional challenges to the statute as overbroad and vague or aid in the defense of artists accused of "lascivious exhibition of the genitals or pubic area" of minors. Recognizing the situated and unique character of this accusation, for example, that not all photographs of nude children are obscene, *Ferber* settles for "a case-by-case analysis of the fact situations" where overbreadth may be an issue (pp. 773, 774). Justice O'Connor, in her concurring opinion, identified examples of possible overbreadth as the statute might be applied to "medical textbooks" and "issues of National Geographic" (*New York v. Ferber* 1982).

Schauer's (1983) analysis of *Ferber* indicates that not all potential questions were addressed by the decision. Furthermore, it is dangerous to underestimate the potential range and types of cases for future prosecution. Certainly the Mapplethorpe photo exhibition in Cincinnati in 1990 illustrates such cases, as does the 1990 ultimately unsuccessful prosecution of the photographic work of Sturges (Heins 1993). O'Brien (1983) cited three cases, probably dating prior to *Ferber*, in which prosecutors unsuccessfully targeted certain sex education materials, or what some would assert to be sex education materials.

SOCIOLOGICAL EXPERTISE AND SEXUALLY ORIENTED MATERIALS

One part of *Miller* requires the comparison of the "suspect" materials to what is accepted or tolerated within contemporary community standards. One may conclude that the jury, representing the community, does not need the results of a community survey. Rather, they would be free to collectively and individually use any and all information they possess. However, jurors specifically must not use their own values and beliefs in the determination of obscenity. Jury instructions used in one Oklahoma case included this admonition: "You must disregard any previous notions you have had and apply the legal definition of obscenity" (*The State of Oklahoma v. [Defendant]* 1989, No. 9). The same instructions also state: "You are further instructed that your personal feeling about these magazine(s) is not a proper basis for determining whether or not these magazine(s) appeal to the prurient interest unless you find your opinion is the same as that of the average person in the statewide community" (No. 7).

Miller calls for the construction of an average person, a composite, and a reasonable person. The jury is instructed to make its determination using this composite person, rather than on the basis of each juror's individual tastes. Scott, Eitle, and Skovron (1990) and Scott (1991) take the position that, to fully and ultimately meet the *Miller* test, it is essential that a survey of community standards be conducted. The inclusion of community standard studies is advocated to achieve fairness in the judicial process and to require that the prosecution "prove" the allegations. Various cases strongly state that the burden of proof is on the state (e.g., *Saliba v. State* 1985) while, at the same time, asserting that the "suspect" material itself represent sufficient evidence for the court's determination of obscenity (*Commonwealth v. Trainor* 1978). However, according to *United States v. Various Articles of Merchandise* (1984), the government's failure to provide evidence of community standards enhances the possibility of appeal.

In effect, the prosecution is required to construct no more than what a layperson would describe as a simplistic case. The state's case consists of the following elements: the display of the alleged obscene materials to the jury, which is done by showing the videotapes or magazines to the court, the allegation that the defendant was aware of the general nature of the material (rather than a requirement that the defendant knew the materials were obscene) (see *Commonwealth v. Trainor* 1978), and testimony from police officers or other witnesses identifying the defendant as the distributor or possessor of the materials. It is difficult to imagine a prosecutor soliciting a survey of community attitudes, even in those situations in which it is publicly known that the defense is conducting its own survey. First, as noted above, the law does not require it. Second, limited resources may not permit it. Third, and perhaps most importantly, survey results often support the defendant's, not the prosecution's, case. The average public, it appears, expresses more tolerance or acceptance of sexually oriented materials than the courts and various moral entrepreneurs (Wallace 1973; Glassman 1978; Diamond and Dannemiller 1989; Winick and Evans 1994). Thus, the interests of the prosecution are served by efforts to prohibit use of surveys in court. This is not to assert, of course, that any and all sexually oriented materials are tolerated or accepted. There are limits to the public's tolerance (Scott, Eitle, and Skovron 1990; Scott 1991), as well as some variations in tolerance based upon community size (Glassman 1978). However, even studies conducted in more local, traditional, rural areas fail to support the repression of sexually oriented materials (Rudolf and Fargo 1988). One can reasonably expect in most instances that the composite public will express toleration of sexually explicit materials sold or rented in their community for private adult use (Winick and Evans 1994).

It is likely, therefore, that the sociologist will be retained by the defendant, not the state. According to a somewhat optimistic (if not idealistic) article that appeared in the *Rutgers Law Review*, "Survey evidence is probably the best such evidence [concerning community tolerance of sexually oriented materials] that a defendant may produce. Such empirical data will tend to reduce the otherwise inevitable battle of the experts" (Miller 1988:485, 486). The results of social surveys are admitted into evidence as exceptions to the hearsay rule under the *Federal Rules of Evidence* (Graham 1986) (see *Pittsburgh Press Club v. United States* 1978; *Commonwealth v. Trainor* 1978). Their utilization in obscenity cases, however, occurs less frequently than common sense might anticipate (Miller 1988). Sociological surveys, it would appear, are difficult for a court to incorporate into its deliberations.

A defense attorney who seeks to qualify a sociologist as an expert witness who intends to testify on the results of a survey is likely to be challenged by a prosecutor, not on the admissibility of the survey, but on its weight or significance for the case. It is not inevitable, however, that any survey is admissible in court (see *Commonwealth v. Trainor* 1978). *Saliba v. State* (1985) identifies the criteria for a proper survey (or poll): "The poll was conducted by an expert in the field of surveying;

the relevant universe was examined; a representative sample was drawn from the relevant universe; the mode of questioning was 'correct' (mail, telephone, personal interview, etc.); the sample, questionnaire, and the interviews were designed in accordance with generally accepted standards; the data gathered was accurately reported; and the data was analyzed in a statistically correct manner."

Saliba (1985:1188) comments: "The adherence to this generally accepted methodology renders the poll's results admissible in the form of expert opinion." Once admitted, any challenges by the prosecution pertain to the weight to be given to the survey results already accepted as evidence.

Three additional points of law should be noted. First, *Carlock v. State* (1980) recognizes the right of the defense to present the best evidence of community standards that can be produced. Thus, surveys that are conducted months after the alleged offense usually are admissible.

Second, as indicated in *Saliba* (1985), if the relevant universe is surveyed and the other conditions are met, the results are admissible. In some courts, the relevant universe for the determination of community standards is the state, while in others it is a county or a metropolitan area or the area of court jurisdiction (Scott, Eitle, and Skovron 1990). For example, the relevant universe in *Saliba* was the county in which the alleged offense took place, while *People v. Nelson* (1980) utilized the entire state for the determination of community standards. Importantly, national "polls" are not considered helpful in determining "local" standards (see *United States v. Various Articles of Merchandise* 1984).

Third, the sociologist need not construct a survey that questions subjects specifically about the "suspect" material. Questions constructed that indicate degree of acceptance of sexually explicit material are ordinarily admissible (*People v. Nelson* 1980), although not all courts agree (see *Flynt v. State* 1980). *Saliba* stated that the results of questions about what is and is not acceptable in the community are helpful to the court in determining community standards and are, therefore, admissible. Likewise, the results of questions inquiring about community acceptance of materials depicting specific sexual activities found in the suspect materials also are admissible. A sociologist retained by the defense whose research design included showing the suspect materials to subjects and subsequently measuring their reactions would perhaps be considered ideal but is certainly not required by the court for admissibility.

SOCIOLOGY AND OBSCENE MATERIALS

I have conducted community surveys for the defense in two cases involving the distribution of alleged obscene materials under Oklahoma law. In 1985, a husband and wife were arrested for renting approximately 30 sexually oriented or X-rated videotapes (located under the counter) from a video rental store that they managed in a small university community. The specific charges alleged seven rental videotapes to be obscene under Oklahoma statutes. Their attorney contacted me with a request that I conduct a community standards survey to be presented at their trial.

I initiated a telephone survey of adult respondents systematically sampled from the local community telephone book (see Lavrakas 1987). A female university student was employed and trained to conduct the telephone interviews.

In the brief interview, two questions relating to community standards — with responses to be "yes" or "no" — were asked. They were: Would you say that people have a right to do certain things in private but not in public? Do you think adults have a right to watch films including sexually explicit acts in the privacy of their homes? The results were presented in frequency distributions and percentages.

In the end, the defendants decided to plead guilty. I testified at their sentencing hearing as to the results of the survey. I was readily accepted as an expert, and my survey was admitted into evidence, although it should be stated that testimony at sentencing is less stringently regulated than at trial. The defendants were sentenced to a small fine, with no jail or prison time.

In 1989, a male employee of an adult bookstore in a large metropolitan area in Oklahoma was arrested for renting two videotapes alleged to be obscene. His attorney retained me to conduct a survey of community standards and to testify at the trial.

In this case, the attorney and I determined that the population representing the local community would be the metropolitan area. Thus, we systematically sampled adult respondents from the telephone book for the metropolitan area. A former female student was employed and trained to do the interviewing. After collecting information from the respondents on length of residence in Oklahoma, age, ethnicity, and sex, five questions were asked that were used to indicate community standards. All questions were approved by the attorney in advance of the interviews. Would you say it is okay for adults to do certain things in private but not in public? Would you say that it is okay for adults to view movies, videocassettes, and magazines in private that show sexually explicit acts? Would you say that it is okay for your neighbor to view sexually explicit movies, videocassettes, and magazines in private, even if you would not want to view them yourself? Would you say it is okay for your neighbor to buy or rent sexually explicit movies, videocassettes, and magazines for viewing in private, even if you would not want to yourself? Do you understand that sexually explicit means exposure to the naked body, male and female genitals, erect penises, physical contact between males and females, including intercourse, oral sex, homosexual and lesbian activities, and masturbation? The questions were to be answered with a "yes" or "no." Seeking to provide the data in simple, easy to grasp terms, we reported using frequencies and percentages.

I was accepted by the court as an expert witness following the presentation of my credentials, with no objection from the prosecution. The court admitted the survey results as evidence. During cross-examination, the prosecutor initially attempted to challenge the research methodology and sampling. Unsuccessful, he resorted to asking such (in my opinion) marginal questions as whether or not "hearing impaired" or "deaf" persons were included in the interviews.

After reporting the findings of the survey, I was questioned by the defense attorney as to whether the two videotapes — one graphically depicting male masturbation, the other of the soft-core variety, portraying heterosexual as well as some lesbian activity — have "educational" or scientific value. (The Oklahoma statutes add "educational" value to the list in *Miller*.) I testified to the educational value of the materials for individuals as well as couples interested in learning opposite-sex behavior as well as variety in sexual acts. The jury deadlocked, with the judge declaring a mistrial. Subsequently, a plea arrangement was reached, with the defendant paying a fine.

In 1985, a man residing in a small town in Oklahoma was charged under federal statutes relating to child pornography. The case involved nude photographs of two young girls — one age 9 and the other age 11 — allegedly taken by the defendant and submitted to a retail establishment and shipped out of state for processing. Neither masturbation nor any other sexual activity was depicted in the 24 photographs. Some, but not all, of the photographs showed the girls nude, with their genitals exposed. I testified in a hearing challenging the constitutionality of the statute as vague and overbroad. Accepted by the court as an expert, my testimony included opinions related to the vagueness of the portion of the law referring to the "lascivious exhibition of the genitals" as well as legitimate depictions of sexually explicit conduct of minors for purposes of sex education. The federal district court ruled that the statute was neither vague nor overbroad and, therefore, was constitutional. The defendant was later tried by a jury, found guilty, and sentenced to prison.

INDIRECT SOCIOLOGICAL CONTRIBUTIONS

The impact of the sociologist carrying out community standards surveys may go well beyond the case at hand. Although a particular defendant does not achieve exoneration, illustrated by the case with the plea bargain following the deadlocked jury, the survey conducted for this case influenced at least two other cases. Coincident with this case, the same attorney was in the process of representing another defendant arrested for the possession of two allegedly obscene magazines. Although I was prepared to testify in this case, the prosecution dropped the charges. The attorney was able to use the survey results in negotiations on what was undoubtedly a weaker case (i.e., the magazines in question were soft-core).

Additionally, the evidence resulting from the survey was made available to another attorney representing a female employee of a convenience store located in the same metropolitan area arrested for the sale of a soft-core magazine alleged to be obscene. Negotiations between the state and the defense continued to the morning of the 1990 trial, where I was present and prepared to testify, when the defense attorney persuaded the client to plead guilty, requiring only the payment of a small fine.

Two consequences seem likely from the utilization of community standards surveys by defense attorneys. First, prosecutors appear less likely to pursue cases involving materials that are best described as soft-core. Considerable resources would be required for an uncertain return on the investment. For example, because *Playboy* has successfully fought obscenity charges in the past, it is unlikely that any prosecutor would allege it to be obscene, unless its contents radically changed. Exceptions may include situations where citizen activists or moral crusaders demand prosecution of the materials. Threats of prosecution may follow, however (Heins 1993). Second, the prosecutor cannot expect a jury to automatically convict the defendant, even when the materials in question are hard-core, if an obscenity standards survey documents the statistical acceptance of the materials by the local or regional community.

ADVOCACY, RESISTANCE, AND NORMALIZING: THREE CONSEQUENCES OF JOINING SOCIOLOGY AND OBSCENITY

The benefits of agreeing to serve as an expert witness are several: the opportunity to conduct sociological research and to apply one's expertise and research findings to the law, to "teach" sociology to those in the courtroom, including jurors, and to work in collaboration with attorneys, experts from other disciplines, and, at times, defendants themselves. However, I perhaps derive my greatest satisfaction in knowing that, when I demonstrate that allegedly obscene materials fall within the moral boundary of a local community, I am resisting the power of the state to decide what is appropriate reading and viewing materials while also challenging the antipornography crusaders who are dedicated to imposing their restricted standards on the general community. In remarks to follow, I discuss the advocacy, resistance, and normalizing consequences of a sociologist who serves as an expert witness in obscenity cases.

Advocacy for the Defendant

Sociologists educated in the rarefied world of the research university are not accustomed to thinking of themselves as advocates for this or that embattled group. Though they may harbor sympathies for a particular group, the demands for objectivity and detachment in research ordinarily preclude proactive support. The sociologist as an expert witness, however, enjoys a much closer fit to the old adage that to know something is to change it. I conduct research and construct arguments that are likely to have serious consequences for a defendant's future life. The work of the sociologist influences whether the defendant receives a felony conviction or, upon a guilty plea, the nature of the punishment imposed by the court.

I would find it difficult to serve the interests of the client and the attorney if I was not convinced that the defense's case is substantially legitimate. It is true, of course, that a survey of community standards could be conducted with no knowledge of the particulars of a case. Belief in the legitimacy of a case, however, is necessary for me to render a genuine or persuasive courtroom performance. Therefore, I make the decision to participate in obscenity cases on a request-by-request basis. I ask and answer the following questions before I agree to participate in a case: Is the charge possession rather than sale or rental of the materials? Is the defendant an employee of an establishment, rather than the owner? Is the material soft-core rather than hard-core? Is the material nonviolent rather than violent? Without a community standards survey, would the defendant likely be convicted? Without a community standards survey, would a conviction likely be followed by a fair and just punishment?

Even with these criteria, however, determining what and where the dividing line is between cases with and without merit remains difficult. Reviewing the cases in which I participated illustrates one sociologist's decision-making strategy. All but one of the cases involved soft-core material, which was the most compelling factor for me. I accepted one case that did involve hard-core material on the basis that no violence was depicted and the court required that a community standards survey be performed to determine guilt or innocence.

Child pornography cases are particularly troubling and challenging. Child sexual abuse and child exploitation by visual depictions remain serious social problems (Campagna and Poffenberger 1988; Tyler and Stone 1985; Pierce 1984). Factors I consider when deciding whether or not to participate in an alleged child pornography case include: Are the materials in question depictions of nudity as compared with actual sexual activities? Is the child older, rather than younger? Is there any evidence the child was sexually abused, as commonly defined in the child abuse literature? Are there reasonable or legitimate assertions by the accused of medical, scientific, educational, or artistic value to the material? Are there large or small amounts of the suspect materials?

There are child pornography cases in which I would never become involved. On the other hand, there are cases that merit the involvement of the sociologist. In the one child pornography case in which I participated, the defendant was alleged to have taken a 24-exposure roll of film of two young girls in various states of dress and undress, including a few photographs in which the girls were nude or partially nude, some of which exposed their genitals. No sexual activity was depicted. There was no evidence that the defendant had ever sexually abused either of the girls, nor was there evidence of any attempts. With these facts, I decided to participate in the case.

When I accept a case, my focus is on the legal and social issues it represents. That the defendant possesses or lacks certain personal qualities is irrelevant to my work in the case. Indeed, I routinely accomplish my work as an expert without establishing a personal relationship with the defendant. I never met the defendant in the child pornography case, for example, and was only briefly introduced to the defendants in the other cases. The most contact I had was a brief chat with one of the defendants. A criminal charge is a serious life event for defendants, with serious repercussions for their lives. As a sociologist working on obscenity cases, however, my primary interest is in the relationships between the suspect materials and community standards.

Challenge to Antipornography Crusaders

My work in the courtroom resists both antipornography attitudes and the activities of antipornography crusaders. Despite the *Attorney General's Commission on Pornography: Final Report* (1986), there is little social and behavioral science literature to support the drastic censorship of sexually oriented materials (Scott 1985; Heins 1993). When I conduct a community standards survey that documents the tolerance of public opinion for allegedly obscene materials, I am challenging the legitimacy of the crusaders and their prosecutorial allies. Despite being both "right-wingers and liberals" (Bright 1992:11) and variously drawn from both "feminists and the religious right" (Heins 1993:162), the antipornography crusaders neither speak for nor represent the majority of persons in a typical community — even, I might add, an Oklahoman community in which moral standards are comparatively more numerous and visible than in other geographic regions. Although people may strongly believe that pornography is harmful, if a community's standards tolerate or accept sexually oriented materials, the materials cannot be found obscene (i.e., pornographic) and, therefore, be banned from the community. Even if scientific evidence were to conclusively demonstrate that children and certain susceptible adults are likely to be harmed by exposure to sexually

oriented materials, jury instructions specifically exclude these categories, requiring instead that the use or effects of use of "suspect"
materials be related to the "average person," not a special group or age
category (*The State of Oklahoma v. [Defendant]* 1989, No. 7).

From a societal perspective, the most important function of obscenity and child pornography laws is a symbolic one (Galliher and Cross
1983; Gusfield 1963, 1981). In reality, few people are charged under
these statutes. For example, far less than 1 percent of federal inmates
were sentenced in 1992 for both "pornography and prostitution"
(Maguire, Pastore, and Flanagan 1993:520). In 1993, 89 federal inmates
were sentenced (out of 41,810 total cases) for "pornography and prostitution," representing 0.2 percent of all cases (Maguire and Pastore
1994:528). It is not likely that state courts see much more activity on
obscenity statutes than their counterparts at the federal level. The
symbol that community values prohibit sexually oriented materials and
child pornography is sufficiently upheld and reinforced by occasional
prosecutions. Not unrelated to resisting the moral panics generated by
zealous antipornography crusaders, my testimony in obscenity cases is
a public discourse along the lines of "sex is not dirty."

Normalizing Sexuality and Nonobscene
Sexually Oriented Materials

Sex and sexually oriented materials are normalized in the testimony
of a sociologist. The message is simple: some sexually oriented materials are obscene, and some are not (Heins 1993). Explicit and graphic
materials may have legitimate educational, scientific, or other value
and cannot be defined as obscene, despite the disapproval of the
crusaders.

The case of the deadlocked jury (see above) illustrates the normal-
ization of sexuality and sexually oriented materials. Two videotapes,
one depicting male masturbation and the other depicting various sexual
activities, including mouth-genital contact between males and females,
were alleged to be obscene. Both, of course, were shown in their entirety
to the jury and those in the courtroom. When questioned, I discussed
the educational and entertainment value of these materials. The flam-
boyant defense attorney, taking every opportunity to exclaim how
"bored" he was while watching the videos, asked me if I was bored, a
question that had not been planned and for which I was not prepared. I
replied in the affirmative — watching a video of six males masturbating
in sequence was boring. Boredom, of course, denotes disinterest and
perhaps apathy, not shock, disgust, or horror. I gave further evidence
regarding the frequency of participation in masturbation and oral sex in
this culture, arguing that such behaviors are common and that the
videos may benefit viewers. My intention was to convey the idea that
sex is fun, that sexual desires are normal, and that it is okay for

individuals and couples to rent, view, and enjoy videos and other materials that are sexually explicit.

My capacity to normalize this sexual material for the court was intentionally aided by the defense attorney, who emphasized that not only was I qualified to discuss the community standards issues in the case but also I am married and a religious person. Thus, I was presented to the court as neither a radical nor an atheist with a vendetta against religion. Moral boundaries — what is accepted or tolerated and what is not accepted or tolerated in the group or community — are at issue in obscenity and child pornography cases. Moral entrepreneurs or crusaders, specifically represented by the prosecutor, seek to establish — perhaps redefine and narrow — or enforce a boundary through the prosecution of the defendant. The sociologist serves as a mirror to reflect, rather than create, community values. These are not the sociologist's values that are reported, nor are the survey results guaranteed to be consistent with the values of the sociologist. Rather, the sociologist testifies to the survey results, giving interpretation and explanation where the court permits. Despite Henshel's (1990) concerns about intellectuals and experts, the sociologist as expert witness acts as neither moral entrepreneur nor juror. The role of the sociologist is that of facilitating the work of the jury or judge — as final rule interpreters (O'Sullivan 1994) — by providing necessary and useful information.

It is the intent of the law that the decision of guilt or innocence be made by reasonable, rational persons working in a fair and just way. Furthermore, jury instruction clearly prohibits jurors from using their own values to determine whether the material is defined as obscenity or child pornography. Reid indicates that, although juries consist of peers, they do not necessarily reflect the community as far as race, sex, and so on are concerned (1990:404). The 12 jurors are not reflective of community values. Therefore, the sociologist provides essential evidence about the community for the members of the jury. Testimony of the sociologist says to the jurors that their individual views neither determine nor reflect community standards. When a sociologist is involved in these cases, the establishment of the moral boundary is likely to follow from a reasoned, rational process, devoid of the spurious influence of values of the individual juror, the prosecutor, zealous police, citizen activists, or the sociologist. In a specific sense, the evidence from the community survey denotes the existence of a moral consensus, despite the message of a moral crusade.

BY WAY OF CONCLUSION: SOME FUNDAMENTAL CONCERNS

Several concerns have evolved out of my work with obscenity and child pornography cases, mostly derived from the numerous constitutional questions that remain unanswered in censorship crusades. For example, obscenity and, to a lesser extent, child pornography laws are so vague (in a nonlegal sense) as to render them inexplicable to artists as well as ordinary citizens (Heins 1993:33). A person is not required to know that the material is obscene to be convicted of obscenity charges, nor must a person have read or seen the materials in question to be charged and convicted. "Knowledge" of the contents of the materials involves knowing the "nature" of the materials, rather than the exact content, which is vague and imprecise.

Moreover, it is remarkable that the courts have not required the prosecution to provide empirical evidence of community standards in obscenity cases. It seems to me that the state should be obligated to introduce evidence that the suspect materials are neither tolerated nor accepted by community standards. Finally, I am troubled by the ability of jurors to objectively evaluate the suspect materials based on community standards in lieu of their own personal views. This requirement assumes a certain sociological sophistication that I often find lacking in a typical juror.

A FINAL THOUGHT

A lesbian artist, radical sex activist, and author of erotica states: "Censors have turned certain States of the Union into blindfolded territories, but they can't stop little minds from fantasizing behind the blinders. You may find it rough to buy a copy of *Susie Sexpert's Lesbian Sex World* in Oklahoma, but you sure can find a lot of lesbians, a lot of sex, and a world of taboo activities circulating throughout the Sooner state" (Bright 1992:11). What is true of lesbians appears applicable to other Oklahomans and, no doubt, to Nebraskans, Ohioans, North and South Carolinians, and so on.

REFERENCES

Attorney General's Commission on Pornography: Final Report. 1986, July. Washington, DC: U.S. Department of Justice.

Ben-Yehuda, N. 1985. Deviance and Moral Boundaries. Chicago, IL: University of Chicago Press.

Bright, S. 1992. *Susie Bright's Sexual Reality: A Virtual Sex World Reader.* Pittsburgh, PA: Cleis Press.

Campagna, D. S., & Poffenberger, D. L. 1988. *The Sexual Trafficking in Children.* Dover, DE: Auburn House.

Copp, D., & Wendell, S. (Eds.). 1983. *Pornography and Censorship.* Buffalo, NY: Prometheus Books.

Diamond, M., & Dannemiller, J. E. 1989. Pornography and Community Standards in Hawaii: Comparisons with Other States. *Archives of Sexual Behavior, 18,* 475–495.

Feinberg, J. 1983. Pornography and the Criminal Law. In D. Copp & S. Wendell (Eds.), *Pornography and Censorship* (pp. 105–137). Buffalo, NY: Prometheus Books.

Galliher, J. F., & Cross, J. R. 1983. *Morals Legislation Without Morality*. New Brunswick, NJ: Rutgers University Press.

Glassman, M. B. 1978. Community Standards of Patent Offensiveness: Public Opinion Data and Obscenity Law. *Public Opinion Quarterly, 42*, 161–170.

Graham, M. H. 1986. *Handbook of Federal Evidence*, 3rd ed. St. Paul, MN: West Publishing.

Gusfield, J. 1981. *The Culture of Public Problems: Drinking, Driving and Symbolic Order*. Chicago: University of Illinois Press.

Gusfield, J. 1963. *Symbolic Crusade, States Politics and the American Temperance Movement*. Urbana: University of Illinois Press.

Heins, M. 1993. *Sex, Sin, and Blasphemy*. New York: New York Press.

Henshel, R. L. 1990. *Thinking About Social Problems*. New York: Harcourt, Brace, Jovanovich.

Lavrakas, P. J. 1987. *Telephone Survey Methods*. Newbury Park, CA: Sage.

Maguire, K., & Pastore, A. L. 1994. *Sourcebook of Criminal Justice Statistics 1993*. Washington, DC: U.S. Government Printing Office.

Maguire, K., Pastore, A. L., & Flanagan, T. J. (Eds.). 1993. *Sourcebook of Criminal Justice Statistics 1992*. Washington, DC: U.S. Government Printing Office.

Miller, N. 1988. Facts, Expert Facts, and Statistics: Descriptive and Experimental Research Methods in Litigation, Part II. *Rutgers Law Review, 40*, 467–520.

Nobile, P., & Nadler, E. 1986. *United States of America vs. Sex*. New York: Minotaur Press.

O'Brien, S. 1983. *Child Pornography*. Dubuque, IA: Kendall/Hunt Publishing Company.

Obscenity, Oklahoma Statutes, Title 21, § 1021–1024. 1991. St. Paul, MN: West Publishing.

O'Sullivan, R. G. 1994. Moral Entrepreneurs, Local Morality, and Labeling Processes. *Free Inquiry In Creative Sociology, 22*, 73–77.

Pierce, R. L. 1984. Child Pornography: A Hidden Dimension of Child Abuse. *Child Abuse & Neglect, 8*, 483–493.

Reid, S. T. 1990. *Criminal Justice*, 2d ed. New York: Macmillan.

Rudolf, D. S., & Fargo, M. 1988, November. The Obscenity Trial in Rural America: Preparing to Win. *The Champion*, pp. 5–15.

Schauer, F. 1983. Codifying the First Amendment: New York v. Ferber. In P. B. Hurland, G. C. Casper, & D. J. Hutchinson (Eds.), *The Supreme Court Review, 1982* (pp. 285–317). Chicago, IL: University of Chicago Press.

Schlafly, P. (Ed.). 1987. *Pornography's Victims*. Westchester, IL: Crossway Books.

Scott, D. 1985. *Pornography — Its Effects on the Family, Community and Culture*. Washington, DC: The Child and Family Protection Institute.

Scott, J. E. 1991. What Is Obscene? Social Science and the Contemporary Community Standard Test of Obscenity. *International Journal of Law and Psychiatry, 14*, 29–45.

Scott, J. E., Eitle, D. J., & Skovron, S. E. 1990. Obscenity and the Law: Is It Possible for a Jury to Apply Contemporary Community Standards in Determining Obscenity? *Law and Human Behavior, 14*, 139–150.

Sexual Exploitation of Children, 18 United States Code, § 2251–2257, 1988 ed. 1989. Washington, DC: U.S. Government Printing Office.

Tyler, R. P., & Stone, L. E. 1985. Child Pornography: Perpetuating The Sexual Victimization of Children. *Child Abuse & Neglect, 9*, 313–318.

Wallace, D. H. 1973. Obscenity and Contemporary Community Standards: A Survey. *Journal of Social Issues, 29*, 53–68.

Winick, C., & Evans, J. T. 1994. Is There A National Standard with Respect to Attitudes Toward Sexually Explicit Media Material? *Archives of Sexual*

Behavior, 23, 405–419.
Zurcher, L. A., & Kirkpatrick, R. G. 1976. *Citizens for Decency: Antipornography Crusades as Status Defense.* Austin: University of Texas Press.

CASES CITED

Carlock v. State, 609 S.W.2d 787 (Tex. Cr. App. 1980).
Commonwealth v. Trainor, 374 Mass. 796, 374 N.E.2d 1216 (1978).
Court's Instruction, The State of Oklahoma v. [Defendant], Nos. 6, 7, 9, (1989).
Flynt v. State, 264 S.E.2d 669 (Ga. App. 1980).
Miller v. California, 413 U.S. 15 (1973).
New York v. Ferber, 458 U.S. 745 (1982).
People v. Nelson, 410 N.E.2d 476 (Ill. App. 1980).
Pittsburgh Press Club v. United States, 579 F.2d 751 (3d Cir. 1978).
Roth v. United States, 354 U.S. 476 (1957).
Saliba v. State, 475 N.E.2d 1181 (Ind. App. 2 Dist. 1985).
United States v. Various Articles of Merchandise, 750 F.2d 596 (7th Cir. 1984).

12

Toxins in the Environment, Damage to the Community: Sociology and the Toxic Tort

J. Steven Picou

Sociologists are contributing to a growing body of literature on the deleterious effects of toxic contamination on the person, family, neighborhood, and community (see, e.g., Levine 1982; Kroll-Smith and Couch 1993; Erikson 1994). The social and psychological damages to residents of Love Canal, Buffalo Creek, Times Beach, Three Mile Island, Centralia, Bophal, and Chernobyl, to name a few of the more prominent environmental disasters, are documented in detail in a number of well-known studies (see, among others, Erikson 1976; Levine 1982; Baum, Fleming, and Singer 1982, 1983; Baum and Fleming 1993; Kroll-Smith and Couch 1990).

It is reasonable to expect that oil spills, train derailments, plant explosions, and other sudden, massive toxic releases will continue to result in toxic tort litigations. In addition, as residents of neighborhoods and communities gradually become aware of toxic waste sites located in and around their communities, the emergence of what Couch and Kroll-Smith (1985) call "chronic technical disasters" will also trigger lawsuits on behalf of residents who claim a variety of tort damages.

Sociologists with research interests in disasters, environmental sociology, social impact assessment, and applied sociology are likely to be recruited by legal representatives of plaintiffs, defendants, and the courts to assess and evaluate health, economic, social, and psychological damages resulting from damage to local habitats. One theme in this chapter is the increasing use of sociology in toxic tort litigation to identify and assess losses not routinely envisioned by the courts. A second and related theme is the tension between expanding and limiting models of loss assessment. The high degree of scientific uncertainty haunting toxic pollution incidents combined with the opportunity to claim social and cultural, not just physical, losses makes the questions "What evidence?" and "What types of losses?" hotly contested legal issues in most toxic torts. Whether the expert works to expand or limit the assessment of loss or is permitted to work independently of such pressures depends on his or her particular relationship to the courts, a point I will make throughout this chapter.

A brief overview of toxic tort doctrine identifies the legal basis for damage or injury claims under tort law.

TOXIC TORT LITIGATION: AN OVERVIEW

"Tort," of course, is a derivative of the verb "to torture." Toxic torts are filed when there is alleged damage to "persons, to property, or to the environment" that results from the "toxicity of a product, a substance or process" (Madden 1992:2). Plaintiffs seek financial compensation for this type of noncontractual civil damage. Toxic tort suits often draw on more general tort law. The decision to use a broader tort framework is likley to occur when toxic exposure to property or person results in plaintiffs' claims for damages of trespass, assault, battery, nuisance, negligence, and misconduct regarding abnormally dangerous activities.

Toxic tort litigation generally involves plaintiffs issuing a number of claims against defendants regarding possible multiple violations of tort doctrine. For example, homeowners in a neighborhood may assert that water draining from an adjacent chemical plant has polluted their property with dioxins, ethylene glycol, and perchloroethylene. These homeowners can bring tort claims to the court that involve nuisance, trespass, and negligence. The nuisance violation declares that the chemical contamination directly interferes with residents' enjoyment of their home and property. The trespass violation declares that the contaminants reflect a direct invasion of plaintiffs' possession of the property. The negligence violation declares that the owners and operators of the chemical plant failed to exercise proper precautions in their plant operation that would have prevented the contamination. Taken together, such claims most often provide the evidentiary context for toxic tort cases (Madden 1992).

However, it should be noted that proof of negligence and proof of actual harm may be unnecessary in many cases in which trespass, assault, and battery charges are claimed (Greer and Freedman 1989). Proof of actual harm often is impossible to demonstrate in toxic contamination cases because of the long latency period between some types of chemical exposure and disease. In short, in the absence of immediate health effects, "characterizing such events as an assault and battery on their person or a trespass on their property may make a great deal of sense" (Greer and Freedman 1989:1). Furthermore, given the possibility that plaintiffs may recover damages for emotional distress and fear of future illness, toxic tort doctrines grant physically injured plaintiffs opportunity to recover for mental suffering. It is in this nebulous area of "emotional distress" and "mental anguish" that I use the tools of sociology to identify compensable damage.

TECHNOLOGICAL ACCIDENTS AND TOXIC CONTAMINATION: THE CONVERGENCE OF SOCIAL SCIENTIFIC EVIDENCE

Kai Erikson notes that toxins in local environments often result in psychosocial trauma for victims that produces "(a) changed sense of self and (b) a changed way of relating to others [and] (c) a changed world view altogether" (1994:241). Implied in Erikson's indicators of change is the importance of sociology in accounting for the variable effects of environmental contamination.

Sociology has a longstanding interest in community structure and psychosocial disorganization. Over the past 25 years, a number of case studies have demonstrated clearly the importance of these areas for understanding the social impacts of technological disasters. Case studies of well-known disasters, such as those that occurred at Love Canal, Times Beach, Three Mile Island, Bophal, Chernobyl, and Prince William Sound, all provide evidence of the breakdown of community structure and both acute and chronic psychosocial reactions by victims (Levine 1982; Baum et al. 1982, 1983; Kroll-Smith and Couch 1990; Picou, Gill, Dyer, and Curry 1992; Palinkas, Petterson, Russell, and Downs 1993). Consistent evidence of sociological damage is captured in the concept of the "corrosive community," or the cultural and structural segmentation that occurs in communities impacted by technological disasters (Freudenburg and Jones 1991). According to Kroll-Smith and Couch: "Toxic chemicals leaking through underground sewers or asbestos fibers floating through the air do not destroy buildings or level houses, but they do damage the moral rules for local community life. When the presence of contamination is defined by a segment of the neighborhood as "impact," the high degree of uncertainty accompanying this type of hazard insures that competing definitions will emerge, creating a marked crisis in the local culture" (1993:87).

Edelstein (1988) documents the insidious social and psychological effects of biospheric contamination in several local communities. Brown and Mikkelsen's (1990) case study of a leukemia cluster in Woburn, Massachusetts, identified multiple social and psychological damages for a subset of residents. Using time series data, Andrew Baum and colleagues are documenting recurring levels of social and psychological distress following the radiation accident at Three Mile Island (Baum and Fleming 1993). A court-ordered study of the psychological and social trauma following a train derailment and toxic spill in Livingston, Louisiana, records in detail the miseries experienced by community residents (Picou 1984). Substantial sociological evidence exists to suggest that toxins in the environment contaminate more than air, water, or soil; they also damage the social fabric of a community, its neighborhoods, its families, and its residents' self-esteem.

Environmental contamination, in short, is often both a biospheric and a sociological disaster.

Although most social scientists acknowledge the importance of community loss to the psychosocial health of victims of toxic contamination, the courts are more cautious in their approach to these data. Indeed, the "standards of research" as judged by the sociological community and the "standards of evidence" as accepted by the court are two different issues (see Chapter 1 in this volume).

EXPANDING AND LIMITING MODELS OF IMPACTS

Edelstein found the courts recognizing what he calls "expanding" and "limiting" models of psychosocial effects in toxic tort litigation (1989:157–159). Typically, sociological evidence collected from plaintiffs expands traditional effects research by including problems associated with a diminishing quality of community, neighborhood, and family life. Defendants, on the other hand, typically argue for a limiting model of loss. Directing the court's attention to the methodological limitations of research designs and quantitative data, defendants' experts and attorneys will ask the court to consider only a limited range of losses. The use of sociological evidence in toxic tort cases reflects the continuing tensions between the expanding and limiting models of expert testimony.

These two models also provide a framework for understanding basic approaches to various expert witness roles that sociologists may assume in toxic tort cases. The expanding model begins by collecting original data on plaintiffs. It, too, is limited, of course, by the amount of capital available to conduct the research (Berk and Oppenheim 1979:128). In general, the expanding model is used by sociologists when they serve as expert witnesses for the courts or plaintiffs and as independent third-party researchers. The limiting model, on the other hand, often is used by sociologists who represent defendants in toxic tort litigation, because this approach reduces the chances for the discovery of information leading to additional claims for damages (Edelstein 1989). Ostensibly, sociological information introduced by plaintiffs' experts will be scrutinized by defendants' experts for any deficiencies in order to raise doubts about its validity. The limiting model recognizes the point that "even when scientifically sound applied research is introduced into advocacy proceedings attacks will likely follow" (Berk and Oppenheim 1979:130).

Most important, the limiting model focuses on discrediting both the expert and his/her testimony, and "it matters little whether genuine flaws surface as long as they appear to be genuine flaws" (Berk and Oppenheim 1979:137). Challenges from the limiting model often are made merely to raise doubts regarding the credibility of the researcher, data collection procedures, sample generalizability, application of statistical techniques, and appropriateness of theoretical framework. Indeed, the adversarial nature of toxic tort litigation rekindles many epistemological arguments in sociology.

There is a third role that experts can play, however, one that does not mandate an expanding or limiting model of loss. Once in a while, the courts appoint experts who then are responsible for reporting directly to judges rather than to adversarial attorneys. Working for the courts, betwixt and between plaintiffs and defendants, sidesteps the tension between expanding and limiting models of loss. I am fortunate to have served in such a capacity.

Keeping in mind the idea of expanding and limiting evidence, consider the following three cases that illustrate the complicated relationships of an expert witness to the courts: the court-appointed expert, the expert for the plaintiffs, and the third-party or unwilling expert. In each case, sociological knowledge is introduced into the court via a distinct path, and the knowledge itself plays a different role in each case, depending upon the relationship of the expert to the court. Consider first the court-appointed expert.

EXPERT WITNESS FOR THE COURT

On September 28, 1982, at 5:12 A.M., an Illinois Central Gulf Railroad (ICGR) freight train derailed in Livingston, Louisiana, a small rural community located approximately 20 miles east of Baton Rouge. A total of 43 cars derailed. Thirty-six were tank cars that contained hazardous and toxic materials such as methyl chloride, sodium, tetraethyllead, toluene disocyanate, perchloroethylene, styrene, and vinyl chloride. Most of these tank cars caught fire, leaked, burned, or exploded. Massive fires broke out after the derailment and continued to burn for almost two weeks. All 2,500 residents of the community were evacuated within hours following the accident. Most were officially evacuated for approximately 14 days. A ten-acre site was contaminated, and over 96,000 cubic yards of contaminated soil were removed and transported to a waste storage site. The excavation and restoration of the contaminated site, including the establishment of recovery wells, was completed in 20 months.

Although there were no deaths or serious injuries and the amount of physical destruction to private property was relatively minimal, residents of the Livingston community perceived the situation as a disaster and responded accordingly. They were concerned in particular with the threat of permanent contamination to the community's water supply, economic damages, emotional distress damages, and negligence on the part of ICGR's transportation operations. A class action lawsuit was filed by the community against the railroad. Among other charges, the railroad was cited for negligence: the engineer was inebriated, and an unauthorized person allegedly was operating the train. The train also was exceeding the speed limit. The suit was filed in the Twenty-first Judicial District Court of Louisiana. E. Gordon Causey, district magistrate, ordered an objective, impartial scientific investigation of the physical, ecological, economic, psychological, and sociological impacts of the derailment. Attorneys for the ICGR appealed to the supreme court of the state of Louisiana, seeking to overrule Causey's order. The Louisiana Supreme Court, however, upheld the order. An interdisciplinary research team was organized, and my work as an expert witness for the courts officially began.

The research proposed by the judge and the Twenty-first District Court of the state requested that an interdisciplinary team of scientists utilize appropriate methodological techniques to estimate the physical, ecological, economic, psychological, and sociological impacts of the derailment and toxic spill. In December 1982, the team met for the first time at Gulf South Research Institute in Baton Rouge, Louisiana. Everyone attending the meeting had prepared a proposal for evaluating various physical and social impacts that reflected accepted measurements and methodologies in the various scientific disciplines. These preproposals were discussed, modified, and revised during a number of sessions. Expanded proposals were developed, and over the following months, a final damage assessment proposal was completed by the various experts and Gulf South Research Institute.

The expectations that the court established for expert testimony were consistent with expectations in the various scientific disciplines for generally accepted methodologies. The interdisciplinary team of court-appointed experts relied directly on their respective disciplines' research literatures for identifying appropriate methods and procedures for assessing the impacts of the Livingston accident (Picou 1984). The sociological damage assessment required a control community, whereas the psychological and economic assessments did not.

I vividly recall objections to my demand for a demographically matched control community. Team members argued that it would cost too much and waste precious time. I relied on the good work done by sociologists who study natural disasters to convince the research team that a control community was necessary (Drabek 1986).

I used a quasi-experimental design to conduct an ex post facto analysis that contrasted the impact community with a demographically matched control community (Picou 1984). Households were selected by a stratified, random sampling procedure, and actual selections were made by court-appointed statisticians. Aided by the matched control community, I confidently summarized my sociological assessment for the courts.

The derailment and subsequent evacuation activities resulted in a long-term (19 months) negative impact on the Livingston area community. This negative impact, which is characteristic of a technological accident, is manifested in terms of Livingston area residents' perceptions that their community is a less desirable place to live, raise children, and (in general) have a happy life. The consequences of the derailment continue in terms of the residents' concerns about inadequate court settlements, fears of a similar accident occurring in the future, perceptions of the railroad as presently being a threat to their families, and increased awareness of the possibilities of experiencing a variety of technological accidents in the future.

The negative impact is more pronounced for residents who lived closest to the site of the derailment, who were evacuated for the longest period of time, and who were separated from family members during the evacuation period. These residents want to move out of the area because they continue to be upset by the railroad, perceive that they have increased risks of getting cancer, and fear that their drinking water will be contaminated in the immediate future. (Picou 1984:109–110)

As I reflect on my later experiences in toxic tort cases, it is obvious that the Twenty-first Judicial Court of the state of Louisiana, with the leadership provided by Causey, was innovative and effective in the manner that it organized a resolution to the legal claims of plaintiffs. Expert testimony was presented by independent, third-party scientists who collected data utilizing generally accepted discipline methods. All reports were completed by the time the trial was scheduled to start. Data in the reports were used to negotiate a relatively quick settlement between the community and ICGR. Such an informed and organized legal response to technological disasters and victims of such events is rare, indeed.

In my opinion, the legal response of the Twenty-first Judicial Court of the state of Louisiana could serve as an example for organizing and resolving legal disputes in future technological disasters. A number of difficulties, however, including costs, time, problems in locating experts, and so on, plague such an enlightened resolution to toxic tort cases (Rosenberg 1994). In spite of these difficulties, a legal strategy that allowed experts to operate between the limiting and expanding demands of plaintiffs' and defendants' interests would likely work in the service of all interested parties. At the very least, it would make the job of the expert easier.

EXPERT WITNESS FOR THE PLAINTIFFS

Almost a decade after Love Canal, toxic contaminants were discovered in an upper middle-class neighborhood south of Houston. In the early 1980s, residential developers constructed a large subdivision adjacent to a hazardous waste landfill, known as the Brio site. A wide variety of toxic and hazardous chemicals were buried in Brio's 89 acre area. Over the decade, residents of the neighborhood known as Southbend were spurred to action by reports of numerous rare childhood illnesses within the area. Community action intensified when the Brio hazardous waste site was officially placed on the nation's Superfund list.

Many Southbend residents blamed the hazardous waste site for their children's unusual illnesses. When federal and state governments did not organize a buyout of residents, a citizens' group emerged to pressure local officials to take action. In its first official action, the local government closed the elementary school. Class-action lawsuits were filed on behalf of the children in Southbend against various chemical companies known to have used the Brio site as a dump. After three years of litigation, the lawsuits were settled out of court. The damage award totaled $207 million. In addition, developers were ordered to assume all mortgages, allowing families to move from the neighborhood. Lawsuits filed by the school district for damages because of the closing of the elementary school have been litigated only recently.

In a bizarre turn of events, however, Southbend houses were once again for sale (at below market prices) shortly after the first families moved out, in spite of the fact that the volatile and dangerous chemicals were still in the Brio site. The reason for this bit of regulatory foolishness was the failure of the Environmental Protection Agency to officially list the neighborhood as an immediate health hazard.

I was approached by attorneys for the plaintiffs and asked to collect data on the emotional distress experienced by the Brio children and their families. There were certain restrictions regarding the selection of respondents for interviewing that reflected court procedures and the data needs of the attorneys. Data were collected from the 30 children and approximately 60 parents identified as trial plaintiffs. The issue of generalizability of empirical findings was resolved by the fact that an equal number (15) of trial plaintiffs were selected by attorneys representing both plaintiffs and the defense. A design similar to the one used for the Livingston research was proposed, and a research team of sociologists was assembled to collect the data. Control neighborhoods were demographically matched and identified and households randomly selected. Not surprisingly, however, although the design for the Brio study was similar to the design for Livingston, the Brio design used a more expanded field of damage indicators.

I was expected to testify on the loss and stress measured by the survey. The survey instrument was designed from previous studies of contaminated communities, and whenever possible, measures were selected that would allow comparisons to national norms and previous research on emotional distress and trauma. The research instrument was approved by plaintiffs' attorneys, and a pilot test determined that the instrument was appropriate for representative plaintiffs.

The measurement of psychosocial damages was comprehensive and detailed. Attorneys for the plaintiffs encouraged an expanded effects model. Indicators for emotional distress claims included measures of fear, depression, trauma, stress, anxiety, family disruption, and health problems. National norms were used to assess the responses of parents whose children were plaintiffs in the case. Compared with this baseline, parents were less happy as individuals, had unhappy marriages, held low evaluations of their personal health, and had greater financial problems. Southbend residents also expressed high levels of worry and fear regarding increased cancer risks. When compared with data on victims of violent assaults and patients seeking bereavement therapy, Southbend residents were found to have levels of psychosocial distress comparable with those of victims of violent assaults and patients seeking bereavement therapy. In summary, the social-psychological evidence collected and presented to the plaintiffs' attorneys documented that both children and parents suffered from chronic emotional distress sufficiently severe to result in personal disorganization and impairment (for a report of this study, see Picou and Gill 1993). Although depositions were scheduled, this case was settled prior to any depositional or trial testimony on my part.

THIRD-PARTY RESEARCHER: SOME
PROBLEMS OF AN UNWILLING EXPERT

Sociologists doing independent investigations of a particular trouble may publish a paper or issue an academic report that is interpreted by one side or the other in litigation as expanding or limiting possible claims to damages. Should this happen, we may find ourselves defending our research as well as our professional integrity against attorneys representing one or the other contentious group.

On March 24, 1989, the supertanker Exxon *Valdez* ran aground on Bligh Reef in Prince William Sound (PWS), Alaska, spilling approximately 11 million gallons of crude oil. The spill occurred at the beginning of the bioregion's most biologically active season and had a devastating impact on the natural environment and the human communities that rely on renewable natural resources. An inadequate response to the spill exacerbated the situation, and a massive oil slick formed and washed ashore on the western edge of PWS days later. Eventually, over 1,200 miles of pristine Alaskan coastline were oiled (Lord 1992). Risking the charge of hyperbole, the spill was called "another Hiroshima" by a federal judge; the catastrophic annihilation of resources and culture resulting from the largest oil spill in North American history has persisted over the years (Davidson 1990; Keeble 1991).

The bioregion's commercial and subsistence fisheries were severely damaged. The pink salmon season, a major component of PWS's commercial fishing industry, was curtailed in 1989. Returns of pink salmon were above average in 1990, severely disrupted in 1991, and weak in 1992 and 1993. The commercial herring season was closed in 1989. It opened again in 1990, but catches were officially limited for the next three years. The commercial herring fishery in PWS closed in 1993 (Ott 1994). Likewise, local Alaskan native subsistence harvests of marine resources registered sharp declines for years after the spill.

In late summer 1989, I put a research team together to initiate a longitudinal study of the community impacts of the oil spill. I was, simply, a sociologist interested in research questions regarding disaster agents and occupational communities. I received initial funding from the Natural Hazards Resource and Applications Information Center, located in Boulder, Colorado. In 1991, the Polar Social Science Division of the National Science Foundation and the Center for Field Studies, Earthwatch, provided additional funding to expand the initial project into a 4-year longitudinal study.

As an independent, third-party researcher, I directed the collection of interdisciplinary data in three small Alaskan communities in 1991 and 1992. The selection of communities was based on a comparative theoretical sample that isolated a renewable resource community (Cordova) and an economically diversified community (Valdez) in the impact area of the spill. A third community in southeast Alaska, Petersburg, was identified as a control community.

Respondents were selected by random procedures and guaranteed anonymity and confidentiality. Some respondents were reinterviewed for four years, and others were reinterviewed over a 2-year period. The study was guided by a theoretical framework that focused on various issues of community and occupational change. It is important to note that this research was not an empirical assessment of social and psychological damages; rather, it was an attempt to theorize the empirical relationships between chronic technological disasters and community change. Two peer-reviewed articles were published from our 1989–90 data in 1992 by members of the project team (Dyer, Gill, and Picou 1992; Picou et al. 1992). The papers focused attention on patterns of community disruptions following the Exxon oil spill. Disruption levels between impacted and control communities highlighted the devastating effects of the spill on coastal settlements. Unknown to me, however, plaintiffs' attorneys referred to these papers as well as public presentations I had made on the topic in written documents presented to the courts during initial phases of the litigation.

Shortly after these papers appeared in print, I was contacted by an attorney representing the Exxon Corporation and another representing a group of plaintiffs. Both men were courteous in our conversations and requested that I send them copies of the papers and other reports I might have. I agreed to supply each side with several documents.

On October 1, 1992, I was issued a civil subpoena by attorneys representing the Exxon Corporation, commanding that as a nonparty, unretained expert, I produce and permit inspection and copying of a litany of documents that were deemed as being under my direct posses-- sion and control (civil subpoena A89-095, October 1992). More specifically, the eight page subpoena demanded that I produce at deposition on November 5, 1992, over 20 categories of documents, summarily defined as:

Originals or any exact copies of every writing or record of every type and description that is or has been in the possession, control, or custody of J. Steven Picou, that he has knowledge of or to which he has access, including without limitation, contracts, agreements, correspondence, memoranda, stenographic or handwritten notes, reports, records, telegrams, telexes, facsimiles, schedules, diaries, notebooks, logbooks, invoices, accounting records, work sheets, data sheets, ledgers, journals, charts, notes, drafts, scribblings, recordings, visual displays, photographs, minutes of meetings, tabulations, computations, summaries, inventories, and writings regarding conferences, conversations or telephone conversations, and any and all taped, recorded, written, printed or typed matter of any kind or description, including all computer-generated or stored data. (U.S. District Civil Subpoena 1992)

Following the receipt of this subpoena, I met with the dean of my college and the university attorney on several occasions, and it was agreed that the University of South Alabama would file a protective order on my behalf. The primary concerns of this protective order involved issues of researcher privilege and the protection of respondent confidentiality.

With a subpoena in hand, I was forced to refocus the research project from data analysis to protection of the data from interests who may purposefully misrepresent results to support a particular legal claim. The issue of confidentiality was particularly important because some respondents were also plaintiffs who were scheduled to be deposed by attorneys representing the defendant. The protective order filed by my university argued for modifying the subpoena, claiming that it required the submission of confidential materials and, thus, placed an undue burden on the researcher. A protection order was granted by Federal Magistrate William Cassady on October 14, 1992, with the caveat that the court would consider the appropriateness of the protective order or the need to modify the original subpoena (U.S. District VII Court 1993). Exxon challenged the protective order on March 18, 1993, filing a motion to compel production of certain documents.

My unfortunate encounter with Exxon and subsequent efforts to protect the confidentiality of those people who participated in this social scientific study sparked debate among sociologists concerned with ethical issues regarding the ownership of sociological evidence (Busch 1991; Rent 1993), the appropriateness of methodological procedures (Lodwick 1994), the involuntary surrender of data prior to project completion (Marshall 1993), and the protection of human subjects (Picou 1995).

On July 1, 1993, Cassady ordered that the defendants' motion to compel be granted in part and denied in part with the provision that the granted portion of the motion to compel be specifically governed by a protective order entered on the same date. The protective order limited access regarding the 1989–90 computer data to the defendants' designated experts. Hard copies were for experts' eyes only. Reproduction of data was prohibited. Any paper documents were to be stamped "HIGHLY CONFIDENTIAL, PURSUANT TO DR. J. STEVEN PICOU PROTECTIVE ORDER IN THE EXXON VALDEZ OIL SPILL LITIGATION." Defendants' experts were required to complete an understanding of confidentiality agreement prior to access of the material. The data were to be produced solely for statistical analysis, and attempts to identify individuals listed on the computer documents were prohibited. The defendants' motion to compel production of the 1991–92 data was denied.

On July 2, 1993, Exxon filed a motion to amend the "Court's order of July 1, 1993," because it did not "distinguish between Plaintiffs and non-Plaintiffs" regarding the produced material. Exxon wanted "all information as to individuals who were Party Plaintiffs or a member of any class of Plaintiffs without any reaction." This motion to amend was denied.

The court also denied Exxon's motion to secure the names of any plaintiffs who may have been participants in the original survey. This motion suggested that the defendant's attorneys had at least one hidden agenda, that is, to secure information that could be used to embarrass, intimidate, or contradict the testimony of plaintiffs (Marshall 1993). In retrospect, I take some pride in knowing that my independent research on Alaskan villages affected by the Exxon oil spill was perceived by both legal parties as relevant to their case. For the plaintiffs, my data were most provocative, suggesting an expanded effects model, documenting cultural, economic, and social infrastructure losses following the spill. For the defendant, on the other hand, my data were a public embarrassment, a potential liability and, thus, became the target of sharp, sustained attacks. I easily can imagine a quite different scenario, however, if my data had revealed only limited effects from the spill. The lesson here is simple but worth recalling: sociologists who independently research problems and issues that are in litigation may find themselves in the uncomfortable position of defending an expanded or limited effects model in the uncharted territories of the courts.

CONCLUSION

Illustrated in this chapter are some of the ways toxic tort litigation and the sociology of technological disaster impacts now are being joined. The use of sociological evidence in toxic tort litigation reflects the documentation of numerous deleterious social, behavioral, psychological, and health effects resulting from technological disasters. Sociology, in other words, is perceived as important in its capacity to assess the kinds and degrees of losses individuals and communities are likely to incur when local environments become sources of danger. In its capacity to imagine effects that are greater than the body or the personality, sociology complements medicine and psychology in assessing the stresses and traumas of biospheric contamination. Sociology is in a unique position to conceptualize the damaging effects of environmental toxins on sociocultural resources and to provide convincing accounts of how blows to the tissues of community life shake a person's confidence and reduce his or her ability to cope effectively. The opportunities for sociology to inform a court's deliberations, however, as I have attempted to show in this chapter, are shaped by the various relationships of the expert to the legal proceedings.

ACKNOWLEDGMENT

The completion of this chapter would not have been possible without the support of the College of Arts and Sciences (Larry Allen, Dean) and the Office of Academic Affairs, University of South Alabama. I am grateful to Don South, Mark Mobert, Dave Johnson, Duane Gill, and Maxey Roberts for comments and discussions regarding earlier versions of this chapter. The technical assistance provided by Linda Burcham, Dan Dennard, Jan Bolton, and Pat Picou is also acknowledged. Any errors contained herein are solely my responsibility.

REFERENCES

Baum, A., & Fleming, I. 1993. Implications of Psychological Research on Stress and Technological Accidents. *American Psychologist*, 48(6), 665–672.

Baum, A., Fleming, R., & Singer, J.E. 1983. Coping with Victimization by Technological Disaster. *Journal of Social Issues*, 39(2), 117–138.

Baum, A., Fleming, R., & Singer, J.E. 1982. Stress at Three Mile Island: Applying Psychological Impact Analysis. In L. Bickman (Ed.), *Applied Social Psychology Annual*, Vol. 3., (pp. 217–248). Beverly Hills, CA: Sage.

Berk, R. A., & Oppenheim, J. 1979. Doing Good Well: The Use of Quantitative Social Science Data in Advocacy Proceedings. *Law and Policy Quarterly*, 1(2), 123–146.

Brown, P., & Mikkelsen, E. J. 1990. *No Safe Place: Toxic Waste, Leukemia, and Community Action*. Berkeley: University of California Press.

Busch, L. 1991, May 10. Science Under Wraps in Prince William Sound. *Science, 252*, 772–773.

Couch, S. R., & Kroll-Smith, J. S. 1985. The Chronic Technical Disaster: Toward a Social Scientific Perspective. *Social Science Quarterly, 66*, 564–575.

Davidson, A. 1990. *In the Wake of the Exxon Valdez*. San Francisco, CA: Sierra Books.

Drabek, T. E. 1986. *Human System Responses to Disaster: An Inventory of Sociological Findings*. New York: Springer-Verlag.

Dyer, C. L., Gill, D. A., & Picou, J. S. 1992. Social Disruption and the Valdez Oil Spill: Alaskan Natives in a Natural Resource Community. *Sociological Spectrum, 12*, 105–126.

Edelstein, M. R. 1989. Psychosocial Impacts on Trial: The Case of Hazardous Waste Disposal. In D. Peck (Ed.), *Psychosocial Effects of Hazardous Toxic Waste Disposal on Communities* (pp. 153–176). Springfield, IL: Charles C. Thomas.

Edelstein, M. R. 1988. *Contaminated Communities: The Social and Psychological Impacts of Residential Toxic Exposure*. Boulder, CO: Westview.

Erikson, K. 1994. *A New Species of Trouble: Explorations in Disaster, Trauma, and Community*. New York: W. W. Norton.

Erikson, K. 1976. *Everything in its Path: Destruction of Community in the Buffalo Creek Flood*. New York: Simon and Schuster.

Freudenburg, W. R., & Jones, T. R. 1991. Attitudes and Stress in the Presence of Technological Risk: A Test of the Supreme Court Hypothesis. *Social Forces, 69*(4), 1143–1168.

Greer, E., & Freedman, W. 1989. *Toxic Tort Litigation*. New York: Prentice Hall Publishers.

Keeble, J. 1991. *Out of the Channel: The Exxon Valdez Oil Spill in Prince William Sound*. New York: Harper Collins Publishers.

Kroll-Smith, J. S., & Couch, S. R. 1993. Technological Hazards: Social Responses as Traumatic Stressors. In J. P. Wilson & B. Raphael (Eds.), *International Handbook of Traumatic Stress Syndromes* (pp. 79–91). New York: Plenum.

Kroll-Smith, J. S., & Couch, S. R. 1990. *The Real Disaster is Above Ground*. Lexington: University of Kentucky Press.

Levine, A. 1982. *Love Canal: Power, Politics and People*. Lexington, MA: Lexington Publishing.

Lodwick, D. 1994, Spring. Attacks on Sociological Research. *The Useful Sociologist, 16*, 3,5,13.

Lord, N. 1992. *Darkened Waters*. Homer, AL: Homer Society of Natural History and Pratt Museum.

Madden, M. S. 1992. *Toxic Torts Deskbook*. Boca Raton, FL: Lewis Publishers.

Marshall, E. 1993, July 16. Court Orders "Sharing" of Data. *Science, 261*, 284–286.

Ott, R. 1994. *Sound Truth: Exxon's Manipulation of Science and the Significance of the Exxon Valdez Oil Spill*. Anchorage, AK: Greenpeace.

Palinkas, L. A., Petterson, J. S., Russell, J., & Downs, M. A. 1993. Community Patterns of Psychiatric Disorders After the *Exxon Valdez* Oil Spill. *American Journal of Psychiatry, 150*(10), 1517–1523.

Picou, J. S. 1995, October. Sociology and Compelled Disclosure: Protecting Respondent Confidentiality in the Court. Presidential address, Mid-South Sociological Association, Mobile, AL.

Picou, J. S. 1984. Ecological, Physical, Economic, Sociological and Psychological Assessment of the Illinois Central Gulf Train Derailment. *Sociological Assessment*, Vol. 5. Baton Rouge, LA: Gulf South Research Institute.

Picou, J. S., & Gill, D. A. 1993, October. Socio-Toxic Syndrome at a Suburban Superfund Site: A Case Study. Paper presented at the annual meeting of the Mid-South Sociological Association, Montgomery, AL.

Picou, J. S., Gill, D. A., Dyer, C. L., & Curry, E. W. 1992. Stress and Disruption in an Alaskan Fishing Community: Initial and Continuing Impacts of the Exxon Valdez Oil Spill. *Industrial Crisis Quarterly, 6*(3), 235–257.

Rent, G. 1993. Confidentiality in Social Research Threatened. *The Southern Sociologist, 25*(2), 1,2.

Rosenberg, M. 1994. Science in the Courthouse. *Technology in Society, 16*(1), 1–7.

U.S. District Civil Subpoena, No. A89-095 (Alaska 1992).

U.S. District VII Court, Southern Division, No. 92-0072-RV-C (Alabama 1993).

13

Housing the Homeless: The Sociologist as Expert and Activist

Hilary Silver, Steven Fischbach, and Judith Kaye

Americans have no constitutional right to housing. Indeed, many cities legally limit the time people may remain in shelters or withhold shelter altogether to minimize their homeless populations. In response, advocates for the homeless have devised innovative legal strategies to compel state and local governments to insure adequate shelter for those who have none. For example, a consent decree compelled New York City to shelter the homeless on the basis of state, rather than federal constitutional, law (*Callahan v. Carey* 1981; *McCain v. Koch* 1986). Local ordinances in Minnesota, West Virginia, Philadelphia, New Haven, and the District of Columbia are providing some shelter rights, although litigation often is necessary to enforce them. People receiving public assistance in Massachusetts and New Jersey now are also entitled to shelter. (Roisman 1991:203–226; Smizick and Stone 1988).[1]

Although the federal government does not have to construct low income housing where it is needed, it may not discriminate once it embarks on such projects (*Acevedo v. Nassau County* 1974); 42 USC 3612 (1982); 42 USC 3608(d)(5). Therefore, housing lawyers argue: "Viable, race-based claims may be made under state or federal equal protection clauses if discriminatory government policies can be shown to be responsible for the fact that disproportionate numbers of the people who suffer homelessness and hunger — the extremes of poverty — are minorities" (Roisman 1991:210).

In this chapter, we describe a creative use of federal civil rights law — specifically, the Fair Housing Act — to house the homeless (Gelber, Hopp, and Cana 1983). This law was used to deflect racially motivated attempts to scuttle a proposed homeless shelter in Providence, Rhode Island. The plaintiffs in the case, advocates for the homeless, recruited a sociologist committed to racial justice and the provision of affordable housing to serve as an expert witness. Because homeless persons themselves are rarely heard in the courtroom, the sociologist, by attesting to "facts" *on their behalf*, implicitly advocated their position that the shelter should be built and, thus, was acting as a "surrogate activist." Without ever expressing a political opinion about racism or the shelter issue per se, the expert's testimony as to the racial composition of the homeless would have conveyed this intent.

Although the case might have exposed potential tension between community activism and sociological objectivity, the manner in which this dilemma was resolved illustrates the centrality of sociological knowledge in legal findings of racial discrimination. Because the Supreme Court has recognized statistical evidence as a basis for establishing a prima facie case for racial discrimination, sociologists who are certified to present and evaluate statistical information qualify as experts in discrimination cases. Although opponents of the shelter may have sought to discredit the methods by which the statistics were obtained or to introduce statistical evidence about the homeless other than that bearing on "disparate impact," previous rulings in discrimination cases have tended to discount these sorts of objections, especially when supplementary evidence of discriminatory intent exists. In establishing the latter, a sociologist qualified as an expert in race relations also could lend credence to the plaintiffs' argument that shelter opponents were motivated by racial animus.

SOCIOLOGY AND ADVOCACY

A sociologist may choose to study homelessness because he or she deems the problem compelling, but the research itself must conform to methodological requirements. Indeed, innovative sociological methods have been crucial for counting the homeless, thereby giving policy makers an estimate of the problem's scope and causes (Burt 1992; Rossi 1989; Culhane, Dejowski, Ibanez, Needham, and Macchia 1994). That others make use of these findings for purposes of advocacy has no bearing on professional procedure, nor does rendering sociological findings in scientific language mean that they lack rhetorical or persuasive functions (Gusfield 1989). Sociological evidence may yield multiple interpretations and serve varying interests. The symbolic content of social scientific discourse conveyed to others often reflects the social setting in which it is expressed. Thus, when the sociologist presents the "facts" as part of an advocate's case in court, the sociologist indirectly serves as an advocate.

The legitimacy of sociological method and the privilege accorded to scientific discourse bestow greater authority on sociologists than on nonacademic housing advocates even when statistics are being cited that are widely available to the public. Whether in the press, public forums, or open court, sociologists bring an academic imprimatur to bear on "facts" that those without academic credentials find difficult to discover, articulate, interpret, or defend. For example, a content analysis of articles on homelessness in the national press found that "the homeless themselves rarely find a voice in newspapers" and "supportive statements on behalf of the homeless come predominantly from advocacy groups" (Wolch and Dear 1993). Similarly, in the courtroom, sociologists can assist civil rights activists and advocates for the homeless to force municipalities to comply with fair housing laws when deciding on sites for homeless shelters. As the case described below indicates, sociologists can add their technical skills to those of other professionals to advocate for social change on behalf of poorer citizens.

Advocating for the disadvantaged is not, strictly speaking, the sociologist's role. Indeed, one of the fundamental tenets of sociological method is value neutrality. Although critical theories have attacked the assumption of objectivity in social research, sociologists generally have proceeded as if the requisites of scientific method were operative. Sociological evidence often is probabilistic; yet, it also is legitimated if gathered in conformity with disciplinary methodological procedures. *Castaneda v. Partida* (1977) laid out the legal requirements that statistics on racial disparities must meet in order to establish an equal protection violation: "the degree of underrepresentation must be proved by comparing the proportion of the group in the total population to the proportion . . . over a significant period of time" who were affected by a government action. This case itself referred to a major fair housing precedent, *Arlington Heights v. Metropolitan Housing Development Corporation* (1977), that established the "rule of exclusion" in discrimination law: "if a disparity is sufficiently large, then it is unlikely that it is due solely to chance or accident and, in the absence of evidence to the contrary, one must conclude that racial or other class-related factors entered into" the process. Thus, expertise in statistical methods makes it credible to introduce sociological findings as legal evidence of discrimination and to call on sociologists, rather than homeless plaintiffs themselves, as expert witnesses in the courtroom.

This is not to say that sociological knowledge is indifferent to legal or policy issues. Sociological knowledge can and perhaps should serve practical and political purposes (Lynd 1939; Wilson 1993). Rather, moral judgments should not undermine the validity of sociological conclusions. Weber (1949) argued that, although distinguishing between empirical statements of fact and value judgments is difficult, the sociologist's preferences are expressed with special force by letting the facts speak for themselves. To accomplish this, the establishment of empirical facts must be separated from their ethical evaluation. To use Hempel's (1965) terminology, categorical value judgments may dictate the choice of sociological subject matter, but instrumental value judgments, drawing out the expected implications of empirical relationships for policy, can be made without moral or normative bias.

In the shelter suit described below, categorical value judgments influenced both the sociologist's areas of expertise and her decision to testify on behalf of advocates for the homeless. Note that such decisions excluded other categories of evidence that could have been introduced to the detriment of the advocates' argument, such as the mental health, substance abuse, and other behaviors of the homeless. Because these subjects lay outside the sociologist's expertise, it was unnecessary to make a moral judgment about omitting them. Had they been introduced by opposing counsel, the sociologist truthfully could testify that the literature suggested that "client problems" developed as a consequence of severe poverty and homelessness and that the statistics locally available at the time could not distinguish between cause and effect (Jencks 1994).[2] However, if questioned about the policy implications of the statistical evidence she was to present, the opinion that racial minorities would be disproportionately impacted without the shelter would constitute an instrumental value judgment that did not require compromising professional standards of objectivity or the sociologist's normative position. In brief, because sociological knowledge reinforced rather than contradicted the witness's political position, it would not have been necessary to experience a conflict between the roles of professional sociologist and surrogate activist. Before proceeding, a brief comment is in order regarding the use of personal pronouns in this chapter. When we refer to "me" or "my," it is the sociologist expert Hilary Silver speaking.

THE SETTING

Like most cities in the United States, Providence, Rhode Island, experienced a rise in homelessness during the 1980s. Although Providence has a colder climate, more vacant housing, and a smaller minority population than many cities with more homelessness, the city's official shelter population reached 2,119 persons by 1990. During 1987, the city of Providence reported to the U.S. Conference of Mayors that the number of homeless families seeking emergency shelter increased 70 percent, the second highest rise of any major U.S. city (Rhode Island Emergency Food and Shelter Board 1992).[3]

The major force behind this trend was Providence's real estate boom. In the mid-1980s, Providence was among the "hottest" real estate markets in the nation. Housing prices rose more than 30 percent in 1986 and 1987, the largest increase of all major U.S. urban markets. Soaring real estate values rapidly inflated homeowners' perceptions of their wealth and increased their personal stakes in maintaining high property values, but the boom also resulted in rising rents, so that many families could no longer afford their homes. Consequently, the homeless population mushroomed. Although housing values rose in all Providence neighborhoods, the city's homeless population was disproportionately composed of racial minorities.

The largest city of the smallest state was slow to respond to rising homelessness. Sheltering the homeless was largely relegated to an overburdened nonprofit sector supported with federal monies and private donations. Ten small, special purpose shelters sprang up in Providence, usually filled to capacity. Some, like Advent House and the Salvation Army, were restricted to men; others, like Interim House and Sojourner House, sheltered women or, more specifically, battered women and their children. No facility accepted "runaway" youths. The largest shelter housed only 60 persons. Some shelters were church sponsored; others, like those established by organizations dating from the War on Poverty, were supported by charities like the United Way.

In order to disburse private donations and federal emergency or McKinney funds for the homeless, the United Way assembled representatives of these shelters and other social service organizations to form the Rhode Island Emergency Food and Shelter Board (Burt 1992; Rossi 1989:132).[4] In 1988, the board set up its own research committee, still in existence. After a pilot project, the committee collected data on all homeless persons who were shelter residents in the state between July 1989 and June 1990. Each shelter conducted an intake interview to collect basic demographic information, assigning clients an identification number to track them over time and among various shelters in the state. Each shelter also prepared a monthly service record of the number of nights a person was resident in the facility. The monthly data were then centrally compiled to produce an annual report. The tabulated information was made available to the public and to advocates seeking to increase the local supply of shelter.

Statistics based on these data were the foundation for the expert testimony discussed in this chapter. Sociologists specializing in homelessness will recognize that the board's methodology produced figures only on the "sheltered" homeless during the course of one year, not the total number of homeless or potentially homeless persons (Burt 1992:132).[5] The descriptive data also suffer from self-reporting biases. Many seeking shelter may be reluctant to admit to domestic violence, substance abuse, and medical problems.

However, race is probably one of the most reliably recorded characteristics, because the intake interviewer could confirm the client's report. Available data revealed that African-Americans, for example, comprised 14.8 percent of Providence's population but 37.7 percent of the city's homeless (Table 13.1). The racial composition of the homeless population was the key variable in my expert testimony.

TABLE 13.1
Percentage Distribution of Total Population and Sheltered Homeless Population by Race, 1990

	White	Black	Asia	Native American	Other	Hispanic	Total Minority
1990 Census Population							
Rhode Island	89.8	3.9	1.8	0.4	2.5	(4.6)	7.7–14.8
City of Providence	69.9	14.8	5.9	0.9	8.3	(15.5)	21.8–45.6
Sheltered Homeless							
Rhode Island[a]	59.6	24.7	0.7	2.3	3.7	9.1	36.7–40.4
Rhode Island Women	60.0	24.6	0.9	2.7	2.9	8.9	37.1–40.0
Providence Families and Children[b]	38.4	33.8	0.004	3.9	5.2	18.4	56.4–61.6
United States[c]	42.0	44.0	1.000	2.0	1.0	10.0	58.0
U.S. Families and Children	47.0	40.0			5.0	8.0	53.0
Eastern U.S.	30.0	52.0			3.0	15.0	70.0

Sources:
[a]Rhode Island Emergency Food and Shelter Board (1990).
[b]Providence Community Action Program (1988).
[c]U.S. Department of Housing and Urban Development (1989).

THE CASE: FIGHTING NIMBY
TO HOUSE THE HOMELESS

The case under discussion involved a controversy over a proposed homeless shelter that reflected race and class tensions in a gentrifying inner-city neighborhood. To address rising homelessness and the overwhelming burden it placed on nonprofit agencies, a prior mayor, Joseph Paolino, Jr., announced plans in January 1988 to use city funds to develop a comprehensive emergency shelter. Six months later, the city unveiled its proposal to site a shelter for 15 homeless families and 40 homeless single women on Broad Street, a major commercial thoroughfare on Providence's South Side.

The Broad Street site, then occupied by a vacant motorcycle sales and repair shop, was located in the racially mixed neighborhood of Elmwood. In that neighborhood, real estate speculators and gentrifiers had been buying up properties, particularly those with historic or architectural value. The Providence Preservation Society began to funnel national historical preservation funds to local homeowners. Median single-family housing prices in the neighborhood rose rapidly, by as much as 117 percent between 1985 and 1986. Moreover, the profit margin for houses purchased and resold in Elmwood between 1984 and 1986 was 208 percent, the highest of any of the city's neighborhoods during that period.

Shortly after the mayor's announcement, local opposition to the shelter site surfaced. The opponents were mostly young, single, white, middle-class professionals who recently had moved into the neighborhood to purchase and restore historic properties. A group of Elmwood homeowners and business persons organized themselves as the South Side Residents and Business Coalition (SSRBC). The SSRBC mounted a petition drive and letter-writing campaign to city officials and sent out flyers to rally neighborhood opposition to the shelter. Arguing that Elmwood already had enough homeless shelters, the SSRBC maintained that the shelter would cause an influx of crime and prostitution to the area, causing property values to fall. In its literature, the SSRBC reasoned that this decline in property values would turn the neighborhood into "a permanent ghetto" of homeless shelters and public or subsidized housing. Most significantly, they contended that the proposed shelter would lead to an influx of homeless persons who would "upset the precarious balance of social, economic and racial diversity" in the area.

The SSRBC might be viewed as a classic not in my backyard (NIMBY) movement of relatively advantaged citizens rejecting the city-wide "public good" of housing the homeless. NIMBY refers to "the protectionist attitudes of, and exclusionary/oppositional tactics adopted by community groups facing an unwelcome development in their neighborhood" (Wolch and Dear 1993:179). The opposition did reflect the familiar dynamics of "defended neighborhoods" (Suttles 1992). As Fischer has argued, "Many Americans value and enjoy the congeniality of a local community. They often resist that same local community, yet, when it constrains their interests. . . . Neighborhood organizations, for example, typically awaken when outsiders threaten residents' safety or wealth. Otherwise, the energy that drives them usually rests dormant" (Fischer 1991:89).

NIMBY conflicts exhibit certain regularities. During the initial stage, a small, vocal minority living within a few blocks of the proposed development expresses its antagonism to a project "in the rawest, bluntest terms, often reflecting an irrational, unthinking opposition" (Wolch and Dear 1993:181). Local residents and businesses may write letters, distribute petitions, demonstrate, and form neighborhood opposition groups. Surveys provide a standard profile of the NIMBY opponent as "a high-income, married, male homeowner, well educated and with a professional position, living in a large city or its suburbs" (Wolch and Dear 1993:191). As the conflict matures, supporters and opponents move to a public forum, like a zoning hearing, in which "the rhetoric of opposition becomes ostensibly more rational and objective," making reference to property values, personal security, and neighborhood amenity (Wolch and Dear 1993:181). It is said that facilities act as magnets for undesirables or that the neighborhood is already saturated or overburdened with low income housing or service institutions. Finally, victory in NIMBY disputes may be inconclusive, but it tends to go to the group with the most perseverance.

NIMBY opposition is not confined to homeless shelters. Local residents have mobilized against the siting of jails, drug treatment centers, halfway houses, group homes, boarder and AIDS babies, highways, garages, incinerators, and other "noxious" land uses. As Plotkin's analysis of land use control conflicts shows: "When it comes to potential changes in the class composition and economic value of neighborhoods, residents turn sharply against public and private developers who want to bring in people of a higher or lower social rank or, often as not, people of a different color or background" (Plotkin 1987:21, 31). Survey evidence provides the standard profile of the client least acceptable to the public: "a young, single male of minority status and low income, with a social disability that is chronic and visible, is associated with dangerous and unpredictable behavior, and for which he himself can be blamed" (Wolch and Dear 1993:189) — in short, the stereotypical homeless person.

Providence was not the only city to experience conflicts between residents and the homeless. For example, Fort Lauderdale homeowners considered spraying chemicals on beachfront trash cans to keep out "transients." In Los Angeles, the homeless and homeless shelters were targets of widespread vigilante action and police harassment.

However, the SSRBC went beyond the typical class-oriented NIMBY movement in one important respect, namely, the racial innuendo of their discourse. Opponents of the shelter used rhetoric that implied a keen awareness that a disproportionate share of the homeless in Providence were African-American, Native American, and Latino. Since 1989, as the total homeless population in the state began to decline, the number of homeless Hispanics increased sharply, from 8.8 percent to 12.8 percent of all shelter clients. Native American and African-American representation fell slightly (Rhode Island Emergency Food and Shelter Board 1992).

This also is true nationally. Because poverty is higher among minorities, so, too, is homelessness. African-Americans are three times more likely to be homeless than one would expect from their population size (Burt 1992:67, 79; Rossi 1993).[6] In New York City, 94 percent of single shelter residents are members of minority groups. There, too, local communities have increasingly resisted the siting of homeless shelters (New York City Commission on the Homeless 1992).

When the Providence Community Action Program (ProCAP), the city agency Providence designated to develop the shelter, called a community meeting to discuss it, SSRBC members turned out in force. The opponents who testified, virtually all whites, demanded that the agency cancel its plans, advancing the same arguments expressed in SSRBC literature.

Shelter supporters also attended to urge the city to continue with its plans for the shelter. They included members of Project BASIC (Bring Advocacy and Strategy into the Community), a community organization affiliated with John Hope Settlement House and dedicated to improving housing conditions for low income and minority citizens.[7] The spokesperson of Project BASIC, in urging the ProCAP to build the shelter, suggested that the opponents were motivated by racial bias because they feared that an influx of homeless persons would "tip" the neighborhood from its current racial balance into a predominantly minority-inhabited "ghetto." However, opponents shouted down the BASIC spokesperson and other supporters of the shelter, even interrupting the city-hired architects during the presentation of the shelter's architectural plans.

Eventually, the community opposition pressured the city of Providence to withdraw its commitment of public funds to construct the Elmwood shelter. Despite intensifying homelessness, the ProCAP took no action until three months after the community hearing. At that time, the mayor announced a new site for the homeless shelter: a playground adjacent to a public housing project in another area of Providence. By agreeing to develop the shelter on the new site and cancelling its development plans in Elmwood, the ProCAP forfeited more than $400,000 in federal and state funds earmarked for the Broad Street shelter. This loss of money proved fatal. The sponsors never again were able to raise the $400,000 once allocated for the Broad Street shelter, and to this day, no shelter — even on the new site — has been built. Opposition to the Broad Street shelter was not unique. In the two years preceding and following the announcement of the Broad Street shelter, five other facilities proposed for homeless families and individuals in Providence encountered stiff community opposition. Of those five projects, only two were completed.

In the past, NIMBY opposition to publicly subsidized housing was successfully combated with fair housing legislation. Thus, legal precedents from housing segregation suits were readily available for resisting opposition to homeless shelters. The decision to abandon the Elmwood shelter led Project BASIC to file a civil suit against the city of Providence and the ProCAP to compel them to honor their commitment. Two of us, Steve Fischbach and Judith Kaye, were the legal services lawyers who devised and pressed the case for their client; they recruited Hilary Silver to serve as an expert witness. Like many other suits to shelter the homeless, the case was successfully settled on the morning of the trial date, resulting in a consent decree.

THE ROLE OF "EXPERTS" IN
RACIAL DISCRIMINATION CASES

Most NIMBY opponents argue their case as if it were a traditional land-use dispute. Zoning and similar laws tend to favor private property owners and arguments about public health and safety (Plotkin 1987). As mentioned, however, the NIMBY sentiment that fuels community opposition to homeless shelters often is motivated by racial prejudice. During the days of new public housing and Section 8 construction, such opposition to siting low income housing in white middle-class communities was common (*Rizzo v. Residents Advisory Board* 1977; *Project B.A.S.I.C. Tenants Union v. R.I. Housing and Mortgage Finance Corporation* 1986). As funds for constructing new low income housing developments were virtually eliminated in the Reagan years, racial opposition to low income housing in white middle-class areas subsided but resurfaced when funds were made available for building temporary shelter for homeless low income individuals and families.

In the past, racial opposition to low income public or Section 8 housing was overcome when supporters and sponsors of that housing sued under the federal Fair Housing Act to get the housing built. The Fair Housing Act bans both intentional and effective discrimination on the basis of race or color, sex, religion, country of national origin, handicap, and familial status. If the supporters of low income housing can prove that opposition is motivated by racially discriminatory intent, (*United States v. City of Parma* 1980) or if a decision to cancel proposed low income housing has a discriminatory effect, that is, the decision "actually or predictably results in racial discrimination" (*Huntington*

Branch NAACP v. Town of Huntington 1988),[8] they will have established a prima facie violation of the Fair Housing Act.

Project BASIC and their lawyers had experience in challenging decisions to cancel low income housing projects in the face of racially motivated community opposition. Three years prior to the Broad Street shelter controversy, Project BASIC brought suit under the Fair Housing Act to restore funding for a 42-unit Section 8 housing project proposed in Providence's whitest neighborhood. This approach proved successful, and the funds for the project were restored a few years after the lawsuit was filed. Thus, Project BASIC decided to use the same strategy to restore funds for the canceled Broad Street shelter.

Project BASIC's innovative decision to use the Fair Housing Act was not without its risks. The host neighborhood for the shelter, Elmwood, was not a predominantly white neighborhood, and shelters were located in adjoining neighborhoods. However, almost all of the shelter opponents were white, and many of the white opponents had moved recently into the neighborhood to purchase and restore historic houses. In order to prevail at trial, Project BASIC needed to produce certain evidence to establish a prima facie Fair Housing violation. First, Project BASIC had to produce evidence showing that the opponents to the shelter were motivated by racial animus. It did not need to establish that race was the only reason for changing the site. Second, Project BASIC needed to furnish evidence showing that the homeless population was disproportionately composed of racial minorities and that the decision to cancel the Broad Street shelter would have been of more harm to racial minorities than whites.

The use of the Fair Housing Act also had its legal risks. Advocates had successfully used the Fair Housing Act to challenge discriminatory siting decisions of low income housing, but the Fair Housing Act never had been used to challenge discriminatory siting decisions of shelters that provided temporary housing for the homeless. Project BASIC and their attorneys made the innovative legal argument that shelters provided "housing" regulated under the Fair Housing Act. Citing cases in which the Fair Housing Act was applied to less traditional forms of housing, such as group homes for children (*United States v. Hughes Memorial Home* 1975) and rooming houses (*Williams v. Adams* 1985), Project BASIC urged the court to allow it to present its case under the Fair Housing Act.

Prior to trial, the defendants filed a motion to dismiss Project BASIC's complaint, arguing that the shelter decision did not fall under the purview of the Fair Housing Act. The court rejected the defendants' arguments, ruling that "the plaintiff's claim that Pro-CAP gave in to racially motivated pressures when it decided to relocate the shelter does state a recognized theory under the Fair Housing Act" (*Project BASIC v. Kemp* 1990).

Having survived the defendants' attempt to have the case thrown out of court, the shelter advocates had to gather evidence to establish a Fair Housing Act violation. Project BASIC, from its own experience in housing issues, understood the racial nature of the statements made by shelter opponents. To demonstrate discriminatory intent, Project BASIC collected copies of letters sent by shelter opponents to city officials and copies of leaflets and petitions circulated by the SSRBC. As evidence of the discriminatory effect of changing the shelter site, Project BASIC also gathered available statistics on the racial composition of persons and families who sought emergency shelter in Providence and Rhode Island.[9]

All of the data initially were collected by third parties for purposes other than the lawsuit. Aside from local needs assessment, the main impetus to create a centralized clearinghouse for information on the homeless of Providence came from the federal government's reporting requirements in return for shelter subsidies. Thus, public and nonprofit agencies surveyed the homeless primarily for financial reasons. However, once statistics were compiled and published, their interpretation could serve other goals as well. Specifically, reading the racial composition of the homeless as evidence that the absence of a shelter would have discriminatory impact required bringing legal, political, and sociological sensibilities to the raw data.

Although Project BASIC members and staff were prepared to testify on the issues of discriminatory effect and intent, the lawyers were concerned that the court would not give their testimony sufficient weight to establish a Fair Housing Act violation. The lawyers urged Project BASIC to find a person with sufficient academic credentials who could interpret the shelter opponents' statements and relevant statistical data in a convincing matter. Consequently, Project BASIC approached me and asked if I would interpret and vouch for the accuracy of the compiled information. I agreed to assist them.

THE SOCIOLOGIST AS EXPERT

By shifting the terms of the shelter conflict from a land-use dispute to a question of discrimination, sociological knowledge became more central to the case. As mentioned, fair housing law has recognized statistical information as evidence of discrimination, and experts commonly are used in major fair housing cases to prove both discriminatory impact and intent. The social scientist's statistical skills are particularly well suited to demonstrating discriminatory impact, that is, the differential effect of policies or actions on racial or other groups. For example, in *United States v. Yonkers Board of Education* (1985), expert testimony was used to establish the degree of racial segregation in Yonkers in support of the plaintiff's contention that city officials acted to preserve existing patterns of racial segregation when approving sites for subsidized housing. The sociological rhetoric of "segregation" was, thus, influential in establishing the recognition of data on the racial composition of a city's census tracts as legal evidence. Similarly, in *Rizzo v. Residents Advisory Board* (1976), plaintiff's expert explained that the cancellation of a public housing project in a white Philadelphia neighborhood had a discriminatory effect on racial minorities, given both the racial composition of the public housing waiting list and the existing patterns of racial segregation in Philadelphia. The sociologist in the Providence shelter suit was needed to make a similar statement about the discriminatory effect of a policy, namely, not to build a homeless shelter.

The value of the sociologist as an expert witness in this discrimination case was the facility with which I could document and account for group differences with statistical data (differential impact) and my general expertise in social group relations in U.S. society (discriminatory intent). Although sociologists may subscribe to one of any number of race relations theories, the law recognizes only one standard — a statistical one — for demonstrating discriminatory effect. However, sociologists may testify to many different causes for deliberate racial discrimination. For example, some theories emphasize the historical sources of racial bias, particularly in slavery or colonialism. Others locate the causes in economic or status competition among groups. Social psychological theories of prejudice may be relevant, especially the role of racial preferences in "tipping" integrated neighborhoods toward resegregation. Institutionalized forms of racism, such as those taken for granted in language and cultural practices, also can illustrate how group subordination persists in U.S. society. Thus, sociologists can attest to the systematic sources of discrimination that individuals can experience only on a personal basis.

In the shelter case, the sociologist could be called upon to comment on the use of racial code words, such as "ghetto," referring to the levels, sources, and meanings of racial segregation in U.S. society. Based on my previous research, I could testify to the extent of racial inequality in income and housing conditions. It was also helpful that I was acquainted with the problems of homelessness and low income housing in Providence and the nation as a whole. In this area, too, facility with numbers was helpful to the advocates' case. My firsthand research experience with public housing tenants, my published articles on public housing, limited-equity cooperatives, homelessness, and poverty, and my more general facility with statistics were resources I could use in testimony. I also had some prior experience as an expert witness at a Congressional hearing, where I presented evidence to protect the rights of public housing tenants from privatization policies pursued by the Reagan administration.

The plaintiffs expected the judge to rule that statistical data were useful, in fact, essential, to decide whether or not the shelter site would have a disparate impact on minorities. It was agreed that the parties did agree that the plaintiffs could submit to the judge various homelessness reports and statistics upon which I would have relied. This simplified and shortened the testimony that would be needed. However, the legal services attorneys reasoned that the sociologist's contribution would be to present and interpret the data in such a way as to persuade the judge that racial discrimination did, indeed, take place. Project BASIC also hoped that having an expert testify in person would give their case more credibility and, in contrast to mere statistical documentation, would humanize the problems of homelessness and racial disadvantage, persuading the court to assume a moral responsibility toward people without shelter.

The lawyers prepared me for direct examination. I was to explain why the opinion of a doctor in sociology would be helpful to the court in determining whether canceling the shelter constituted unlawful discrimination. If I failed to convince the court of the usefulness of my testimony, I would not be permitted to testify. The following line of questions illustrates how the lawyers would likely have proceeded to demonstrate the usefulness of my testimony to the issues at trial.

Discriminatory Intent

Q: You have testified as to your educational background in sociology, and your professional work in that field of study. As a result of your educational background and professional work, are you aware of any problems that sponsors of homeless shelters have had in finding suitable sites for their facilities?

Q: And has one of those problems been community opposition to siting shelters?

Q: Is there a body of scholarly literature on the subject of community opposition to siting homeless shelters?

Q: Please summarize for the Court, if you can, what the literature on this subject is.

Q: Have you yourself conducted any research on the subject of community opposition to siting homeless shelters?

Q: Could you explain to the Court what your research on this subject has revealed?

Q: Based on your experience and training, has some of the community opposition to homeless shelters been motivated by the race of the prospective residents?

Q: What facts would you look for to make a determination as to whether community opposition to a homeless shelter was racially motivated?

Q: How do persons motivated by racial bias express their opposition to homeless shelters?

Q: Typically, is there a particular point in the siting process when racial opposition begins to manifest itself?

Q: Can you give the Court some specific instances where you determined the presence of racial opposition to the siting of homeless shelters?

Discriminatory Effect

Q: You have testified that experts in your field typically rely on certain statistical data to show that certain practices have or do not have a discriminatory impact on racial minorities, and that the study of such statistics is referred to as "disparate impact analysis." Based on your experience and training, is disparate impact analysis utilized to prove racial discrimination in housing?

Q: Could you list the types of housing controversies in which disparate impact analysis would be appropriate?

Q: Would disparate impact analysis be appropriate to determining whether the decision to cancel the Broad Street Shelter had a discriminatory impact on racial minorities?

Q: Is disparate impact analysis the best method of determining whether the decision to cancel the Broad Street Shelter had a discriminatory impact on racial minorities?

Q: What other methods would someone of your training and experience utilize to determine whether the decision to cancel the Broad Street Shelter had a discriminatory impact on racial minorities?

Q: In siting the Broad Street Shelter, what body of data would you examine in performing a disparate impact analysis of the cancellation of the Broad Street Shelter?

Q: Of what relevance is that data to your performance of disparate impact analysis of the Broad Street Shelter?

Although the testimony would refer to relatively simple data in the form of frequency distributions and cross-tabulations, the numbers still left some room for misinterpretation. For example, the attorney — the layperson in this context — needed some clarification about certain concepts basic to the discipline. For example, cross-tabulations can be read with either marginal distribution as the basis for the cell percentages. During trial preparation, it initially was unclear whether, in examining the association between homelessness and race, I should refer to the representation of minorities among the homeless or the representation of the homeless among minorities. I examined the row numbers with Kaye to determine if the relative proportions of the minority and white populations that were homeless were irrelevant to the question of differential impact, under the criteria outlined in *Castaneda*. Obviously, even if the numbers of white and minority homeless persons were identical, a smaller *share* of the majority population than of the minority population would be homeless.

A majority of the homeless in Providence, a city with a small minority population, did not need to be members of minority groups to show that the shelter decision disproportionately affected minorities. To argue that resiting the shelter would negatively affect minorities, it was necessary to compare a specific racial differential: the percentage of the Providence homeless who were minority (as opposed to white), to the minority share of the Providence population. It also was necessary to compute chi-square statistics to indicate the level of probability at which the racial differential could be attributed to chance.

Other than this occasional clarification, the task of preparing testimony in this case was fairly straightforward. Although the sociologist's presentation at the trial would be brief, it would be essential to the case, providing the judge with a road map to the statistical evidence. The lawyers' role then would be to connect the "facts" presented by the sociologist and other witnesses to the legal conclusion that unlawful discrimination had occurred.

However, in the crush of preparing for trial, the lawyers overlooked the need to prepare me for cross-examination. I was simply advised to "tell the truth" as I knew it. Fischbach told me, "your first obligation to the truth is in your role as U.S. citizen. Advocacy comes in with the choice of client, not with the content of the testimony." Nevertheless, my "truth," like all truths, was selective. First, there were limits to my knowledge of the sociological evidence and literature. Second, the statistics were limited by the nature of the data, whose quality rested upon third parties. There was no way to ascertain whether the racial composition of the unsheltered homeless was similar to that of the shelter population, nor could I testify directly about the rigor and reliability with which shelter statistics were collected.

Third, there is the issue of what Weber called "inconvenient facts" (Weber 1949:145). Sociologists could conceivably use statistical evidence omitted from my testimony to argue that characteristics of the homeless other than their race were the basis for the opponents' objections to the shelter. In *Castaneda*, for example, the population differential between Hispanics and Anglos was challenged unsuccessfully on the grounds that the census counted undocumented aliens and that only literate citizens above a certain age should be considered. Analogously, the defendants could have asked me about the incidence of mental illness, drug abuse, or criminal records among the homeless to deflect the issue from race. I did not need to volunteer these "facts," but on cross-examination or rebuttal, any of these reservations could have weakened my testimony. Although I had considered how I might respond to these issues, the defendants could, under certain conditions, have forced me to choose between sociological objectivity and advocacy for the homeless.

Happily, such a decision was unnecessary. Most lawsuits, including civil rights cases, are resolved without a trial, either through settlement or because of a judge's determination that one side prevails on purely legal grounds. In this suit, the parties did not settle the case until the last minute, and both sides had to prepare for trial. To accommodate the sociologist's teaching duties and because court proceedings are often delayed or canceled at the last minute, the attorney agreed to have the sociologist "on call," ready to come to court at a phone call's notice. However, as it turned out, the parties in the litigation ultimately did negotiate a settlement on the morning of the trial.

The settlement involved an agreement by the city to commit $200,000 and a vacant building to Homeless Action for Necessary Development for creation of a new transitional housing facility. The original shelter was to be completed by October 1992, although it was to be on the playground adjacent to the public housing project in the Hartford Park area rather than on the initially planned Elmwood site. Finally, the city agreed to write into its housing plans and policies stronger language about nondiscrimination in siting homeless facilities and low income housing and agreed to give Project BASIC, the plaintiffs, more formal input into its planning decisions. The attorneys had little doubt that the readiness to go to trial was a major factor leading to the successful settlement and that the sociologist played a key role in this outcome.

Unfortunately, several years later, the city has yet to live up to the consent decree. As is common in discrimination cases, the defendants made symbolic changes and halfhearted efforts to fulfill their obligations. Although project BASIC is formally involved in city plans for homeless and low income housing, neither shelter has been built. Winning a judgment does not guarantee its enforcement.

CONCLUSION: SOCIOLOGICAL TESTIMONY AS ADVOCACY

The denouement of the homeless shelter lawsuit illustrates the need for perseverance in the pursuit of housing for the homeless. Despite the successful legal settlement, the case has yet to produce any shelter for the homeless of Providence. Community activists, like sociologists and attorneys who assist them, must be patient and relentless in pursuing their goals outside the courtroom as well as within. Fischbach and Silver continue to work together for a South Providence community development corporation developing low income cooperative housing for the formerly homeless.

In the public sphere, the political struggle proceeds. The very construction of a social problem called "homelessness" reflects the political strategies of community activists and organizations providing services to those without shelter. Combating homelessness selectively directs attention to the inadequate supply of affordable housing, a theme "with a wide appeal, especially to those who experienced high housing prices directly as would-be purchasers or renters in the housing markets of the 1980s" (Rossi 1993:296). Although this discourse is useful in winning allies for the cause in court and the larger society, it also downplays individual problems, like substance abuse, and, especially, the ultimate cause of homelessness, that is, destitution. The strategic omission of these "facts" from the sociologist's testimony — their irrelevance to the legal case — was yet another, more subtle, form of advocacy.

Serving as a "surrogate activist" need not come into conflict with the role of expert witness. In the shelter case, the evidence of minority overrepresentation among the homeless largely spoke for itself. Insofar as the federal government was willing to accept it, the information collected was recognized as legitimate. To counter objections to shelter-based data, the sociologist could have referred to studies of the unsheltered homeless in selected cities and the newly collected 1990 census data. If arguments that poverty causes the subsequent personal problems of the homeless had been insufficiently persuasive, one could have always pled to ignorance. Sociologists in general and this expert witness in particular could not be expected to know everything that may be necessary to advocate a case for the homeless.

Nevertheless, poorer citizens are at a greater disadvantage than the professional sociologist in terms of the financial resources, time, political influence, and technical expertise necessary to influence the delivery and spatial distribution of urban public services. As Fischer notes, "Although new politics and new laws, such as required 'impact' assessments, empowered many low-income neighborhoods — it is hard to imagine that Robert Moses could bulldoze the Bronx today — neighborhood power is still more easily and more often exercised by the same sorts of advantaged people who protect their exclusive suburbs, some of whom now live in gentrified city quarters" (Fischer 1991:88). When low income community residents lack the formal credentials of their adversaries, they cannot qualify as expert witnesses on their own behalf. They also may lack the resources to hire others who do qualify as such. In such circumstances, the sociologist can serve as a surrogate community activist and, with legal guidance, offer his or her expertise in preparing an antidiscrimination case on behalf of disadvantaged minority communities.

Antidiscrimination laws, such as the Fair Housing Act, are an important but frequently overlooked resource in attempts to pressure city governments into equitable redistribution policies and to fight NIMBY politics. Such battles often take place around issues in which the law protects private property to the disadvantage of the poor. Civil rights legislation can even the playing field and serve as a political tool empowering the minority poor. Although the goal of the shelter lawsuit was to increase the supply of housing for the homeless, the case was made possible by the homeless' racial composition and the opponents' injudicious use of racial code words in fighting the siting decision. Thus, a sociologist conversant with the dynamics of racial inequality or discrimination can contribute to the enforcement of civil rights laws and to the redistribution of local resources for housing or other public uses.

By serving as an expert witness on behalf of low income community advocates, even in the language of "science," sociologists themselves fill the role of community activist. However objective and scientific the sociological interpretation of legal evidence may seem, expert testimony in an adversarial legal system serves a cause by definition. It publicly reveals one's political preferences — to the joy of some and the dismay of others. Attempts to portray a sociologist as an advocate rather than an expert may be unavoidable, if only because the advocates invited the testimony. However, credible sociological testimony must strive for objectivity, or the purpose of requesting it will be undermined. Allowing political passions to overwhelm professional judgment then becomes self-defeating.

The shelter case presented here was constructed around an argument about racial discrimination, not homelessness per se. This largely excluded uncomfortable lines of questioning about the behavior of the homeless. Nevertheless, if I had been cross-examined about "inconvenient facts" and placing professional integrity into conflict with political judgments, I would have come down on the side of professional integrity. Trying to twist the "facts" on one aspect of the homeless would not help the cause when the same source of data was the basis for another assertion about the homeless.

In bringing the discipline to bear upon community affairs, sociologists may face other choices between the role of surrogate activist and that of impartial professional expert. If they serve as expert witnesses, sociologists should anticipate such cross-pressures and, as Weber (1949) insisted, seek clarity and inner consistency in their own political positions.

NOTES

1. In the New Haven case, a historian served as an expert witness as to the traditional inclusion of shelter among the provisions that a community must provide for its indigent people.

2. This was the consensus at the time of the lawsuit. Since then, a few notable sociologists have attributed homelessness partly to deinstitutionalization and crack usage.

3. By 1991, the number of clients in Greater Providence was 2,260. Since 1989, the number of clients seeking shelter in the state has fallen somewhat, from 6,035 to 4,912. However, the number of shelter nights provided and the average length of stay rose.

4. Prior to the passage of the Stewart B. McKinney Homeless Assistance Act of 1987, federal funds to support the homeless were provided under the Federal Emergency Management Agency. Under the McKinney Act, the Department of Housing and Urban Development disburses federal funds through a local agency

United States v. City of Parma, 494 F. Supp. 1949 (N.D. Ohio 1980), aff'd 661 F.2d
    576–77, reh'g denied, 669 F.2d 1100, cert. denied, 456 U.S. 926, reh'g denied,
    456 U.S. 1012.
United States v. Hughes Memorial Home, 396 F. Supp. 544 (W.D. Va. 1975).
United States v. Yonkers Board of Education, 624 F. Supp. 1276, n. 8 (S.D. N.Y. 1985).
Williams v. Adams, 625 F. Supp. 256 (N.D. Ill. 1985).

Afterword

Kai Erikson

As one can see from the very interesting set of chapters gathered here, the range of issues on which sociologists are now invited to testify in courts of law is immense. On the evidence presented here alone, sociologists are being called upon:

To design and conduct surveys. (What is the community standard against which a book or film can be judged obscene? How far has prejudicial pretrial publicity reached out into a given locality?)

To analyze and evaluate existing data. (Do public records reflect patterns of age or race discrimination in hiring practices? Do they suggest that women are being paid less for work requiring equivalent skill and effort?)

To draw life history profiles of persons whose fates are being decided in legal arenas. (Do special circumstances in the life of a convicted felon argue for a reduced sentence? Can one find common themes in the lives of battered women that help explain particular acts or patterns of behavior?)

To describe the cultural basis of given social practices and to interpret the meaning of those practices for people of varying ethnic backgrounds. (Should a person be prosecuted for first-degree murder if she commits a homicide that the norms of her native culture proscribe? Do the terms "alcoholic" or "abusive" mean the same thing in Irish Catholic as in Iranian Muslim households?)

To develop models that can portray and predict behavior (as in the crime foreseeability model noted in Chapter 10 in this volume).

In my own case, to add one more item to the list, I have spent a good deal of time over the past 20 years doing research on and then testifying about the traumatic injuries that both individual persons and communal structures can sustain as the result of widespread disasters.

The variety of sociological contributions to the life of the law, then, has been very considerable, but I think it is fair to say that those of us who get involved in these matters share an intellectual perspective — a disciplinary mind-set — that is often hard to get across in legal settings. This is partly because we have developed a way of describing concepts and of reporting findings that is not easily converted into the languages of the courtroom, but it is mainly because it is our task to look for patterns and consistencies in everyday social life that are not obvious to people who peer through different sets of disciplinary lenses. The chapters in this volume offer a number of examples. I would like to offer two more by way of bringing things to a close, both of them instances in which the sociological mind-set suggested conclusions that stood in sharp contrast to other mind-sets that had been introduced to the proceedings in question.

First, it is a well-known and easily established fact that people in general share a pervasive fear of radiation. A question often raised in legal hearings dealing with nuclear power or nuclear wastes is whether or not that dread should be understood as "irrational." The usual legal mind-set, informed by the cold calculations of cost-benefit analysis, reasons more or less as follows: Radiation has produced very few certi-fied injuries or deaths when compared, say, with automobile accidents, and that being so, the apprehension people feel is out of all sensible proportion. It is, thus, irrational. The problem with that reckoning, as it happens, is that people would much rather risk straightforward auto-mobile collisions than the slow invasion of cancer cells and, more to the point, would do almost anything to avoid the toxic poisoning of their children, those born and those yet to be born. Is this unreasonable? Clearly not. However, how can one convey this to a jury that has just been exposed to the confident cadences of an economist explaining what "the science of" cost-benefit analysis shows? I once guessed out loud in a courtroom that most parents would rather board an airplane that had one in 100 chances of crashing than place one of their own children on an airplane that had one in 1,000 chances of crashing. It seemed to me that everyone in the courtroom nodded in agreement, even though what I was describing was, technically, irrational. The heart simply operates by a different arithmetic. Now, this parallel is far from exact, as the opposing attorney did a good job of pointing out, so I was lucky to get away with it, but even with as obvious a device as this one, the point is hard to make.

Second, lawyers are paid to make expert witnesses look foolish, even when, as in the above instance, they know all too well what the expert is trying to say. However, there are times when the opposing lawyers genuinely do not understand the social drift of the expert's testimony. The following is an exchange between a truly frustrated attorney and a sociologist he was deposing in preparation for a court trial. At issue was the Exxon *Valdez* oil spill and the amount of damage it had done to native villagers who live along the southern coast of Alaska and depend upon fishing both for sustenance and for cultural coherence.

ATTORNEY: Do you know whether salmon were affected by the spill or not?

SOCIOLOGIST: I know that many native people were afraid to harvest salmon and to eat them because they thought they had been contaminated by the oil.

ATTORNEY: Do you have any information as to whether, in fact, salmon were safe to eat?

SOCIOLOGIST: I don't. But I need to add that you are using the word "safe" as it comes from your own vocabulary. Natives judge the quality of the fish by different standards. To them the salmon were not safe no matter what scientists from another culture thought. So I have no idea whether the fish were safe in the first sense, but I know that they were perceived as unsafe in the second.

Whereupon the attorney, exasperated, tries a new approach:

ATTORNEY: Would it make any difference to the opinions you expressed in your report if the natives were *mistaken* as to whether the salmon was safe to eat?

SOCIOLOGIST: I can't answer the question. I don't know what you mean by "mistaken." . . . If white toxicologists in Anchorage declared the salmon to be free of contamination, that would not change the fact that the native people judged the fish to be contaminated and treated it as if it were contaminated. The villagers had a different view of it. *Their* experts declared the fish inedible.

And, after a lunch break:

ATTORNEY: Do you know whether ingestion of crude oil will cause damage to people?

SOCIOLOGIST: We're moving into that same difficult territory again. I'm going to ask you to define "damage."

ATTORNEY: Illness, physical harm.

SOCIOLOGIST: I do not know whether crude oil causes illness by the medical standards of the white residents of Alaska, nor do I know whether it causes illness by the medical standards of the native villagers.

And so it went. From the sociologist's point of view, it was essential to establish that Alutiiq culture had been compromised seriously by the fact that these natives, who have known the ways of salmon for centuries, judged the fish to be diseased and unsafe. From the attorney's point of view, it was essential to establish that the natives were being wrongheaded and superstitious and, thus, were bringing harm to themselves. (It came to me a little later that one of the attorneys sitting on my side of the table came from an Orthodox Jewish family, and if I could live that moment over again, I would say something like, "If toxicologists from Anchorage give Mr. Stein's parents the good news that there is nothing wrong with pork, they are still going to regard it as polluted and corrupt." Alas, the best lines always come after the fact.)

So, our biggest problem, frequently, is to find ways to describe things that seem wholly self-evident to those of us who share a sociological way of looking at the human world. It can be hard. However, I often am amazed at how receptive judges and lawyers and, especially, juries can be to the oblique wisdoms we bring to court, and when that happens, I take real comfort from the thought that our ways of looking at social life sometimes make more sense than we remember.

Cases Cited

42 U.S.C. 3608(e)(5) (1986).

42 U.S.C. 3612 (1982).

Acevedo v. Nassau County, 963, Docket 74-1235 (U.S. Ct. App. 2d Cir. 1974).

Ake v. Oklahoma, 470 U.S. 68 (1985).

Arlington Heights v. Metropolitan Housing Development Corporation, 429 (U.S. Supr. Ct. 252 1977), p. 266, n. 13.

Callahan v. Carey, No. 42582/79 (Sup. Ct. N.Y. County 1981).

Carlock v. State, 609 S.W.2d 787 (Tex. Cr. App. 1980).

Castaneda v. Partida, 430 (U.S. Supr. Ct. 482 1977), p. 1280, n. 18.

Commonwealth v. Trainor, 374 Mass. 796, 374 N.E.2d 1216 (1978).

Court's Instruction, The State of Oklahoma v. [Defendant], Nos. 6, 7, 9, (1989).

Daubert v. Merrell Dow Pharmaceutical, 113 S. Ct. 2786 (1993).

Flynt v. State, 264 S.E.2d 669 (Ga. App. 1980).

Frye v. United States, 293 F.1013,1014 (D.C. Circuit 1923).

Gannilli v. Howard Johnson's Motor Lodge, Inc., 419 F. Supp. 1210, 1212 (E.D.N.Y. 1976).

George v. ISKCON, No. 27-65-75 Orange County Supp. Ct., altered in Cal. App. Ct. No. 0007153 (Cal. App. Ct. 4th Dist., 1989), vacated in 3 S. Ct. 1299 (1991).

Huntington Branch NAACP v. Town of Huntington, 844 F.2d 926 (2d Cir. 1988), aff'd (109 S.Ct. 276 1988).

Isaacs v. Huntington Memorial Hospital, 38 Cal. 3d 112, 211 Cal. Rptr. 356, 695 P.2d 653 (1985).

Katz v. Superior Court, 73 Cal. App. 3d 952, 141 Cal. Rptr. 234 (1977).

Lockhart v. McCree, 106 S. Ct. 1758. (1986).

Lopez v. McDonald's, 193 Cal., App. 3d 495, 23, Cal. Rept. 436 (1987).

McCain v. Koch, 117 A.D.2d 198 (1986), rev'd on other grounds, 70 N.Y. 2d 109 (1987).

McClesky v. Zant, 580 F. Supp. 338 (1984).

Miller v. California, 413 U.S. 15 (1973).

Molko and Leal v. Unification Church, 46 Cal. 3d 1092, 762 p.26 46 (1988).

Molko and Leal v. Unification Church, 179 California Appeals 3d 450 (1986).

New York v. Ferber, 458 U.S. 745 (1982).

People v. Nelson, 410 N.E.2d 476 (Ill. App. 1980).

Pittsburgh Press Club v. United States, 579 F.2d 751 (3d Cir. 1978).

Project B.A.S.I.C. Tenants Union v. R.I. Housing & Mortgage Finance Corporation, 636 F. Supp. 1453 (D. R.I. 1986).

Project BASIC v. Kemp, C.A. 89-0248P (D. R.I. 1990), reprinted in Fair House Fair
    Lending (PH) 15,634.
Residents Advisory Board v. Rizzo, 564 F.2d 126 (3d Cir. 1977), cert. denied, 435 U.S.
    908 (1977).
Rizzo v. Residents Advisory Board, 425 F. Supp. 987 (E.D. Pa. 1976).
Roth v. United States, 354 U.S. 476 (1957).
Saliba v. State, 475 N.E.2d 1181 (Ind. App. 2 Dist. 1985).
Siebert v. Vic Regnier Builders, Inc., 850 P.2d 1332 (Kansas 1993).
United States v. Beneveniste, 564 F.2d 335 (9th Cir. 1977).
United States v. City of Parma, 494 F. Supp. 1949 (N.D. Ohio 1980), aff'd 661 F.2d
    576–77, reh'g denied, 669 F.2d 1100, cert. denied, 456 U.S. 926, reh'g denied,
    456 U.S. 1012.
United States v. Fishman, No. CR-88-0616-DLJ (Northern District of California 1990).
United States v. Hughes Memorial Home, 396 F. Supp. 544 (W.D. Va. 1975).
United States v. Kosminski, 108 S. Ct. 2751 (1988).
United States v. Various Articles of Merchandise, 750 F.2d 596 (7th Cir. 1984).
United States v. Yonkers Board of Education, 624 F. Supp. 1276, n. 8 (S.D. N.Y. 1985).
Vang v. Toyed, 944 F.2d 476 (9th Cir. 1991).
Williams v. Adams, 625 F. Supp. 256 (N.D. Ill. 1985).
Wollersheim v. Scientology, (260 Cal. Rptr. 331, 1989), vacated 3 S. Ct. 1298 (1991).

Selected Bibliography

Acker, J. 1990. Social Science in Supreme Court Criminal Cases and Briefs: The Actual and Potential Contribution of Social Scientists as Amici Curiae. *Law and Human Behavior, 14,* 25–42.

Anthony, D., & Robbins, T. 1992. Law, Social Science and the "Brainwashing" Exception to the First Amendment. *Behavioral Sciences and the Law, 10*(1), 5–29.

Blackman, J. 1986. Potential Uses for Expert Testimony: Ideas Toward the Representation of Battered Women Who Kill. *Women's Rights Law Reporter, 9*(3/4), 227–238.

Bowker, L. H. 1993. Does the Battered Woman Syndrome Exist? In R. J. Gelles & D. R. Loseke (Eds.), *Current Controversies on Family Violence* (pp. 154–165). Beverly Hills, CA: Sage.

Bursik, R. J. 1988. Social Disorganization And Theories Of Crime And Delinquency: Problems And Prospects. *Criminology, 26,* 519–551.

Chesler, M. A., Sanders, J., & Kalmuss, D. S. 1988. *Social Science in Court: Mobilizing Experts in the School Desegregation Cases.* Madison: University of Wisconsin Press.

Choi, C. 1990. Application of a Cultural Defense in Criminal Proceedings. *UCLA Pacific Basin Law Journal, 8,* 80–90.

Erikson, K. 1994. *A New Species of Trouble: Explorations in Disaster, Trauma, and Community.* New York: W. W. Norton.

Evans, S. S., & Scott, J. E. 1983. Social Scientists as Expert Witnesses: Their Use, Misuse, and Sometimes Abuse. *Law and Policy Quarterly, 5,* 181–214.

Faupel, C. E. 1991. *Shooting Dope: Career Patterns Of Hard-Core Heroin Users.* Gainesville: University of Florida Press.

Gelber, B., Hopp, R., & Cana, S. 1983. Recent Developments in Housing Discrimination Law. *Clearinghouse Review, 16*(8), 806.

Giannelli, P. C. 1993. "Junk Science": The Criminal Cases. *Journal of Criminal Law and Criminology, 6,* 105–128.

Glassman, M. B. 1978. Community Standards of Patent Offensiveness: Public Opinion Data and Obscenity Law. *Public Opinion Quarterly, 42,* 161–170.

Greer, E., & Freedman, W. 1989. *Toxic Tort Litigation.* New York: Prentice Hall Publishers.

Hall, M. G., & Brace, P. 1994. The Vicissitudes of Death By Decree: Forces Influencing Capital Punishment Decision Making In State Supreme Courts. *Social Science*

Quarterly, 75, 136–151.

Harris, D. A. 1992. The Constitution and Truth Seeking: A New Theory on Expert Services for Indigent Defendants. *Journal of Criminal Law and Criminology, 83*, 469–529.

Jacoby, J. E., & Paternoster, R. 1982. Sentencing Disparity and Jury Packing: Further Challenges to the Death Penalty. *Journal of Criminal Law and Criminology, 1*, 379–387.

Jasanoff, S. 1993. What Judges Should Know About the Sociology of Science. *Judicature, 77*(2), 77–82.

Kawanishi, Y. 1990. Japanese Mother-child Suicide: The Psychological and Sociological Implications of the Kimura Case. *UCLA Pacific Basin Law Journal, 8*, 32–46.

Kroll-Smith, J. S., & Couch, S. R. 1993. Technological Hazards: Social Responses as Traumatic Stressors. In J. P. Wilson & B. Raphael (Eds.), *International Handbook of Traumatic Stress Syndromes* (pp. 79–91). New York: Plenum.

Miller, N. 1988. Facts, Expert Facts, and Statistics: Descriptive and Experimental Research Methods in Litigation, Part II. *Rutgers Law Review, 40*, 467–520.

Picou, J. S. 1984. Ecological, Physical, Economic, Sociological and Psychological Assessment of the Illinois Central Gulf Train Derailment. *Sociological Assessment*, Vol. 5. Baton Rouge, LA: Gulf South Research Institute.

Richardson, J. T. 1994. Dramatic Changes in American Expert Evidence Law: From *Frye* to *Daubert*, with Special Attention to Implications for Social and Behavioral Science Evidence. *Judicial Review, 2*, 13–36.

Roesch, R., Golding, S., Hans, V., & Reppucci, N. D. 1991. Social Science and the Courts: The Role of Amicus Briefs. *Law and Human Behavior, 15*, 1–11.

Roisman, F. 1991. Establishing a Right to Housing: A General Guide. *Clearinghouse Review, 7*(16), 203.

Scott, J. E. 1991. What Is Obscene? Social Science and the Contemporary Community Standard Test of Obscenity. *International Journal of Law and Psychiatry, 14*, 29–45.

Scott, J. E., Eitle, D. J., & Skovron, S. E. 1990. Obscenity and the Law: Is It Possible for a Jury to Apply Contemporary Community Standards in Determining Obscenity? *Law and Human Behavior, 14*, 139–150.

Shinn, L. 1992. Cult Controversies and the Courts: Some Ethical Issues in Academic Expert Testimony. *Sociological Analysis, 53*, 272–285.

Smizick, F., & Stone, M. 1988. Single Parent Families and a Right to Housing. *The National Lawyers Guild Practitioner, 45*(3), 74.

Walker, L.E.A. 1993. A Battered Woman's Problems Are Social, Not Psychological. In R. J. Gelles & D. R. Loseke (Eds.), *Current Controversies on Family Violence* (pp. 133–153). Beverly Hills, CA: Sage.

Walker, L.E.A. 1986. A Response to Elizabeth Schneider's Describing and Changing: A Woman's Self-Defense Work and the Problem of Expert Testimony on Battering. *Women's Rights Law Reporter, 9*(3/4),223–225.

Walker, L.E.A. 1984. *The Battered Woman Syndrome*. New York: Springer.

Williams, K. D., Bourgeois, M. J., & Croyle, R. T. 1993. The Effects of Stealing Thunder in Criminal and Civil Trials. *Law and Human Behavior, 17*, 597–609.

Wilson, W. J. 1993. Can Sociology Play a Greater Role in Shaping the National Agenda? In William J. Wilson (Ed.), *Sociology and the Public Agenda*. Newbury Park, CA: Sage.

Winfree, L. T., Jr. 1987. All That Glitters is Not Necessarily Gold: Negative Consequences of Expert Witnessing in Criminal Justice. In P. R. Anderson & L. T. Winfree, Jr. (Eds.), *Expert Witnesses; Criminologists in the Courtroom* (pp. 138–153). Albany: State University of New York Press.

Wolfgang, M. E. 1974. The Social Scientist in Court. *Journal of Criminal Law & Criminology, 65*, 239–247.

Woo, D. 1989. The People v. Fumiko Kimura: But Which People? *International Journal of the Sociology of the Law, 17*, 403–428.

Name Index

Subject Index

About the Contributors

Lee H. Bowker is Dean of the College of Behavioral and Social Sciences at Humboldt State University. Among his books in the area of criminology are *Prison Victimization* (Elsevier 1980), *Corrections: The Science and the Art* (1981), *Beating Wife-Beating* (1983), and *Ending the Violence* (1986). He serves as an expert witness in homicide and child custody cases involving battered wives, as well as on a variety of other sociological and criminological topics.

Kai Erikson is the William R. Kenan, Jr., Professor of Sociology and American Studies at Yale University. He is the author of *Everything in Its Path: Destruction of Community in the Buffalo Creek Flood* and *A New Species of Trouble*.

William E. Feinberg is a Professor of Sociology at the University of Cincinnati. His current research interests include an empirical assessment and a computer simulation model of social behavior during escape from the Beverly Hills Supper Club fire, in which 165 persons died; that research is being conducted in collaboration with Norris Johnson. Feinberg also is currently working with a simulation model that considers the potential for neighborhood-based hate crimes, elaborating on Blau's macrostructural theory of intergroup relations.

Steven Fischbach is a staff attorney with Rhode Island Legal Services.

Craig J. Forsyth is a Professor of Sociology at the University of Southwestern Louisiana. He is the author of over 80 journal articles, books, and book chapters. He has worked as a defense mitigation expert in more than 40 first-degree murder cases.

Philip Holley is Associate Professor of Sociology and Criminal Justice at Southwestern Oklahoma State University. Recent research has focused on boot camp programs, lesbian mothers, and rib joints.

Joseph E. Jacoby is a member of the Department of Sociology at Bowling Green State University. He taught in human sciences and criminal justice programs at the University of Houston/Clear Lake and the University of South Carolina before taking his present position. He currently is conducting a study of the transition of mentally ill criminal offenders after release from prison.

Pamela J. Jenkins is an Associate Professor of Sociology at the University of New Orleans. Her work as an expert witness coincides with her own research on incarcerated women convicted of homicide in the death of their intimate partner. Her other interests include the relationship between community violence and domestic violence (in *Preventing Violence in America*, edited by Robert Hampton, Pamela J. Jenkins, and Tom Gullotta).

Judith Kaye has a training and consulting practice specializing in work force diversity and antibias education.

Barry Kinsey is a Professor of Sociology at The University of Tulsa. In February 1977, he was granted a leave to serve as Senior Analyst for Health on the Staff of the U.S. Senate Budget Committee, which was continued through the fiscal year 1978, 1979, and 1980 budget cycles. He specializes in medical sociology with interests in health policy, especially in the areas of alcohol and drug abuse, health financing, and health delivery systems. In addition, he coordinates the university's crime and justice studies programs and has teaching and research interests in the sociology of law, criminology, and criminal law and procedures.

Steve Kroll-Smith is Director of the Environmental Social Science Research Institute and Professor of Sociology at the University of New Orleans. He coauthored *The Real Disaster Is Above Ground: A Mine Fire and Social Conflict*. His latest book, *Bodies In Protest: Environmental Illness in Late Modernity* is forthcoming.

J. Steven Picou is Professor of Sociology and Chair of the Department of Sociology and Anthropology at the University of South Alabama. Over the past 15 years, he has been studying the social-pyschological impacts of technological disasters. Most recently, he has served as the director of several research projects on chronic community impacts of the Exxon *Valdez* oil spill in Prince William Sound, Alaska. His most recent publications on this topic have appeared in *Sociological*

Spectrum, *Industrial Crisis Quarterly*, and the Exxon *Valdez* Oil Spill Symposium Proceedings. Picou and his colleagues are currently editing a volume entitled *Technological Disaster at Valdez*.

James T. Richardson is Professor of Sociology and Judicial Studies at the University of Nevada, Reno, where he also directs the Master of Judicial Studies Program. He teaches Social and Behavioral Science Evidence in the Master of Judicial Studies Program, Social Psychology and Law in the Interdisciplinary Doctorate Program in Social Psychology, and Sociology of Law and Sociology of Religion for the Sociology Department. He has published approximately 100 articles and book chapters, as well as six books in his areas of interest. His most recent article appeared in *Judicature*.

Hilary Silver is Associate Professor of Sociology and Urban Studies at Brown University. Her research focuses on poverty and inequality in the United States and Europe. She recently completed a study for the federal government on racial disparities in dismissals and several articles for the International Labour Office on social exclusion.

Patricia G. Steinhoff is Professor of Sociology and Director of the Center for Japanese Studies at the University of Hawaii at Manoa. She regularly teaches courses in social organization, symbolic interaction, and comparative studies. Among her research interests is the treatment of political radicals in the Japanese criminal justice system. She has served as an expert on Japanese culture in several legal proceedings involving Japanese nationals in U.S. courts.

William E. Thornton, Jr., is a Professor of Sociology and Director of Criminal Justice at Loyola University, New Orleans, and a practicing criminologist. His specialty areas include security, crime foreseeability, and crime trend analysis. His research and publications have been in the area of juvenile crime and delinquency, crime prevention and control, and crime analysis.

Lydia Voigt is a Professor of Sociology at Loyola University, New Orleans, and a practicing criminologist specializing in premise liability litigation. Her interests include international criminology; she has been examining crime and justice in Russia. She is coauthor (with William E. Thornton, Jr.) of *Criminology and Justice*, (1994), *Delinquency and Justice* 3rd ed. (1992), *The Limits of Justice: A Sociological Analysis* (1984), and numerous other publications about crime in the United States and Russia.

Marvin E. Wolfgang is a sociologist and criminologist at the University of Pennsylvania and Director of the Seilin Center for Studies in Criminology and Criminal Law. He is the author of numerous books and publications on the issues of crime, criminal law, and violence including *Patterns in Criminal Homicide, Crime and Culture,* and *Crime and Justice* (3 volumes).

ISBN 0-275-94852-8

90000>

EAN

9 780275 948528

HARDCOVER BAR CODE